"Andrew Pierce turns  thoroughly entertai— I've known him —"
DAME JOAN COLLINS

"A warm and vivid read that shows how untidy life can be but that everything can be healed with love. This wickedly gossipy journalist will melt your heart with his own story."
JEREMY VINE

"A genuinely heartbreaking, heartwarming, heartstopping story of one man's search to find his long-lost birth mother. Andrew Pierce's account will bring tears to your eyes – tears of sadness but tears of joy, too."
RICHARD MADELEY

"*Finding Margaret* is a moving odyssey of disappointment, yearning, seeking, detective work and ultimately self-discovery. Andrew Pierce's crisp prose propels the reader on a perilous voyage, sometimes verging on the unbearable. Purchase a box of tissues before embarkation."
VANESSA FELTZ

"Everything that makes Andrew Pierce a brilliant reporter is present here – a gripping story, bracing opinions, emotional honesty and, of course, a big reveal."
DANIEL FINKELSTEIN

"A very human and emotional story which was unpredictable. Searingly honest."
IAIN DALE

"A sensitively written book that is both touching and moving and deserves a wide audience."
JEFFREY ARCHER

To Betty and George, my real mum and dad.

PROLOGUE

It was a typically autumnal Birmingham day: dreary grey skies overhead and drizzling with soft rain. I'd barely slept a wink before setting off early that morning from London's Euston Station, along with my good friend Amanda, on what had felt like the longest train journey of my life.

The same agonising question that had kept me awake last night was still hammering away in my head: *Was I doing the right thing…?*

For weeks I'd been organising this trip with all the precision of a military operation. I had known it might not be straightforward, but I'd never expected to find myself feeling so incredibly anxious. Sitting in the stationary black cab – its engine running and with the back window steamed up – my stomach was churning with nervous tension. Almost breathless with fearful anticipation, I could feel my emotions beginning to oscillate out of control. I was obviously in danger of becoming a complete nervous wreck.

Struggling to ignore waves of nausea, I brushed a damp, clammy hand through my hair. I could feel my heart pounding. Hard and fast. Oh my God! Was I in danger of hyperventilating? Or even having a heart attack?

But it seemed that I wasn't the only one worried. Because the taxi driver, who'd been glancing at me in his mirror, now turned to gaze at me with concern. 'Are you feeling OK, mate? You're looking very pale.'

Catching a quick glimpse of my reflection in his mirror, I realised he was right. My face was waxen.

Desperately trying to calm down and pull myself together, I picked up the newspaper I'd bought to read on the train. But it was no good. I couldn't seem to concentrate on anything. So, almost for something to do, I used the paper to clear the cab's rear window…

And there she was.

Suddenly I knew, with total certainty, precisely *who* I was looking at. The approaching figure was still too far away for me to discern either her age or her features. Nevertheless, I had absolutely no doubt that the small, elderly figure with the distinctive shock of white hair was the reason I was here.

At the age of forty-eight, I had finally found my birth mother.

CHAPTER ONE

From a very early age, I'd known that I was adopted. My mum and dad had always told me that at birth, I'd been placed in Nazareth House, an orphanage – or what would nowadays be called a 'children's care home' – in Cheltenham. From there, they had adopted me, when I was known by my first two Christian names, Patrick James, at the age of two years old.

However, although it might seem unbelievable, the truth is that it wasn't until I had left home and was working as a journalist that I realised I had no idea about the first name, let alone the surname, of the woman who'd given birth to me. Even when I had finally managed to discover those important details, it wasn't until much later that I decided to make a serious attempt to track down my birth mother.

So why, for so many years, had I made no effort to delve, even superficially, into my past? Well, the truth is that I was very happy and much loved by my parents, who treated me in exactly the same way as my elder brother and two sisters. And, of course, I'd grown up as Andrew James Pierce, the names my adoptive parents had given me. I was perfectly happy with my new name, and as everyone knew me as Andrew Pierce, there seemed no reason why I should want to change it or dig into the past.

Besides which, I was the only adopted one in the family. On the very rare occasions when the subject arose, normally just in passing, I used to joke to my siblings, 'I'm the special one!' (I've always suspected that José Mourinho pinched the idea from me.) But, on the other hand, no matter how loved and cherished you are in a family – and I most certainly was – if the blood that courses through your veins is entirely different to that of the rest of them, it is possible that natural curiosity will cause you to occasionally wonder where you came from.

For instance, I was slightly built, with dark hair and a pale, sallow complexion, while my three siblings were all heavily built, fair-haired and had distinctive Swindon accents.

Swindon is where I grew up, but I never looked or even sounded like my brother and sisters. So, if anyone had to guess which one of us was adopted, there is no doubt that they would have immediately picked me out of a lineup every time!

The background to my life with my adoptive parents began in 1956, when George and Betty Pierce and their two-year-old daughter Susan arrived in Swindon as part of a major exodus of Londoners to the Wiltshire town. They had spent the first three years of married life with my dad's parents, Daisy and George Pierce, in a 1930s tenement block of council flats on the Isle of Dogs. It's still there today, dwarfed by the adjacent gleaming towers of multi-million-pound opulence, a testament to the regeneration of London's Docklands by Margaret Thatcher's government.

Dad's sister, Fran, also lived in the flat, along with their brother John and his wife Molly. So, when Mum and Dad's daughter arrived a year after their marriage in 1953, to say that the flat was crowded would be an understatement. Dad had grown up on the Isle of Dogs, leaving only briefly when he was evacuated at the very beginning of the war, but returning with his five siblings in September 1940, the day the first bombs were dropped on London.

Dad's father, George, who'd lost a leg in the Battle of the Somme during the First World War, was still living dangerously by working as an auxiliary firewatcher in the Second World War. During the Blitz, the government became particularly worried about the Luftwaffe dropping incendiary bombs, so over 6,000 people were recruited to the Auxiliary Fire Service. It was extremely dangerous and exhausting work. Especially for our family, as the Isle of Dogs appeared to be a prime target.

Basically, as far as the enemy was concerned, the Pierce family were a sitting duck. Around the edges of the island and close to the river were timber yards, paint works, various factories, and other businesses producing jams, pickles and confectionery, all highly combustible products. The top of the island contained the three large West India Docks, while down the middle were the Millwall Docks, with most of their docksides lined with shipping from all over the world, together with warehouses stuffed full of the cargoes those ships had carried. At the bottom of the Millwall Docks were the McDougall flour mills, whose tall silos provided an outstanding landmark for the enemy bombers, all of which made the island a highly flammable and thus tempting destination.

Other than the guns operated by the Royal Airforce, the island's defences consisted of only four anti-aircraft guns, manned by the Royal Artillery. But all fire-fighting – whether spotting enemy bombers, reporting incendiary bombs or desperately trying to deal with raging fires or operating the ack-ack guns – was an extremely dangerous occupation. At the height of the Blitz – between

September 1940 and May 1941 – an estimated 430 people were killed defending the Isle of Dogs. Moreover, the men and women of the Auxiliary Fire Service were expected to go on duty after having worked at their normal jobs during the day, before trying to stay awake and keep watch over the skies at night.

We were all very proud of Dad's father. 'Granddad Pierce', as we called him, proudly wore his First World War medals throughout the London Blitz. He was also an amazingly modest man. Born in Brighton in June 1895 to a family of fishermen, at the age of nineteen he'd enlisted at the very beginning of the Great War and was posted to the French front in 1915.

Apparently, he never spoke about the horrors he'd witnessed on the battlefield and in the trenches. After losing his leg at the Somme and being mentioned in dispatches, he was evacuated back to England and, following a long spell in a field hospital, was eventually discharged after a year's convalescence in 1917. He always reckoned that he'd been one of the lucky ones. But besides his war service in the Second World War, Granddad Pierce was known for his favourite party trick. This consisted of pulling up his trouser leg to enable his delighted grandchildren to see, touch and even rap their knuckles on his large, bright-pink false leg.

My mum, Betty Cornish, had grown up in Dagenham. She lived at 8 Elm Gardens, a mid-terraced house on the Becontree Estate, which was one of the largest public-housing estates in the world and was built between 1921 and 1935. Always headstrong and opinionated, Betty was born in January 1934, followed by her two younger brothers, Tony and Mike, who both rose well above their humble beginnings to become high-powered electronics engineers with Reuters in London. Their father John, my granddad, was a meter reader for the London Electricity Board, while their mum,

CHAPTER ONE

Anne, worked at a Lyons Corner House in Fleet Street. I still own my granddad's clock, which he was awarded after thirty years of service to the Electricity Board. Mum's early claim to fame was that the 1966 World Cup-winning England manager Sir Alf Ramsey's mum lived across the road.

All three Cornish children were clever, with Mum winning a scholarship to the Ursuline Convent in Brentwood in Essex. It was a huge achievement, but it wasn't a happy experience for her. Most of the girls were fee-paying pupils. Unfortunately, even if it wasn't true, my mother always felt they looked down their noses at the working-class scholarship girl from a Dagenham council estate. The school, which had opened in 1900, was strict and my mother regularly clashed with the nuns who ran it. Although easily clever enough to go into further education or university, she simply wasn't interested. Because she had always loved looking after children, Mum had already decided to train as a nursery nurse in Stepney, in the East End of London.

Often, on the way home from work or on the weekends, she would take the bus to a roller-skating rink in Forest Gate. The building, originally a theatre and cinema, had a very large auditorium, stage and dance floor. The Art Deco building closed for good as a cinema just before the outbreak of the Second World War, but soon reopened as a roller-skating rink. It's where my mum and dad first met in 1950, when she was sixteen and he was twenty-three. She'd dropped her ticket. Dad picked up the ticket, saying as he did so, 'I think I should look after this – and you!' In fact, he did indeed look after her for the rest of their married life – until he was struck down by Alzheimer's disease when she, in turn, looked after him. It was a love affair that was to last for more than fifty years.

They often went to the rink on a wet Saturday afternoon, loving the roaring sound produced by thousands of clay wheels clattering across the hard wood and particularly enjoying the background organ music that blared out songs from the hit parade. For a while, in the early 1950s, roller skating was all the rage. Then, when the craze for roller skates died down, the rink became a music venue, hosting, among others, The Who and Jimi Hendrix. Sadly, it was demolished in 2005 to make way for an ugly brick building housing a ventilation shaft for a Channel Tunnel rail link.

Mum and Dad were married in the Holy Family Church in Oxbow Lane in Dagenham. Their wedding day was 4 April, Easter Saturday, 1953. Mum was nineteen and Dad was twenty-six. They married against the wishes of her parents, who thought that she was far too young. However, as they were married for forty-nine years, her parents definitely got that one wrong. Ironically, Nat King Cole's 'Too Young' was one of her and Dad's favourite songs and we played the music at his funeral. We also had Nat King Cole's 'Incredible' – because that's what he was, a point I made in his eulogy.

After their wedding, Betty and George went to Hastings for a week, with Susan, their eldest child, proving to be a honeymoon baby. But unfortunately, following Susan's arrival, Mum lost two children who were both stillborn, a boy and a girl. So, while the loss of those babies devastated Mum and Dad, especially coming so soon after their decision to leave the Isle of Dogs for a new life in the countryside, it also seems likely that if either of those babies had lived, I would never have been adopted by the Pierce family.

When Mum and Dad arrived in Swindon in 1956, in a van containing a mattress and not much else – hired, as neither of them could drive – they were delighted to become the very first occupants of 173 Frobisher Drive. It was not only my family's first home

CHAPTER ONE

of their own but, as the first tenants of the neat three-bedroom, semi-detached house on the bright and newly built Walcot council estate, they were also among the first people to live on Frobisher Drive itself. It subsequently proved to be Betty's home for fifty-nine years. Mum died peacefully in her sleep in the bedroom that she had shared with George for almost half a century.

As far as my parents were concerned, the house was an absolute palace after the cramped flat on the Isle of Dogs. Happy to have escaped the dirt and pollution of London – not to mention the dreaded winter fogs, thick as pea soup – the family were thrilled to find their house surrounded by rolling green fields, complete with grazing cows and sheep. In contrast to London, life in Swindon seemed idyllic, providing an abundance of fresh air and healthy exercise. I still recall Mum sending us off to pick berries and wild plums from the hedgerows in late summer, not just for making jam but also to make her famous apple and blackberry pies. Moreover, to add to their happiness, Dad had obtained a really good job working as a spot welder on the assembly line of the new Pressed Steel Fisher Car Company, which went on to become British Leyland. It had opened in 1955 and at its peak employed 6,600 workers.

Once a small market town, mentioned in the *Domesday Book* and set in some of England's most glorious countryside, when I was a child, Swindon had a population of approximately 60,000. Whereas today, it is nudging towards 200,000, with its close proximity to the M4 and fast trains into London helping to accelerate the town's expansion.

There's no doubt that the factory was the magnet that drew so many Londoners to Swindon, which was also a major railway town, where very few of the town's workforce were ever late for work. This was famously due to the fact that every morning, the railway company's hooter sounded at 6.45 a.m. with a seventeen-second blast continuing intermittently until 7.30 a.m. Not only was the hooter our built-in alarm clock, but according to local legend, it was also possible to hear it well over 25 miles away.

Betty and George loved their new life in Swindon. Following their example, soon after they'd left the Isle of Dogs, two of Dad's brothers, John and Vic, the latter with his wife Maureen, also moved to the town. And, just to complete Mum and Dad's joy, it wasn't long before my eldest sister, Susan, had a sister, Shirley, followed two years later by a brother, Christopher.

Mum, who had been raised as a Roman Catholic – with Dad happily converting to the faith when they married – made sure that they immediately became members of the local Holy Family Catholic church. My parents also joined the choir, although Dad was the more musical of the pair and had the better voice.

One Sunday in 1963, a charismatic priest from the Clifton Catholic Rescue Society officiated at the 11 a.m. mass, delivering a rousing sermon about the importance of the family. He told the parishioners, most of whom worked at Pressed Steel or for the railway, that there were dozens of babies at an orphanage called Nazareth House in Cheltenham, who desperately needed good, loving Catholic homes. He knew that money was tight for most of the congregation. But as he told them, 'Love costs nothing.'

Following the priest's urging, Betty and George began to give serious thought to adopting another son. They talked long and hard about it to each other. They also discussed it with Betty's parents, who by now had also retired to Swindon. Mum's mother Anne and her husband John were divided on the subject. Anne was all in favour, not least because she loved little boys. But Mum's father,

CHAPTER ONE

John, was opposed to the idea, fearing that an adopted child might possess bad genes or could upset her other three children.

However, Betty and George had made up their minds, going through a series of interviews with the Clifton Rescue Society to establish that they were suitable adopters. This is how they came into my life for the first time, via a two-hour bus ride from Swindon to Nazareth House Children's Home in Cheltenham, in early 1963.

As it happened, their own three children, Susan, Shirley and Christopher, were all separated by two years. But, having always wanted four children, Betty and George decided that ideally, they'd like to adopt a second boy, around the age of two, to equalise the numbers. So, in May 1963, they were introduced to me and we all went out for a walk in the local park. They gave me a packet of sweets, Liquorice Allsorts, and they continued to visit Nazareth House regularly, often taking advantage of a lift to Cheltenham from a friend or neighbour as they didn't have a car of their own. They took me out for walks and for lunch in local cafés. It seems that I never said very much, obviously being very shy and reticent with a limited vocabulary (some people might well think that I've made up for lost time since then!).

But whenever Mum and Dad notified Nazareth House that they'd like to come over to Cheltenham to take me out for the day, it always seemed that when they arrived I was dressed in long checked trousers just like Rupert Bear – at that time a popular cartoon in the *Daily* and *Sunday Express*. Puzzled, because it was a hot summer and I was only two years old, they also noticed that I seemed to be constantly scratching my legs. Concerned, they decided to try to solve this mystery. So, when George was walking with me around the gardens of Nazareth House, he ducked behind a tree and rolled up my checked trousers. He was utterly shocked to discover that my legs were a weeping mass of red-raw sores and blisters, bloody from where I had scratched them.

Later, Mum would tell me that she'd never forgotten the note of anger in her normally mild-mannered husband's voice as George told her, 'His legs are in a terrible state,' adding grimly, 'We've got to get the boy out of here, Bet. As soon as possible!' It would be the best part of half a century before I would discover the potentially terrible truth behind *why* the orphanage had allowed my legs to get into such a mess.

There followed a series of weekend visits on the bus or hitching a lift with neighbours and friends who were lucky enough to have cars before Betty and George took a big step, taking me home to meet their own children for the first time. The youngest, Christopher, who was only four years old, was excited at the prospect of having a younger brother to try to boss around. This was a habit that never deserted him as we were growing up.

Mum and Dad also bought me some new clothes. My favourite aunty, Beth, who was married to Mum's younger brother Mike, recalls one of the first times she met me in Swindon. I clambered onto her lap and declared with great pride, 'This is *my* jumper,' as I pointed to it. 'This is *my* shirt. These are *my* trousers. These are *my* socks. And these are *my* pants!' According to Beth, I ran through my entire wardrobe, which, in retrospect, is not surprising as I'd never had my very own clothes before. In Nazareth House, the children's clothes were stored haphazardly in a large cupboard, creating a constant free-for-all so that I never knew which clothes I might find available to wear at any one time.

Luckily for me, it also seemed that Susan, Shirley and Christopher enthusiastically approved of the idea to adopt me, which must have been a considerable relief to my soon-to-be parents. In

CHAPTER ONE

November 1963, I was in Swindon on a weekend visit when the orphanage was suddenly struck by a bout of measles. The home was swiftly put into quarantine, which meant that I wouldn't be able to return to Nazareth House for some time. Ever practical, Betty and George suggested that I should stay with them in Swindon for good and it was agreed with the Clifton Catholic Rescue Society that they would formally become my foster parents. This was a result that suited everyone. Betty and George would no longer have to endure the long and tiresome four-hour round trip to Cheltenham. It would also enable them to more easily integrate me into family life, before the adoption was approved.

Unfortunately, it meant that I never had the opportunity to say goodbye to the nuns and staff at the orphanage, nor to any of the little friends I'd made during the two years I'd spent at Nazareth House, the only home I'd ever known – which must have been hugely unsettling for a toddler and is possibly why, for the next few months, I slept in a cot in Betty and George's bedroom. Apparently, I regularly endured very disturbing nightmares.

Even now, so many years later, I can still see the 'nanny goat', with its menacing horns, gazing down at me from a high arched window, which must have originated from something frightening in Nazareth House. There was also another, terrifying nightmare, where I found myself in a pram, being pushed aimlessly through dimly lit streets by a ghostly female figure whose face I could never clearly see. I've often wondered if that could have been my birth mother.

However, as I became part of the Pierce family, the nightmares woke me up less and less. Every night before bed, Betty slathered cream on my chapped, red legs. Thanks to her tender care, the painful sores gradually disappeared, but she never discovered what had originally caused this problem. My formal adoption was finalised on 11 March 1964, at the county court in Clarence Street, Swindon, just one month after my third birthday. My parents had to pay a £1 court fee. I've always hoped they felt that I turned out to be a real bargain.

As I learned a very long time later, a woman inspector from the Catholic Rescue Society made an official visit to the family home at the end of July 1964 and was delighted by what she saw:

> Patrick appears to have settled happily with this family. He was finishing his lunch when I arrived. He greeted me shyly but talked happily and brightly to Mr Pierce and [his brother] Christopher. He has given no trouble, according to Mrs Pierce. It seems that Patrick has settled sufficiently to display his stubbornness occasionally [an attribute I still have today!] but to no great extent and it has been easily handled apparently. The children are very fond of him and have readily accepted him into the family.

By this time, I called Betty 'Mummy' or 'Mum'. Apparently, the word came easily. As I grew older, I sometimes wondered if I'd ever called my birth mother by the same loving term. But it wasn't the same for George. Try as they might to persuade me to call him 'Daddy' or 'Dad', in those early days, I always referred to him as 'Man', which was probably because there had been only nuns in my life at Nazareth House, apart from a priest at Sunday mass, of course. And my unknown birth father was presumed to be either dead or to have disappeared from my birth mother's life before I was born.

The following month, there was another report by the now renamed Clifton Catholic Children's Society:

CHAPTER ONE

> Patrick, now known as Andrew, seems well and happy. He appears to be one of the family and is obviously loved by them all. He has given no trouble – eats and sleeps well, plays happily on his own and with the other children and seems quite content. His speech has improved and his vocabulary has widened considerably since going to the Pierce family.

Clearly, in the orphanage I had been withdrawn, shy and obviously unhappy. This would explain the absence of any conversational skills, even though there had been dozens of other children to talk and play with. As for now being called 'Andrew', it seems that my new parents had come up with what they thought of as a clever wheeze to introduce me to my new name. 'Patrick's in the cupboard,' they used to say, pointing to the floor-to-ceiling kitchen pantry cupboard whenever I was confused at being called Andrew. They got this idea from me because I refused to allow the toilet door to be closed, constantly saying, 'They shut me in the cupboard.' Warm and loving parents as they were, neither George or Betty realised at the time the amount of potential psychological damage that lay ahead for 'Patrick' – the little lost boy from the orphanage who retreated into the deep and dark recesses of his psyche, only to come tumbling out, with totally unforeseen circumstances, at a distant point far in the future.

There's no doubt that the Catholic Church played a major role in the life of our family. Like my brother and sisters, I went to Catholic junior and secondary schools, which in my case, as I learned much later, would also have been a condition of the adoption agreement with the Rescue Society. And needless to say, our family never missed Sunday mass or a holy day of obligation (often a saint's feast day, when you are expected to attend mass).

As kids, however, one drawback to our religion came when we went on holiday, visiting various seaside locations for a precious two weeks in the summer, which meant that we usually travelled on a Saturday. But no sooner had we reached our destination – and were longing to jump into our swimming suits, before dashing off to play on the beach – than we'd find ourselves dispatched into the local town with stern instructions to find the nearest Catholic church, all because Mum needed to know the time and place for mass the next day, which was always a Sunday.

Along with my brother and sisters, I was sent off at the age of four to the local primary school. Just about all of my friends lived locally and, if Catholic, we all went to the same school. Most of my recollections of that time concern the fun we had in the summer holidays – which, in my memory, were always hot and sunny. Practically living on my push-bike – my most treasured possession – I played the usual childish games with my friends, often thoroughly irritating the local adult population. Our favourite, and the most fun, involved sneaking into gardens and orchards, happily 'scrumping' apples and other fruit before taking to our heels to escape our inevitable discovery; often laughing so hard as we ran away that more often than not we dropped our booty. I was thin, wiry and a fast runner, so luckily I was never caught, unlike some of my friends who were regularly captured and given a good hiding, although somehow this never seemed to stop them joining in the fun. In the winter, we had regular snowball fights during the Christmas holidays and, of course, on our way to and from school.

The subject of snowballing brings the headmaster of my junior school immediately to mind. A Scotsman, James Valleley prided himself on being what he called 'a disciplinarian'. In fact, he was a horrible man. An outrageous snob – with absolutely nothing to be snobbish about – and a cruel bully. He humiliated me by sacking me as a prefect at the end of the two-week probation period in our final fourth year. I was replaced by a new boy at the school, one Rupert Gordon-Walker. A nice boy. A posh boy. Unlike most of the other kids at our junior school. His uncle, Patrick Gordon Walker, was a former Labour Education Secretary. Valleley would have purred with pleasure at the thought of cosying up to a political luminary. It was my first exposure to elitism.

Many years later, I got a message from Rupert Gordon Walker via a journalist colleague whom he had known at university. Now a big hitter in the City, he apologised for his role in my schoolboy humiliation. It was 1998. I was touched and surprised that all those years later he could even remember his short-lived promotion. He was at the school for only one term – how on earth did he connect me with that bruised eleven-year-old some twenty-five years later? As for Valleley, it was well known he was dissatisfied with not having been promoted to a better and more prestigious school. He seemed to delight in thrashing the young children in his care with a long, thick leather belt. I specifically remember him once 'belting', as he called it, over 100 of us for throwing snowballs at one another in the school playground. Looking back now, recalling his flushed cheeks and the manic grin on his face as he excitedly smashed a large piece of chalk on the desk in front of him with the leather belt – to more effectively demonstrate how much it would hurt – I suspect that he was, in fact, gaining some kind of perverse satisfaction from his actions.

After a bit of a rocky start – I struggled with maths, couldn't stand woodwork and technical drawing lessons and was easily distracted – I was fundamentally much happier at my secondary school St Joseph's, a Roman Catholic comprehensive. St Joe's (as it was always known) was the only Catholic senior school in the rapidly expanding area, which meant that it was fast becoming one of the largest schools in the county. In fact, it was so huge that by the time I became a pupil it was split between two sites a good mile apart from one another.

I'd always been in the top stream in primary school, where I had, on the whole, got on well with most of my teachers. Enjoying sports, I was in the junior school relay team and was also a champion hurdler. Besides representing the school in speech competitions, I was also the chief altar boy and, until my voice broke, I sang solos at the Christmas and Easter church services. But, despite being placed in the top stream of the senior school, I appear to have found it hard to cope with the hundreds of strange and unknown faces, both in the classroom and the playground. For whatever reason, I definitely seemed to go slightly off the rails during my first year. Disruptive behaviour, such as answering teachers back (never a good idea!), talking too much and regularly being put on detention during school lunch breaks resulted in a first-year report that made for grisly reading.

A no-nonsense disciplinarian at home, my mother exploded when she read the report. In fact, both Mum and Dad were baffled as to why I was behaving so badly at school. Unfortunately, there was worse to come. Following the disastrous school report, I found myself demoted from the A to the B stream for my second year, something I found utterly humiliating and which provoked yet another eruption from Mum, who deployed a slipper with devastating effect, as she had high hopes that I would make a real success of school and go on to better things.

Crushed at having been so stupid, and vowing that I would not let my parents down again, I worked flat out for the next two years

CHAPTER ONE

and was happy to find myself readmitted to the top stream in my fourth year for the start of my GCE syllabus. However, there proved to be a silver lining to my relegation to the B stream, because I was lucky enough to find myself being taught English by Mrs Bennett. A highly inspiring teacher, Mrs Bennett, among many other projects all designed to inspire her pupils, had set up a class newspaper.

I particularly enjoyed writing about local sporting fixtures. Mrs Bennett was so taken with my match reports on Swindon Town Football Club – languishing, as usual, at the lower levels of the football league – that she demanded to know from which newspaper or magazine I'd copied them. When I managed to convince her that they were entirely my own work, she uttered a few prescient words that, unbeknown to her, helped to shape my future adult life. 'Well, you've definitely got the gift of the gab, Pierce!' she said, before turning to the rest of the class. 'Instead of chatting endless nonsense in my classroom, especially when I'm trying to teach you all to appreciate some decent English literature, you'd do well to follow this lad's example. Because, providing he works hard in my class, he'll be able to chat to his heart's content as a newspaper reporter. I also happen to think,' she added with a grin, 'that he might look quite good in a dirty trench coat and hat.' The class laughed. But it was the first time that an idea of what could be, maybe, my possible future career began to form in my mind.

Mrs Bennett, to whom I obviously owe so much, was also responsible for pointing out that if I was really serious about going into journalism, I should put together a scrapbook of cuttings. In those days I was sports mad (unlike today!), so – with bare-faced cheek – I wrote to the *Daily Mirror*, giving my opinion on the day's burning issues, such as who I thought the next England manager should be after Alf Ramsey was sacked.

In fact, I often succeeded in winning the £10 'Star Letter' prize, which for a schoolboy on a council estate was, at the time, a huge amount of money. I wrote to the *Daily Mirror* because that was the Labour-Party supporting newspaper my parents always read. In fact, just about everyone on Walcot read either the *Mirror* or *The Sun*. As part of my efforts to become a journalist, I continued bombarding the *Daily Mirror* with letters to the editor. One of the letters, published when I was fourteen, even made my mother cry. And this would prove to be instrumental in furthering my future attempts to gain a job as a reporter.

CHAPTER TWO

By the time I was in the sixth form at school and studying for my A-levels, I'd set my heart on joining a newspaper. I was hoping to go straight from school by gaining a job as a trainee reporter, after having already ruled out any idea of going to university. While I knew that my parents would do their very best to support me, they would have to face the likelihood of making a large financial contribution to my university grant. It would have been very tough on them, particularly as none of my siblings had done A-levels, let alone gone to university. Besides, Mum and Dad had never had much spare cash.

To help with the family finances, I took a job in 'Bob's', a local greengrocer's in a little row of shops on the Walcot estate. Every Thursday night I traipsed around Walcot selling lottery tickets for Swindon Town Football Club. I also worked on the giant dish-washing machine in Swindon's BHS. I paid my parents £3 a week housekeeping. So, with three kids off their hands, they could comfortably afford two holidays a year. It was another reason why I didn't want my attendance at university to prevent my parents from having that second holiday, which I knew meant such a lot to them.

So, armed with my book of cuttings, and some six months before my final school exams were due to start, I drew up a list of a dozen newspapers within a sixty-mile radius of Swindon. But the process of applying for a job proved to be very dispiriting. If I managed to get a reply – I'd even enclosed stamped, addressed envelopes with my applications – I had the distinct feeling that the editors were sneering at my efforts. 'We prefer to interview candidates who have a degree' was the usual comment.

Eventually, there was only one newspaper left to write to on my list. Home from school during the Christmas holidays, I told Mum I wasn't going to send off that last letter. 'I've written to eleven papers. And every one of those who've bothered to reply have all been really snotty,' I grumbled, feeling heavily depressed at my failure to succeed in securing even one interview. Especially, as I gloomily told myself, I had no degree and couldn't even guarantee that I was going to get high grades in my A-level exams.

The newspaper I was petulantly refusing to write to was the *Gloucestershire Echo* in Cheltenham. My mother did her best to change my mind, saying that she had an idea that this time I would succeed. But I had an uneasy feeling about Cheltenham itself. I wasn't sure why. Was it due to the fact I'd spent the first two years of my life there, in the Nazareth House Orphanage? Eventually, Mum, who never took no for an answer, persuaded me to write to the *Echo*. But I still remember thinking, as I walked to the post box, that I had little chance of success. Especially for a boy from a comprehensive school, who lived on a council estate and whose dad worked in a local factory, light years away from the likelihood of being employed by a newspaper in a posh spa town like Cheltenham.

So, doing my best to put that last application completely out of my mind, I went back to school, totally unmoved when, about ten days later, I got home one evening to find a typed envelope addressed to me. I was pretty sure that it was from the *Gloucestershire Echo*, and even more certain that it was likely to say something along the lines of, 'Thanks, but no thanks.' But... to my utter amazement I discovered that, against all the odds, I was being invited for an interview. I was ecstatic! All my doubts were immediately forgotten as I realised that my wonderful mum had been proven right, yet again.

On the train to Cheltenham, I felt resplendent in my new sports jacket and slacks. I could even see my reflection in my polished shoes. And, as I was ushered into Tom Hoy's office, I was thrilled to see that the editor was busy leafing through the sheaf of *Daily Mirror* cuttings I had included along with my application. Softly but well-spoken, with slicked-back hair and large glasses, he immediately made me feel at ease. I soon got the impression that he wasn't particularly a sports fan, because the letter he was focused on was the one I had written some four years earlier that had made my mother cry. He asked me to explain the circumstances that had led me to write and send it to the *Daily Mirror*. So, I took a deep breath and told him the story.

It happened that Mum was home from work one day. And in her lunchbreak, as usual, she was engrossed in the *Daily Mirror*. I had noticed she was reading a spread by Marje Proops, the paper's legendary 'agony aunt', who was a regular fixture on TV and radio. But I was surprised to note that Mum's eyes were red. Had she been crying? Before I could say anything, she pushed the paper across the table and said very quietly, her voice sounding wobbly, 'Your dad and I would *never* stand in your way if you ever wanted to track down your birth mother.' I was stunned. What on earth was Mum talking about? I couldn't remember the subject of my birth mother ever having been mentioned. But, before I could gather my scattered wits, my mother rose swiftly from the table and hurried off back to work.

Totally mystified, I picked up the paper to discover that Marje Proops had written an article firmly supporting the government's decision to allow adopted children to track down their birth parents. Upon reading further, I learned that Marje thought it right that people like me should be able to make contact with their birth mothers. The government had acted to change the law because so many children who were given up for adoption in the 1950s and 1960s, when single mothers were social pariahs, wanted to find out who they really were. Harold Wilson's government had proved sympathetic to the idea and the law was being changed.

Basically, the idea seemed to be an attempt to try to piece together the first few days, weeks, months or even years of their lives. It took some minutes for me to grasp the full ramifications of what Marje was saying. And even longer to take on board the fact that I was one of the people she was writing about; one of those people she thought had the legal right to know about their heritage. It was the first I'd heard of the change in adoption law. It had certainly never been mentioned at home or school. Mum and Dad must have been painfully aware of the change in legislation but they never mentioned it to me and I must have missed it on the news.

But while I was intrigued by the idea, I really hated to see my usually tough mum so upset. So, no sooner had she left the house than I dashed off a letter to Marje Proops on my mother's baby Brother typewriter. Among other points, I argued that 'blood wasn't necessarily thicker than water'. And why would I need to find my so-called 'birth mother', when I had the mum I loved at home? I'd thought that I was writing a personal letter to Marje. But, to my astonishment, it was the leading letter on the readers' letters page a few days later. No one from the paper had contacted me, so it came as a complete surprise. Although, to be fair, we weren't on the telephone, so the *Daily Mirror* would have struggled to make contact, even if they'd wanted to.

It was a routine day at work for Mum at WH Smith's supply depot, when one of the girls in the warehouse where she worked exclaimed, 'Ooh, Betty! Your Andrew is in the *Mirror* again.' Instinctively, my mother turned to the sports pages, but her colleague Peggy said, 'No. Not there, Betty. It's here, near the front.' After Mum read the letter, she dissolved into floods of tears. By this time, all the other girls in the warehouse were crying too. Mum was so moved that she even took the rare step of telephoning my dad at British Leyland, where he was a spot welder on the assembly line, to tell him to read the letters page. Always more emotional than Mum, he also burst into tears on reading his son's tribute to his mother.

As for me, the first I knew of the letter's publication was when I went to pick up the front door key from our neighbour, 'Aunty' Maureen Tilsley. Like my parents, she had moved from London to Swindon after the war. So, she told me all about the letter when I knocked at her door after school. Like any typical fourteen-year-old, I was deeply embarrassed by all the fuss. I didn't want to talk about Nazareth House, and certainly not about my birth mother, about whom, at that stage in my life, I knew absolutely nothing. In fact, I could hardly look at Mum, who probably just wanted a big hug from her youngest child, when she came home from work. To be honest, I can remember that my mind was already on school the next day, because I knew the other kids would torment me. And, of course, they did. I had to put up with being called 'Marje' for a few months until another boy made a right fool of himself by calling me that out loud in the classroom, which earned him a stinging rebuke from our form teacher Mrs Greevy and after which I was left in peace. The nickname vanished.

But winding forward to February 1979, it seemed that Mr Hoy, the editor of the *Gloucestershire Echo*, loved the letter for one very good reason. He just happened to be the father of two adopted children. 'I hope my children feel the same way about my wife and me,' he said. A week later, he wrote to offer me a job, starting immediately after my A-level exams.

It was like a dream come true. It was far and away the most exciting thing that had ever happened to me. And, what's more, I had done it on my own, with no help from my school. So, it's no wonder that even to this day, I firmly believe that I got my big break in journalism simply because I was adopted. As for my mum, she cherished that letter I'd written as a fourteen-year-old until the day she died, which is why I could never tell her when I eventually broke my teenage promise: that I was finally making the decision to try to find my birth mother.

Needless to say, after I received that wonderful offer from the *Gloucestershire Echo*, I threw myself even more enthusiastically into my studies, only too well aware that the job offer depended upon my passing at least two exams with good grades. I was studying English, History and Economics and I was pretty sure that if I worked really hard, I could achieve success. The exams came and went in a blur and I was reasonably optimistic that I'd done well. As I was to learn later, I had indeed done so – achieving very good grades in all three subjects. So, as I had two weeks before starting work on the *Gloucestershire Echo*, I joined some friends from school and enjoyed a week on a religious retreat, operated by the De La

CHAPTER TWO

Salle Brothers at their rambling country house in Berkshire. That brief holiday was followed by a week at home which I spent working full-time at Sainsbury's in Swindon, stacking shelves and on the checkout, in order to save some money for the deposit on my new home – a small rented bedsit in a house in Cheltenham.

On the first day of my journalism apprenticeship, I was, as you might expect, a bundle of nerves. After all, I had only left school some two weeks earlier. For the past six years, I'd hoped and prayed for the chance to somehow find my way into journalism. And yet now, almost unbelievably, here I was! Actually standing in the newsroom of a well-established and highly respected local newspaper, while all about me typewriters clattered, telephones rang, reporters shouted at one another and photographers, laden down with cameras, frantically came and went. There was absolutely no doubt about it. I had arrived! And what's more, it was every bit as exciting as I'd dreamed it might be.

I soon found myself pitched straight in at the deep end, being taken to meet the most senior police officer in the town, who chatted to the reporters face to face each morning while updating them on the local crime scene. The 'job', or assignment, was listed in the newspaper's daily diary under the heading 'Police Calls'. Unfortunately, I can't recall anything about the conversation with the chief superintendent, who only had some minor misdemeanours to relay, clearly none of which were deemed interesting enough to be written up in that day's paper. But I do vividly remember a monologue from the deputy news editor Roger Clement, who took me with him as he drove to the police station. On the way, he made a point of advising me to take driving lessons, so that I could buy myself a vehicle like his and thus fiddle the mileage on my expenses. He also talked non-stop about why – if I knew what was good for me

– I should join the National Union of Journalists (NUJ). I listened politely and made no comment, since clearly none was expected or called for. Interestingly, he omitted to mention the fact that only a few months earlier, when I'd already been offered my new job, there had been an NUJ strike at the *Echo*, which had clearly made little difference as the paper had managed to be published and sold as usual.

The next day I was introduced to Albert Shipton, the editor of the *Echo*'s sister paper the *Cheltenham Chronicle*, which was published weekly. Mr Shipton then proceeded to deliver a lecture about why I should join the Institute of Journalists (IoJ) – the NUJ's smaller rival. But I knew that the newspaper had only been published during the NUJ strike because the IoJ hacks had carried on working. His speech turned out to be yet another long monologue with, once again, no response being required from me. So, I listened politely in silence. Little did either of my counsellors know or suspect, but I had absolutely no intention of joining either union. My own, private views on the world of trade unions in general had been coloured by the serious economic damage they'd arbitrarily inflicted on my own family – and hundreds of other households in Swindon – during the 1970s. My dad, George, was on the assembly line at British Leyland – a large company, which was proving to be an industrial basket case. He was constantly coming home early from work after yet another wildcat strike had been decreed by an undemocratic and unrepresentative show of hands. It was always the same scenario, with the militant shop steward declaring, 'It's a vote for our brother unionists. Out, brothers, out!'

One of the many reasons I was privately rooting for Mrs Thatcher concerned her pledge, as Conservative leader, to bring in secret ballots before strike action could be formally agreed. I thought it

CHAPTER TWO

could prove transformative for my family and was thus why I'd decided to vote for the Tory Party in the 1979 general election. Besides which, Britain had just been dragged through the 'Winter of Discontent', when even the dead couldn't be buried because of the strikes paralysing the country. As far as I was concerned, the Labour Prime Minister, Jim Callaghan, had sold out to the militant trade unions. Yet, despite the damage being inflicted on the country, one of our neighbours who had dared to put up a 'Vote Tory' poster in her window had her reputation brutally torn to shreds by the women who came into Bob's – the local greengrocer's store, where I worked on Sunday mornings. 'Who does she think she is?' was the general consensus, which is why I kept silent about my plans to vote for Mrs Thatcher.

Unfortunately, in the polling station in May 1979, my big brother, Chris, loudly and angrily denounced me after looking over my shoulder to see which way I had voted. He was absolutely furious at what I had done, ranting and raving all the way home, loudly telling anyone we passed about how I had, quite deliberately, let down the working class. But, as I'd hoped, Mrs Thatcher duly made history by being elected as our first woman Prime Minister. *And*, what's more, she kept her pledge to tame the excesses of the militant trade unions.

Who would have thought that my first adult, permanent job two months after that historic general election would take me back to Cheltenham? The very same town where I'd spent the first two and a half years of my life in the Nazareth House Orphanage. As it turned out, on the very day I was due to begin my new job, my parents were away on their annual two-week factory holiday. So, my eldest sister Sue and her husband Ian kindly drove me to Cheltenham on the Sunday before I started work.

My sister cried all the way home due to the fact that she'd been utterly repelled by the horrors of my new bedsit accommodation, mainly the overwhelming stench of cats' urine in the communal hallway. For my part, I was never bothered about the bedsit itself. It was by far the cheapest I'd been able to find, but still cost me the princely sum of £12 a week. Nowadays, of course, the rent seems incredibly cheap, but it was a huge chunk from my £19 weekly take-home pay. However, I was young and all I cared about was doing well at my new job. Although, I have to admit that as Sue and Ian drove away, I did feel a cold hand clutching at my insides. Loneliness? Fear? Nerves? Probably a mixture of all three. Moreover, I couldn't help thinking about Nazareth House itself. I'd hardly ever visited Cheltenham, so I knew nothing about the layout of the town, nor whether the orphanage might still be there.

I woke early the next day, Monday 16 July 1979, for my first day at work as a reporter. Looking back now, more than forty years since that warm summer day, I can hardly believe my luck at having been in continuous employment as a journalist ever since; particularly in a profession which is renowned for being unstable and insecure.

At the time, of course, I was as green as grass. But luckily, I had the sense to know it. Also, I was thrilled beyond measure to find myself working with eight highly experienced reporters. Yet, even in the middle of a typical noisy newsroom in those far-off days, I'd immediately noticed the long row of large, grey metal filing cabinets. I already knew that they would contain the life-blood of a journalist: the newspaper's cuttings library. I also remember making a mental note to take a good look, if and when the opportunity arose to do so, because I knew that there was bound to be a file in there on Nazareth House. Although, of course, that would have to wait until I had become an established reporter there. But even then, I knew that I could only have a good look through the filing cabinets when I could be absolutely certain of there being no one around, particularly as I was anxious to avoid any difficult, personal questions.

As the new kid on the block, my first few weeks at the *Echo* were uneventful. I was still a gawky, awkward teenager and suffered the occasional breakout of painful acne. Doing my best to look presentable, I wore a smart jacket, trousers, shirt and tie every day. I had a '60s haircut and went to the launderette every week. I had only one pair of shoes: black, standard lace-ups. Altogether, I was totally in awe of my much smarter, older colleagues, among whom was the extraordinary Harriet Tongue, who had gone to Cheltenham Ladies' College – in those days known to be one of the best schools in the world. In fact, the only other time I'd heard such a cut-glass accent was when the Queen delivered her Christmas message! They certainly never made women like Harriet on the council estate where I came from. However, while I initially found her very intimidating, by the end of my four years on the paper, I was proud to regard her not just as a colleague but as a good friend.

Another colleague was Ros Clarke, who, like myself, had been adopted. But Ros had had a very different start in life, since her family were multi-millionaires and owners of the Heart of England newspaper group, while her father, Sir Stanley Clarke, drove a Rolls-Royce. This was certainly very different to my dad, who drove an Austin Allegro – one of the most mocked cars ever to leave a British car factory production line. My father had worked on the car at his British Leyland car factory and was blissfully unaware of the scorn with which it was regarded by sneering motoring pundits. Ros herself, however, couldn't have been a nicer person, but we rarely swapped notes about our upbringing, other than the fact I knew she'd been adopted as a baby. She came home to Swindon with me once for a family wedding. Mum and Dad were a bit nervous, having never met a millionaire's daughter before. But then neither had I, until I went to live and work in Cheltenham. In the end, they thought she was wonderful and they both absolutely loved her.

Two months after starting work on the *Echo*, I was working late in the office one evening, when I realised that I was quite alone. This was clearly my big chance. I decided to find and take a good look at the Nazareth House file in the newspaper's cuttings library. The *Echo* had been founded in 1873, and I knew that the orphanage had opened around the same time, so there should be no problem in discovering all I needed to know about its history and the current details of the children's home. My heart fluttered as I drew open the cabinet containing the files beginning with 'N'. There were several Nazareth House envelopes. My throat was dry. My stomach was churning. But, as I pulled out a cutting at random, my heart nearly missed a beat…

Yes, there was a photo of Nazareth House, but it had closed in 1965, just one year after my adoption had been finalised. So now, I was looking at a building in the throes of demolition. I felt as crushed as the building: as if someone had punched me hard in the solar plexus. I could hardly breathe as I wondered what secrets had been razed to the ground by the contractors. Try as I might, I couldn't seem to focus on the text. Was I crying? In retrospect, I realise that I was certainly badly upset. Unable to prevent my eyes filling with tears, I hastily thrust the cutting into its envelope before pushing it back into the filing cabinet and slamming the drawer shut.

I felt utterly deflated and bitterly disappointed to learn that Nazareth House no longer existed. Even before starting work in

CHAPTER TWO

Cheltenham, I'd been building up enough courage to revisit the orphanage, aiming to see if I could recall anything of my time there. Or maybe, to see if any part of the building might be familiar in some way. But, after calming down and taking a deep breath, I looked up the old location of Nazareth House on a local map. Realising that it was just a few minutes' walk away from the *Echo*, I decided to make a detour on the way home to my oh-so-salubrious bedsit, via the Bath Road, where the imposing Victorian building had once stood. Only to discover some ten minutes later that in its place there was now a boring, ugly 1970s office block that was owned by an engineering company called Linotype-Paul. It's now a block of flats called Century Court. The image of the *Echo* photograph, which I'd seen only a short time earlier, flooded into my mind, the rubble in that picture representing all that remained of my first home.

I've no idea why it had never occurred to me that the old building might have been torn down a long time ago. Although, with hindsight, maybe I shouldn't have been so surprised. By the end of the 1960s, there was a widespread view that raising children in institutions harmed their emotional, physical and psychological development. Certainly in my time, while children with disabilities were typically the first to be placed in care homes and orphanages, they were frequently the last to leave, all too often ending up entirely forgotten by wider society. Fostering was then regarded as a far more compassionate and loving way to bring up a child, especially in the first few months or years of their lives. But, whatever the reason, within a year of my adoption, it seemed that Nazareth House had closed for good.

Standing opposite the large, ugly office block, I closed my eyes, doing my best to summon up memories of the orphanage. But, try as I might, I couldn't remember anything. All I knew was just hearsay, part of the family legend I'd grown up with. For instance, I knew that if I'd gone around the back of Bath Road, I would have found myself in the park where my mum and dad took me the first time they'd visited Nazareth House. It was in that park that they'd introduced me to Liquorice Allsorts. Apparently, when Mum asked if she could have the lemon sweet (she loved yellow), I popped it straight into my mouth. Clearly I wasn't used to sharing! But this was the beginning of a love affair with what are still my favourite sweets.

Goodness knows why my new parents had fallen for the unusually taciturn two-year-old in his red duffel coat and Rupert Bear checked trousers. But, to this day, I can only be profoundly grateful that they did. Walking home from Bath Road to my digs, I found myself feeling sad that I'd never be able to paint a picture of my early life in Cheltenham because it was obviously destined to remain a blank canvas, or so I thought then.

I had invested some of my £19 weekly wages – paid to me in cash in a brown envelope – in a second-hand bicycle. Because, of course, there was no way I could possibly afford driving lessons, let alone buy a car, particularly when paying my rent left me with only £7 a week to live on. So, quickly coming to the conclusion that if I wanted any extra money, I'd have to find some part-time employment, I got a job working behind the bar at the Cheltenham Squash Club for a couple of years to try to make ends meet.

I enjoyed cycling and used to tour the town and surrounding areas on my days off. One day I decided to explore the London Road, which was the very same route my mum and dad would travel from Swindon to Cheltenham on the bus, or in a friend's car when they first came to visit me, in 1963. Through some dense trees, I spotted what appeared to be a hotel, possibly a hospital, or maybe even a nursing home? I got off my bike to explore. Seconds later, I suddenly felt as though I'd been hit by a thunderbolt. Because, I somehow knew – with total certainty – what the sign at the entrance was going to say. And a minute or two later, as I stared at the sign fixed to the gatepost and proclaiming the words, 'Nazareth House', I realised I'd been quite right.

I later learned that, completely unknown to me and my family, when the orphanage was closed down, the nuns had been moved to a leafy part of town called Charlton Kings. There, housed in a modern, 1970s purpose-built private nursing home and surrounded by beautifully manicured gardens, they looked after elderly people. I can still recall the strange, slightly eerie feeling that there seemed to be far too many coincidences in my life. Not only had Mum and Dad rescued me from Nazareth House, in Cheltenham, but my very first job happened to be in Cheltenham itself. On top of which, the *Echo*'s editor also had children who were adopted, a fact that had clearly led to my employment. And now, I'd discovered that my old orphanage had not only been relocated, but was currently situated in the same road where I lived in a grotty bedsit… in Cheltenham. Was that just a coincidence? Or was it fate, I wondered as I cycled past the rich emerald green lawns towards the large building. Padlocking my bike and placing it carefully against the wall, I walked into the entrance foyer.

The first person I saw was a nun in her almost full-length black veil and tunic. She looked as if she were in her fifties, so she could have been at the orphanage when I was there. But I couldn't summon up the courage to ask her. So I decided to tell the nun, who I think was called Sister Joseph, that I was a Roman Catholic who'd recently moved to live in Cheltenham and so I was wondering if she could find me any chores to do on a voluntary basis. It was clearly the right approach as her face immediately lit up. 'You would be most welcome,' she said. 'Some of our residents get very few visitors. Perhaps you could sit and talk to them when you come here?' I told her that I'd be delighted. And so it was that on my mid-week day off from the *Echo*, I would cycle to Nazareth House, before taking some of the older residents into the gardens for a spin in their wheelchairs. Or, I would talk to them in the communal areas, joining them for their tea and biscuits. I also often used to go into the chapel at the nursing home to pray. It was a very restful place, and also felt strangely familiar.

Among the inhabitants, there was a wonderful old major whom I became very fond of and who always looked out for me. He had a booming voice and was much given to barking out orders, as though he were still on a military parade ground. Unfortunately, his authority was somewhat undermined by the fact that he often bellowed his orders in the communal areas of the home while stark naked. As I recall, the nuns appeared to be very tolerant of and relaxed about this. But it was my first real exposure to the dreaded Alzheimer's disease, which I found very distressing.

After several weeks, I plucked up the courage to say to Sister Joseph, with whom I sometimes prayed in the chapel, 'I was a Nazareth House boy. I was there from 1961 to 1963.' Sister Joseph beamed at me and said, 'I thought that I recognised you. Yes, I definitely can remember you.' But I didn't think for a minute that she was telling the truth. However, in an effort to jog her memory, I told her that I was known as Patrick James when I was in the home. Also the fact that I never knew my surname, but I was sure it sounded Irish. I can also recall asking her once – very casually – if she happened to have any photographs of the orphanage. 'No,' she said, with a sorrowful shake of her head. 'No, I'm afraid there are no old photographs of Nazareth House.' But I didn't believe she was telling me the truth that time, either.

I told Mum and Dad on the telephone that I was spending time at Nazareth House and they were enthusiastic. 'It means you are giving something back,' said Mum, who never asked if anyone was working there from my time. So I told her what the nun had said. My mother was as sceptical as I was. 'I reckon that nun is just being polite,' Mum told me. 'You were a toddler when you left. How could she possibly remember you?' It was a very rare conversation about Cheltenham and Nazareth House. Because, while Mum and I had an excellent relationship, we very rarely talked about my adoption. In fact, I never knew what Nazareth House had looked like, and nor was there ever any mention of my birth mother. I never raised the subject, and neither did my mum.

I kept up my visits to the new Nazareth House for another year or so. During that time, I got to know a nun, whose name I can't remember, but who'd been at the orphanage during my time there. 'Oh, yes, I do remember you,' she said firmly. 'You were a skinny little thing and never said a word.' Even though, to this day, I'm almost certain she had no real recollection of me, she was definitely right about two things. As I discovered much later, I was as thin as a whippet and also a shy, introverted and stubborn child who rarely spoke a word. All of which is highly ironic – particularly when you consider what I now do for a living.

As for my birth mother, Sister Joseph volunteered the information, 'I'm not certain, of course. But I think she went back to Ireland. Or your mother might have died,' she added casually, without a flicker of warmth or emotion. As I later uncovered, it was the standard line given to adopted kids. Mainly, I believe, in an attempt to stop them trying to track down their birth mothers, or delving too deeply into the time they'd spent in the orphanage and potentially opening up a can of worms.

CHAPTER THREE

A few months into my job at the *Echo* I was beginning to feel very lonely. Most of my school friends had gone to university and even if I'd wanted to go home, I couldn't, because Mum had decided that it was best for me to stay away for at least six weeks, to get used to living alone. And even then, to return home only occasionally. Tough love of course, but she was quite right – as usual.

Needless to say, the bedsit didn't have a telephone, which increased my sense of isolation, while most nights the electricity went off, supposedly due to the wiring being so old. Although I always suspected that it was mice – ignored by the landlady's fat, lazy cats – who continually nibbled through the cables. As money was so tight, I took the deliberate decision not to rent a TV, instead listening to Radio 4 around the clock. I also read a lot, particularly political biographies, which led to me becoming increasingly fascinated by Westminster. I was a huge admirer of Margaret Thatcher and never missed *Yesterday in Parliament* on the radio, which is how I became increasingly involved in reporting the affairs of Cheltenham Borough Council. The subject matter might, quite frankly, sound as dry as dust – if not dead boring – but I had developed a knack of peering behind the deliberately convoluted, leaden prose in council minutes and exposing quite a few interesting stories, even occasionally managing to discover some dodgy financial dealings or potential scandals involving councillors.

In my first month of working for the *Gloucestershire Echo*, when I was still obviously a bit wet behind the ears, I had my first encounter with the town's MP, Sir Charles Irving. Everyone in Cheltenham seemed to know that he was gay and, as far as I could see, no one really cared one way or the other. I had never knowingly met a gay man or woman before – although I was already beginning to wonder about my own sexuality. Charles Irving had been the town's Conservative MP since 1974 and wielded a huge influence over local affairs. Three times mayor of Cheltenham, he was also chairman of the borough council's policy and finance committee, where all the council's power rested. He was fifty-nine, dashing and extremely handsome, with a well-deserved reputation for lethal, witty repartee and deadly 'one-liner' put-downs, as I discovered to my cost at our first meeting.

The incident took place when I was attending a charity event on behalf of the *Echo*. As the only reporter present, I was introduced to Irving, who enveloped me in warm words of encouragement and appeared to take an interest in my new career. I can remember thinking, 'What a charmer!' However, during the evening, I happened to overhear him discussing the council's housing department, which he dismissed as second rate and not fit for purpose. Interested, I duly approached the great man, asking him to tell me more about the housing department. Unfortunately, what I'd thought of as a simple question immediately sparked a volley of loud and aggressive abuse, which almost blew me off my feet. 'How dare you eavesdrop on a private conversation!' he raged. 'You've only just started working on the *Echo*. Trust me – you won't have a very long career in journalism at this rate. Especially if people think you're a devious little sneak.' I might have been only eighteen, but I knew how to stand up for myself. Never easily intimidated, I politely pointed out to the MP that I had heard him making the remarks at a public event, to which the *Echo* had been invited. He glared at me, before abruptly turning on his heel and striding away without another word.

My article duly appeared on the front page of the *Echo* the very next day. In the office, the telephone rang and Irving asked for me by name. My more established colleagues looked surprised that the MP was asking for me. I, of course, took a deep breath and braced myself for another broadside. But, to my astonishment, it was 'Irving the charmer' once again. 'Super story today, Andrew,' he gushed. 'Sorry if I was a bit harsh with you last night,' he added smoothly. 'Perhaps we can meet sometime?'

Irving was to become a good friend and contact, regularly inviting me to his home, Drake House, the biggest private dwelling I'd ever set foot in. I gazed around in wonder and amazement. It was full of expensive and highly ornate furniture, gilt-framed oil paintings and luxurious fabrics. There were heavily embossed, solid silver frames containing photographs of Irving with Mrs Thatcher, Michael Heseltine – then a young and ambitious Environment Secretary – and Cecil Parkinson, who was to become the Tory Party chairman. I recall a cheque for £98, apparently a dividend from his shares in Marks & Spencer, casually tossed onto a coffee table. I can still remember thinking that it was over four times my weekly take-home pay. But the 'confirmed bachelor', as the newspapers often referred to him, was rumoured to have made his money in the family hotel business long before becoming a Member of Parliament.

Irving often gave me good advice. But there is one statement he made, possibly confirming his own strong belief and principles, which I've never forgotten: 'Always be yourself, Andrew. Never make the mistake of trying to be something you're not. Because, authenticity always works.' He never married. He never pretended he was 'straight', but on the other hand, he never confirmed that he was gay. As for the Tory Parliamentary Party – they all seemed to know that he was gay and were supremely uninterested. As for Mrs Thatcher, she certainly never took any interest in his sexual orientation; not least because when she became Prime Minister, he sent a huge bouquet of fresh flowers to her office in the House of Commons every week.

A towering figure in the Cheltenham council chamber, he ran rings round the other councillors who were minnows by comparison. Much later in my career, when I got my first job on a national newspaper, working for *The Times* and based in the House of Commons, I had a front-row seat in the press gallery looking down on the government and opposition frontbenchers. It also gave me the opportunity of dining regularly with Irving, who was chairman of the Commons catering committee. Knighted in 1990 and retiring in 1992, he always had a fund of political gossip and I used to help him out with some of his speeches in return for a slap-up dinner in the main dining room of the House of Commons.

But all that lay in the future.

In the meantime, I was kept busy working as a reporter for the *Echo* and thoroughly enjoying my increasing interest in politics, mainly due to Charles Irving. Besides which, of course, I was still heavily involved in the Catholic Church, not just visiting the new Nazareth House Nursing Home regularly, but also dividing my time on Sundays between the three different Catholic churches in

Cheltenham. In fact, I was always pleased if a certain, handsome visiting priest was celebrating mass at one of them.

Brooding, rugged and highly charismatic, there was a touch of Charlotte Brontë's Mr Rochester about this particular priest. He wasn't just handsome. His tall figure was extraordinarily impressive and I noted that conversations stopped when he entered a room. His sermons held the interest of most people in the church. He also seemed to have a great connection with the young, as well as the ability to relate to his parishioners. Moreover, he knew and understood that many of us were struggling with some of the harsher strictures of the Roman Catholic faith. In particular, the Church's intolerant attitude towards divorce and, of course, the important and troubling questions so many people, desperately worried about their sexuality, had. For instance, the Church teaches that homosexuality is 'intrinsically disordered', which is not just outdated, it's also deeply offensive.

Over a period of time, I gradually realised that I had taken an unhealthy shine to the priest, who was probably almost forty. We often talked after mass, or at youth rallies in which he would be heavily involved. One Saturday afternoon, I was thrilled to see him at the church's summer fete, where he easily persuaded me to buy some raffle tickets. Even then, I can recall wondering why I always felt so drawn to him. However, just as I was about to leave the fete, I was amazed to hear my raffle ticket being drawn out of the hat, especially as I'd never actually won anything before. But now, it seemed that I was the proud owner of a bottle of whisky, although, to tell the truth, ever since I made the mistake of drinking far too much Southern Comfort one evening – resulting in being horribly sick at a friend's house, aged eighteen – it wasn't my favourite drink.

However, I felt weirdly elated to have won the bottle. I had just moved into my very first flat after spending the past two years of my life in hideous bedsits. I now had a proper kitchen and – thank God – my own bathroom for the first time. The joy of not sharing a loo with five other bedsits! It was tiny, of course, consisting of a sink, loo and shower, the head of which would frequently fall down onto my head, usually when the water flow was too strong. As if I cared! Especially as I reckoned that shower had definitely changed my life for the better. I was no longer queuing with the tenants of the other bedsits just to use the only bathroom in the building, which was, more often than not, utterly filthy. I also had a separate bedroom with a really comfortable double bed. All in all, the flat was a huge improvement on my previous accommodation and I felt like I was king of the castle. There were still one or two problems, such as the interior décor, which was a bit grubby. However, the whisky I'd won in the church raffle meant that I could at least offer any visitors a drink, even if they did have to run the gauntlet of another hallway redolent of the distinctive aroma of cat pee.

As I was leaving the fete with the bottle of whisky tightly clenched in my hand, the priest stopped me and said, 'I hope you're not going to drink that on your own?' I blushed as I always did when I was in his presence and muttered something about offering it to guests, then I raced away, even though it was clear he wanted to continue talking to me.

Goodness knows why, but all my life I've had this strangely deferential attitude to men and women of the cloth. By then, it was 1981 and the Catholic Church was held in high esteem. For instance, the Polish Pope, John Paul II, was viewed as akin to a rock star, attracting millions of pilgrims and followers to the open-air masses he held around the world.

CHAPTER THREE

Some weeks after the fete, the priest, who was back in Cheltenham after helping out in another parish, buttonholed me after mass and asked if I'd finished the whisky. 'I haven't even started it,' I told him, before agreeing to meet him later that evening for a drink. When I joined him at the pub, I noticed that he was dressed in his trademark priestly garb, complete with his dog collar, which was undone, signifying that he was off duty. When I invited him back to my place for a nightcap, I never thought he would say 'yes'. The whisky must be the attraction, I thought as we walked through the busy streets to my flat. As we mounted the stairs – my flat was on the top floor – I nervously apologised about the hallway décor, which he kindly pretended not to notice. But, for the first time, I was highly relieved that the hooded rays emitted by the solitary light bulb (no light shade of course) concealed the faded, peeling wallpaper.

As we were chatting, I opened up to him about how I had started my life in Nazareth House Orphanage, discovering that he was a regular visitor to the new Nazareth House Nursing Home. He wanted to know all about my adopted family, as well as my birth mother and father, of whom I knew nothing. I also confided to him that I was struggling with my sexuality. When I'd left Swindon, aged eighteen, to work on the *Echo*, it never occurred to me that I might be gay. I liked girls, although I'd had crushes on a few of my male school friends, but I had assumed it was a phase that would pass. In all my years at school, the subject of homosexuality never cropped up in the classroom, and while it might sound laughable to Gen Z, we were never taught that it was possible to live an alternative lifestyle. Moreover, I cannot recall anyone in our large comprehensive school who was known to be gay.

I hadn't actually talked to many people about it, so this was a big step for me and the priest was very sympathetic. He assured me that no one would ever pass judgement on me if I were gay, at which point I felt I had no choice but to blurt out the harsh truth: 'No one, except the Catholic Church!' This was 1981. Homosexuality had only been legal since 1967. There was a gay pub in Cheltenham, the Salisbury Arms, which I only ventured into once – and promptly fled, never to return, mainly because I'd felt totally out of my depth and not at all sure of how I was supposed to behave. On top of which, nobody working in my newspaper office was gay. Although, I had heard vague rumours about a man in the advertising department. According to the office gossip, he was 'in his thirties and lives with his mother, so he must be gay'. Clearly. Guilty as charged!

Charles Irving was gay, but it never affected his numbers at the ballot box and he successfully held the seat for eighteen years, until he retired from Parliament. I'd always admired Charles. He never gave a damn what people thought. He was independently wealthy, comfortable in his own skin and a highly popular figure. Not for him the idea of hiding his sexuality behind marriage – the choice made by so many of his contemporaries at Westminster, on both sides of the Commons chamber. I had spoken very briefly to Charles about it, his wise advice being to follow his example and concentrate on always being highly discreet.

The priest knew all about Charles Irving. Talking into the early hours, we managed to finish off the large bottle of whisky in one go, admittedly with lots of water. When he got up to leave, he staggered and almost fell over. And I have to admit that I was also feeling dizzy and was definitely no steadier on my own feet. But the church was a fifteen-minute walk away. There was no communal telephone in the hall of my building and it was long before the advent of mobile phones, so there was no way he could call a cab.

CHAPTER THREE

Moreover, although he had his car with him, he certainly couldn't get behind the wheel in his current state. So, he asked, could he possibly stay the night?

Once he'd assured me that he was happy to sleep on the sofa, I managed to find a spare blanket, all the while suggesting that I should sleep on the sofa instead. But he wouldn't hear of it. Nor would he share the bed, finding the suggestion 'highly inappropriate'. As for me, the room was spinning and I reeled into bed, instantly falling asleep. I woke in the early hours feeling utterly dreadful. My head was viciously thumping as I dimly realised that the priest was now in the bed too. With my underwear somewhere around my ankles, I could only keep my eyes tightly closed, hardly daring to breathe as he kept pulling my pants up and down.

Oh my God! How many priestly oaths is he breaking? I wondered desperately, somehow incapable of asking him to stop. Was it my deference to the priesthood? Irish Catholic guilt? Embarrassment? Or terror? Was I embarrassed for myself – or was I embarrassed for him? I could not turn round to face him in the bed, so I pretended to be asleep. I feared I knew what might happen if I spoke to him. My first gay sexual encounter…? In a double bed with an ordained Roman Catholic priest…? The possibility of what could happen was utterly dreadful… totally unthinkable… even if I wanted to. How would I ever be able to look him in the eye? And what about the Church? This was close to committing a mortal sin! Would I be allowed to attend mass again…? My head pounded with so many dreadful and terrifying questions and I was in turmoil as I fiercely willed myself back to sleep. It felt like my brain was spinning out of control, probably the effect of so much whisky, which luckily helped me to lapse into unconsciousness once more. As far as I know, nothing happened.

When I woke in the morning, he was on the sofa, looking as if he had been there all night. Maybe I had dreamed the whole hideous episode…? But as he left immediately, without looking me in the eye and not even staying for a cup of tea, I knew that I had not imagined it. In fact, I suspect it was guilt and embarrassment that drove him so quickly out the front door. We only spoke about the incident once, when he said he'd told his parish priest that he had stayed the night at my flat because he would have been over the drink-drive limit. 'If you had been done for drinking and then driving, you would have found yourself all over Andrew Pierce's newspaper,' the older priest had said, apparently warning him to be more careful in future. But if the older priest discovered what had *really* gone on in my flat that night, he could have ended up all over the national newspapers as well, because I was still only nineteen at the time and it was illegal for gay people to have sex until they were twenty-one.

After that, I saw the priest only once or twice and we hardly said anything to one another, merely exchanged pleasantries. Later, I was sad to hear that he'd left the priesthood, especially as he had always been an inspiring preacher, drawing many young people to the Church. I can only imagine that he had lost his battle, both with his sexuality and with his vows of celibacy. However, as the Catholic Church has, very slowly, begun to change its rules, accepting married priests and also those with children – when they broke with the Anglican Church over the acceptance of women priests – it is surely only a matter of time before a pope rings the changes and allows serving priests to marry.

Despite my traumatic experience with the charismatic priest, my Catholic faith remained strong and important to me during my time in Cheltenham, as it is today, so I was incredibly excited to

CHAPTER THREE

be chosen by my newspaper to cover Pope John Paul II's visit to Britain in May 1982. Armed with my press pass and trusty camera, I boarded the overnight train to Coventry and was immediately engulfed by the amazing party atmosphere on board. Nuns, priests and Catholics of all ages were crammed into the carriages as we left Cheltenham railway station, the train stopping frequently throughout the night to collect more and more pilgrims. No one slept. We were all far too excited. Even my family from Swindon, who'd also been determined to join the pilgrimage, were somewhere in the midst of the thousands of people already crowded together at the airport in blazing, early-morning sunshine for the Pope's open-air mass.

I was so lucky! I had a pass for the press stand, where I stood alongside reporters from international newspapers and had an unrivalled view of the altar where the Pope would celebrate mass. As a mere local newspaper reporter, I was secretly thrilled to find myself rubbing shoulders with Fleet Street aristocrats, famous presenters and bigwigs from the BBC and ITV, as well as some US broadcasters like CNN. It was heady stuff for a 21-year-old trainee reporter.

As images of the Pope's arrival by helicopter at Baginton Airport, now Coventry International Airport, flashed up on the giant screen, which was placed high above the altar, a huge cheer went up from the crowd. It was the first ever visit to the UK by a reigning Pope. John Paul II had become Pope four years earlier and was then a truly influential and revered leader, despite his unwavering opposition to demands for change on issues like abortion, birth control, women priests and homosexuality. To cater for his arrival, a 'temporary city' had been built in the airport, using 50 miles of scaffolding and 5.5 miles of chain-link fencing, along with the giant television screen mounted above the altar.

As the Pope stepped from his helicopter to greet his adoring public, there were smiles, cheers and tears of joy. 'This Pope is a genuine "superstar",' I wrote in my notepad. 'A rock star – however famous – would never have had anything like the same reception.' I abandoned my position in the press stand to explore a maze of white marquees near the altar. No one asked me where I was going, or attempted to stop me when I halted in front of one marquee, mainly because I had been struck by a flag fluttering from the top. It bore the image of two crossed keys and a tiara, and I was sure that it was the coat of arms belonging to the Holy See and Vatican City.

As it happened, I wasn't the only one who had worked out who was in that marquee. Standing to my left behind the chain-link fence were two nuns: but not just any old nuns. To my amazement they were Sister Jacqueline and Sister Nuala, who had taught me A-level English at St Joseph's Comprehensive School, back in Swindon. I couldn't believe that out of over 300,000 people crowded into the airport grounds, I would find myself standing next to two of my favourite teachers, whom I had barely seen since I'd left school some three years earlier. They seemed delighted to see one of their former pupils, quietly making a name for himself in newspaper journalism. But even as we were exchanging greetings, the sound of heavenly music emerged from the marquee and was accompanied by the distinctive figure of Cardinal Basil Hume, the leader of the Roman Catholic Church in England and Wales, leading the way out of the tent.

The last time I'd seen Cardinal Hume had been almost exactly a year earlier, in May 1981, at an ecumenical service in the magnificent surroundings of Gloucester Cathedral. At that time, long before the advent of the internet with its ability to provide constant, up-to-date news, I had travelled by bus from Cheltenham to cover the special ceremony for my newspaper. As a result, I'd been well out of touch with radio and newspapers for at least a couple of hours. So when, before the service had even begun, one of the cathedral's deacons stood up in the pulpit and asked the congregation to pray for the health of Pope John Paul, I'd merely thought of it as part of this particular service. It was only when the woman next to me began to sob loudly, swiftly followed by many others around me, that I realised something terrible must have happened. Moments later, someone turned to tell me that the Pope had been shot in St Peter's Square in Rome, before being rushed to hospital where he was, at that very moment, fighting for his life.

I was dumbfounded. 'The Pope has been shot' is not a phrase I ever expected to hear. Certainly not in a large cathedral when I was about to be addressed by a man who could, quite possibly, be a candidate to replace John Paul if he succumbed to his injuries. A deep sense of gloom seemed to descend on those assembled as Cardinal Basil Hume led the prayers for the Pope's recovery. After the service, I had spoken briefly to the Cardinal, before he was surrounded by radio and TV reporters seeking his views on the attempted murder of the Pope.

And here I was, one year later, staring once more at Cardinal Hume, who was followed by the 'great communicator' himself, our Polish Pope Karol Wojtyła. I could hardly believe it. Also, I could hardly believe that the Pope's security was so lax as to be virtually non-existent. The fact that I was able to come within a few yards of the Pontiff without being stopped, searched, or prevented in any way from getting so close to him was shocking. However, despite my fears and worries for his safety, my two former teachers and I were incredibly lucky that day. As all three of us sank to our knees, the Pope stopped to smile and give us his personal blessing. It was one of the most moving moments of my life and I will treasure the memory of that blessing to my dying day. John Paul II was elevated to the sainthood in 2014, nine years after his death. So, not only did I have his personal blessing, but I'm certain it will be the only time I'll ever be that close to a real, live saint.

After three years in Cheltenham, I was fortunate to meet a jobbing actor and theatre stage manager, Colin Stanley, in a pub. He was looking for a lodger and I jumped at the chance of moving, the minute I saw his house. There was a bath, even a bidet, hot running water, central heating, a telephone and a small garden. And definitely no cats. I could hardly believe my luck!

Colin was away working in London for most of the year and I was still regularly attending church. I was painfully aware that I was gay, and yet was conflicted about the Catholic teaching on homosexuality, which was judged by the Church to be 'a sin'. I don't recall there being any discussion about being gay at home, and while I was friendly with one of the priests from our family church in Swindon, he would never discuss the subject; not even when he was technically off duty and we went to the local pub for a drink. This is one of the reasons why I was for many years chairman of the Iris Prize, an international LGBT film festival. One of the subjects the films regularly explores is the many difficulties gay men and women are likely to encounter, especially when 'coming out' in schools, colleges, the workplace and even within their own family; whether in their teens or middle age. It pains me to say that even today, homophobia is still a major problem throughout the world.

It was in Cheltenham, as I moved into my lovely new home, that I met my first boyfriend, Jerry, who was a hairdresser. After six months, when I realised the relationship was serious, I wrote and broke the news to my parents, fearing that they would be devastated. But I had no need to worry, since they proved to be their usual sensible and down-to-earth, pragmatic selves. Mum called a gathering of my brother and two sisters, who were all married and producing grandchildren. 'I've got some important news about Andrew,' she told them. But before she could say another word, my eldest sister Sue quickly chipped in, 'Oh, Mum! Is he going to be a priest?' 'Err... not quite,' Mum told her. 'He's written to tell us that he's queer. Or, to use a more modern term – that he's gay.' A statement which immediately produced floods of tears from Sue.

However, when this was all relayed back to me by my other sister, Shirley, who phoned me at the *Echo* office the next day, she added, 'Everything is going to be absolutely fine, kid. Because the family are right behind you. And I will always love you – whatever you are!' Subsequently, every member of my family met Jerry and he was happily welcomed into their homes, and even though we parted many years later, Jerry still remains a very important friend to me.

I've often wondered if being gay was the reason that St Joe's, my old school, has never invited me back to talk about my career as a successful journalist. After all, I had spoken at Millfield, one of our finest public schools. I'd taken part in discussions with City institutions about the need for employers to be more inclusive and I was also a member of Stonewall, the equal rights organisation. It's amusing to recall that when I was a schoolboy in Swindon, I thought all the gay people were in London. It was only when I began working and living in Cheltenham that I realised they were much closer to home.

CHAPTER FOUR

After five wonderfully happy years in Cheltenham, I decided that it was time to try for a job on a bigger newspaper. My first editor, Mr Hoy, had retired and it seemed like a good time to move on. I had made a name for myself as an experienced local government reporter. Helped, I may say, by my friendship with Sir Charles Irving, whose tentacles extended all over the town hall. It was often thanks to a 'nod and a wink' or a nudge in the right direction from him that I was able to track down and secure some strong front-page stories.

I applied to various newspapers in the Midlands and was lucky to be taken on by the *Birmingham Post & Mail*. This took my career into a different league, as the *Mail* sold 300,000 copies a night compared to the *Echo*'s 35,000. Birmingham was also Britain's second city and a Labour Party stronghold – a total contrast to Cheltenham, a large town and spa, with a solitary Labour councillor on the local authority. At the time, the *Post & Mail* was launching a series of weekly newspapers and I got the job of working for the *Weekly Mail* in Bromsgrove, a few miles south of Birmingham.

While I was working for the *Post & Mail*, I made some great friends. Among them was Jane Moore, who was one of the star writers on the *Mail* and whom I looked up to with awe and admiration as she was clearly destined for greater things. Which, of course, she subsequently achieved as a columnist for *The Sun*, as well as becoming a successful novelist and a panellist on one of my mum's favourite ITV shows, *Loose Women*.

Another good friend was Sandy Hopkins, who ran the newspaper's advertising department, and her husband Tony Flanagan, a brilliant photographer. He was one of the most handsome men I've ever met, with a shock of dark hair, an impish grin and sparkling eyes. Sandy always teased me about the way I spoke, dubbing me 'preppy' because she thought that I talked with a public school accent, which I frequently pointed out was nonsense, citing the fact that my own three siblings, whom I'd grown up with and who had all attended the same comprehensive school as myself, spoke with broad Wiltshire accents. Yet her own son Alex, who at that time was attending the fee-paying Bromsgrove School, had a distinctive Birmingham accent – just like his parents. It just goes to show there's clearly no rhyme or reason why one person in a family can pick up a particular accent when another one doesn't.

I spent a lot of time with Sandy and Flan (as Tony was affectionately known by his friends) at their lovely thirteenth-century house in Feckenham, near Bromsgrove. However, there was no way I could keep up with their alcohol consumption. I remember once driving into their village with Flan and spotting huge swerving tyre marks in the neighbouring field. Of course it was Flan's handiwork after another epic night of partying. Long after I'd left the *Post & Mail*, I often returned to Bromsgrove to visit them and we remained great friends for many years until, very sadly, they both died far too young. They had insisted that if I ever moved to a big national newspaper, I should track down the story of my birth mother. Deep down I knew they were right.

It was entirely by chance that I eventually stumbled upon the name of my birth mother. Nowadays, all details and certificates of public records, such as those for births, marriages and deaths, can be obtained via the internet; that is, by contacting the GRO (General Register Office) online. But, up until 1997, it was still possible to visit the General Register Office, in St Catherine's House on Kingsway in London, which allowed the public direct access to the indexes of births, marriages and deaths and gave them the opportunity to obtain the relevant certificates in person.

By now in London, and working for *The Times* as a general news reporter, I was at the GRO on a routine newspaper project. But, after doing my homework for the paper, I suddenly decided to do some private research of my own. After all, I'd never actually seen my own birth certificate, so it might be interesting to look it up. Hauling down the very large and very heavy index files for the correct date, I flicked through the pages to February 1961 – the month and year of my birth. But, despite scanning the lines of names again and again, I was completely mystified. On my birthday, there was absolutely no reference to, or any trace of, a child bearing my name.

Why no mention of my birth…? I could feel myself becoming slightly breathless, my cheeks flushed as I stared down in confusion at the open pages in front of me. Struggling to control a rising tide of panic, and, if I'm honest, feeling just a little scared, I replaced the weighty volume back on its shelf, before swiftly leaving in search of a strong cup of coffee. After draining it and feeling a lot calmer, I returned to resume my search. Only to achieve exactly the same result. Try as I might, I could find absolutely no mention of Andrew

James Pierce. What in the hell was going on? Had I been the victim of an elaborate con? Or a possible hoax? Was there something about the adoption that I hadn't been told? Did I not really exist? All of these utterly mad, idiotic thoughts flashed through my mind, again and again. In desperation I made my way to the information desk, ashamed to hear myself mumbling and stuttering as I asked the assistant why my name was missing from the register. To tell the truth, I was feeling seriously embarrassed by now. Even more so when the man asked me, in a low voice, 'Are you adopted?'

My first reaction was astonishment. How on earth could he possibly know that? 'Well… er… yes, I am,' I muttered helplessly, feeling like a complete idiot by this time. However, the man gave me a reassuring smile before explaining that the 1961 entry would be registered in the name of my original birth parents, while I, of course, had been searching under my adopted name. Which was not, after all, such a strange action on my part, as it was the only name I'd ever really known. I told the man that I was pretty sure there would be just the one parent's registration. Which was undoubtedly why I'd been put up for adoption. 'I'm sure that we can help you,' the nice guy from the information desk informed me. 'Believe me, lots of adopted people make exactly the same mistake.'

But I knew it wouldn't be that easy. I'd never known my birth mother's name; not even her Christian name, let alone her surname. The only information I'd ever had from my mum and dad was that I'd been named 'Patrick James' and that I'd been born at Bristol Southmead Hospital in February 1961. So, reassured by the presence of the friendly and helpful Geoff – he and I were by now happily on first-name terms – we looked through the list of all the babies born in the Bristol hospital on my birth date. *And there it was!* In black and white. A Patrick James Connolly had been born in Bristol

CHAPTER FOUR

Southmead Hospital in February 1961. It was the only entry for a child named 'Patrick James', so it had to be me.

The birth certificate was printed off and presented to me by Geoff. There were, of course, more details. It was the very first time I'd seen my birth mother's name: 'Margaret Connolly.' On the certificate, next to the father's name, was the terse entry: 'Unknown.' It drew me up short. Even though I had always assumed Margaret was a single parent, the word was flashing in my head like a traffic light. I think it was the brevity of the language I found so shocking. 'Unknown'. Brutal, but factual and there for all to see.

My mind was racing. I wondered whether Margaret Connolly knew who the father was. Presumably she must have done. Had he refused to have anything to do with her? Or, was it the other way round? Had her parents thrown her out of the family home when they discovered her secret? I knew that single mothers were regarded as social sinners in 1961. Or had she withheld his name to protect him? And if so, why?

The vague thoughts I'd had about tracking down my birth mother over the past few years crystallised in an instant. For the very first time in my life, I had her real name. But my head was full with a mass of pressing questions. Was her surname still Connolly? Had she married? I hoped so for her sake. Did she have children of her own? Children that she'd actually managed to keep? I was sure she would have. And if so, they would be my half-brothers and sisters. It was in that moment, staring down at my birth certificate, that I knew I had no choice but to try to find her.

Returning to work, I telephoned my mum. I used to speak to her at least once or twice a week. After catching up on the news from Swindon, I told her about my weird experience and relayed the information that my birth mother was someone called Margaret

Connolly. But there was no response from Mum at the other end of the phone. Absolutely none at all. A total silence. So, feeling incredibly guilty that, somehow, I was letting her down, I immediately dropped the subject and quickly began talking about something else.

Over the years, I'd always feared that if I asked my parents too many questions, they would suspect me of wanting to make contact with my birth family, which is why I didn't want to do anything that might upset them. They had given me everything a child could ask for, so the idea that they might think I didn't appreciate all their loving care had always deeply troubled me. But, at the same time, with the assistance of Geoff, who'd been so helpful in locating my birth certificate, I now knew more about my birth mother than I ever had. So, doing my best to ignore any thoughts of guilt as far as Mum was concerned, I took the big step of registering with a *bona fide* and well-respected charity.

This particular charity's aim was to collate the names of birth parents who were anxious to track down the children they had once, for whatever reason, given up for adoption. I was subsequently sent the list of names. But unfortunately there was no mention of a Margaret Connolly. Of course, I was hugely disappointed. But I convinced myself that Margaret might not know anything about that particular organisation. Besides, I was quite sure that even if she had eventually married and started a family, she would be desperate for some knowledge of the child she'd given away, which is why I included my name on the list of children who'd expressed an interest in finding their birth parents.

I'd read enough to know that many birth mothers were wracked by guilt to their dying day. It seemed that the sadness never left them. Even the birthdays of their adopted children proved to be

CHAPTER FOUR

difficult occasions, with the mothers having to endure the heartbreak in private as so many of them had remained totally silent, never telling anyone about what they had done. Having been a journalist for thirty years, I knew that there were two sides to every story. The stories with happy endings were frequently repeated. Unfortunately, the unhappy ones were not.

But just those two words, 'Margaret Connolly', allowed me to try to draw a picture of my birth mother, and her early life, for the first time. My mental image was that of a teenage girl with long dark hair, a slim figure and high cheekbones – just like myself. I guessed she'd come over to Britain probably from her native Ireland to have the baby, far from the prying eyes of her disapproving family. Had she returned to Ireland after she'd left me in the orphanage? Was I the result of a fumbled sexual encounter with a lad from her school? Possibly a childhood sweetheart?

I had so many questions. To which, as yet, I had no answers. But, as all these ideas and images flooded into my mind, I was certain of at least one thing. It would have been horrendously difficult for Margaret to go through nine months of pregnancy and give birth to her baby without at least one of her family or friends knowing, which meant that, undoubtedly, someone must have helped her. Although, to be honest, part of me did fear that Margaret might be dead. Or, far more likely, had she returned to her birthplace and was now living in Ireland?

But I did suspect there was a chance that if her parents were very strict Catholics – like so many of those I'd known when I was young – she could well have been thrown out of the family home. It was common knowledge then that many young girls were sent to England to give birth, the usual pretext being that they were going to stay with relatives or look for a job.

However, the charity assured me that as soon as they had any information, they would definitely get back in touch with me. Although they did mention that it might take some time. So, while I waited to hear from them, and having given them as much detail as possible, I got on with my very busy, and at times hectic, journalistic career.

I was clearly developing itchy feet, because, after working for the *Post & Mail* for two or three years, I decided to head for 'the big smoke' to try to make it on a national newspaper. I eventually decided to take the risk, accepting a job on a relatively recent innovation for the industry: a newspaper delivered entirely for free through people's front doors. My colleagues in Birmingham thought I was utterly mad. Why leave a well-established regional newspaper to work for what they disparagingly called a 'free sheet'? I must confess, the paper being called the *Yellow Advertiser* didn't help. It was a dreadful name. But, on the other hand, it was a neat little paper – and I had a ball.

Working across Essex and east London, I came across some amazing stories, including one of my favourites – an encounter with a Labour councillor who'd been arrested for being drunk in charge of his wheelchair. That really brightened my day. Another case concerned a local Tory MP, Harvey Proctor, which hit the headlines when he was fined in court for having sex with a man under the gay age of consent of twenty-one. The man was aged twenty, while Proctor was thirty-four, a situation which would be entirely legal nowadays and unlikely to prompt an arched eyebrow from even the staunchest puritan. But at the time, it was enough to destroy Proctor's political career.

Yet so often, politics and journalism are symbiotic. Some thirty years later, in my current job at the *Daily Mail*, I was the first

CHAPTER FOUR

journalist to interview Harvey Proctor after he'd been wrongfully accused of historical sexual abuse and murdering children by a fantasist calling himself 'Nick'. Carl Beech, aka 'Nick', who caused utter misery in his attempt to destroy so many men's lives, was eventually convicted of concocting the entire story and sentenced to eighteen years in prison.

I was proud of the way the *Daily Mail* took up Proctor's case – as well as that of the former chief of the defence staff Lord Bramall and the late Lord Brittan, the former Home Secretary, who died not knowing that the police had exonerated him. But, during Proctor's original problems in 1986–87, I'd made some good contacts in Fleet Street and began supplementing my income by freelancing for national newspapers. I had a couple of good hits with the *News of the World*, who invited me to work from their newsroom on Saturdays. It was a big breakthrough, and the £120 fee for a day's work was almost as much as I earned in a week on the *Yellow Advertiser*.

In those days I had a battered red Mini Metro. Sent off one Saturday to the village of Dummer in Hampshire, I had to pursue an increasingly well-known redhead: Sarah Ferguson, who was apparently dating Prince Andrew. There was no sign of the prince when I got there, but I did find Sarah Ferguson. We had an energetic walk across the village green as she cleverly and politely dodged my questions about her blossoming relationship with the Queen's second son. They were married a few months later.

The *News of the World* had given me my first mobile phone. It was early days for this particular piece of modern technology, so it resembled a large, heavy brick and was *very* cumbersome. It also kept ringing – a lot! The office news desk had shown me how to make a call on the phone but unfortunately, no one had explained how to answer it. In my trusty Metro, I grappled with the ringing phone, all the while swearing violently under my breath. I momentarily took my eye of the steering wheel, then… CLUNK! I had shunted into a parked car in front of me. Now it looked as if my £120 fee from the newspaper was going to be spent in a garage repair shop, which was bad news. Though – fortunately for me – at least it wasn't Sarah Ferguson's car. I spent a couple of years freelancing for the paper and then got lucky when I was offered a job as a parliamentary reporter in the press gallery for *The Times*. It helped that I had learned the traditional Pitman New Era shorthand, which meant that I had passed 110 words a minute as a trainee reporter. Court reporters and the Hansard writers in Parliament can manage 180.

By 1988, my regular salary combined with the extra money I earned from freelancing equated to the magnificent sum of £22,000, which meant that I could afford to buy a house. It was in Forest Gate, east London, which thrilled my parents, who'd met on the roller-skating rink there in 1950. In fact, when Mum and Dad came to stay at my house they could hardly believe the property was just one minute's walk from the old rink, and that the Princess Alice pub (named after one of Queen Victoria's many daughters) where they'd had their first date was still there on the corner – and it was now my local.

When I started in the parliamentary press gallery that year, my hero Mrs Thatcher was at the peak of her powers. I had a bird's-eye view from the front row of the gallery, overlooking the government and opposition front benches. And I was still there when she made her dramatic resignation statement, after suffering a fatal wound in the first round of the November 1990 Tory leadership contest against Michael Heseltine. 'I'm enjoying this!' she proclaimed, in what was, for the House of Commons, an absolutely outstanding,

CHAPTER FOUR

bravura performance. And I knew then that I was privileged to witness history in the making.

Many years after her fall from power, I would often take her to lunch at the Ritz Hotel. She always liked to have the same menu: chicken bisque followed by lemon sole and just one glass of white wine. As we left, the pianist always played the famous tune 'A Nightingale Sang in Berkeley Square'. A sweet smile would flit across her face as she'd squeeze my arm and say, 'Do you know, dear, that's my favourite song.' Of course I knew, which is why the pianist would play it for her whenever she had lunch there, in what is regarded as one of the loveliest dining rooms in London.

After a couple of years in the gallery, I was promoted to 'The Times Diary', an upmarket gossip page. It brought me into contact with the likes of Jeffrey Archer, one of my favourite novelists, who's now a great friend. I never miss his memorable shepherd's pie and Pol Roger champagne Christmas parties, hosted with his wife Dame Mary in their magnificent penthouse overlooking the River Thames. I even got a mention in his *Prison Diaries*. Published after his two years in jail for perjury, Archer wrote two bestselling diaries and yet another bestselling novel based on his experience behind bars. The great thing about Jeffrey is that he just keeps bouncing back, while still writing bestsellers in his eighties.

On the diary, I worked in *The Times*'s office in Wapping in London's East End, which was just a few miles from where my dad, George, was brought up in the Isle of Dogs. I also worked from *The Times*'s office in the House of Commons, where I continued to increase my political contacts. I was in and out of the House of Lords, as well as being invited to some of the swish clubs in Whitehall beloved of civil service mandarins and government ministers.

I also found myself outside Conservative Party HQ on election night in 1992, when John Major's government was fully expected to be defeated, killed and buried by Neil Kinnock's Labour Party. This wasn't an unreasonable assumption, as the Tories had already been in power for thirteen years. In fact, I thought my copy for the next day would end up somewhere near the back of the paper with the sports pages. After all, who cares about the losers? But, of course, as we all know, John Major managed to upset the odds, squeaking home to victory with a majority of twenty-one. So, I was there to record his triumphant arrival at Conservative Party Headquarters, and my copy made page three, as I revealed that many senior Cabinet ministers, convinced that they were facing the humiliation of losing their prestigious posts, had hurriedly sent out for champagne in the early hours of the morning, then suddenly realised – to their great surprise – that the party was actually heading for victory.

I have fast-forwarded some of the highlights of my career, to illustrate that my long journey – to the point where I finally decided to try to find my birth mother, Margaret Connolly – had started after years, if not decades, of total denial on my part. *Why should I be even vaguely interested in who she was?* I used to ask myself. *Why would I want to trace her? What was the point in doing so?* I knew nothing about the woman who, after all, had given me up to a couple of complete strangers. She'd put me in a children's home, almost 50 miles from the hospital where I was born. So it was clearly a case of out of sight, out of mind, right?

Actually, I don't think that I ever really believed any of those statements. But, over the years I have learned that they are very common thoughts and reactions for so many who were, for whatever reason, given up for adoption – and indicative of the very real fear that somehow it was their fault they were rejected or abandoned,

CHAPTER FOUR

which in just about every case was totally untrue. It was generally the financial pressure – the inability to provide for their child – that had forced parents to reluctantly agree to adoption.

Like so many others, my problem was further complicated by the fact that I already had a great mum and dad whom I loved very much. So why would I need another parent figure in my life? But logic does not always rule the heart. In the end, my natural curiosity – I was a journalist after all – got the better of me. I had begun to fear that Margaret might be dead or becoming infirm, and that was the key factor which prompted me to finally take the plunge.

I was forty-eight and assumed that Margaret was a young teenager when she had me. If I was right, Margaret would be in her early sixties, which meant that the clock was ticking. I was also compelled to take action by the fact that shortly after taking redundancy from British Leyland, my own dad – gentle as a lamb and loved by everyone – had shown the first signs of Alzheimer's in his early sixties. Clearly there was no time to lose. What if the same had happened to Margaret?

So finally, with the help of my old journalist friend from my Birmingham days, Jane Moore – who, among her other talents, was apparently a whizz at tracking people down – I decided to try to find my birth mother. Jane and I discussed it over breakfast in a branch of the Balans café chain in Soho. Jane ordered the 'Full English', to help with the hangover she was nursing after partying with David and Victoria Beckham the night before. For my part, I couldn't eat anything. I was already fretting over whether I was making the right decision. Having spent the night tossing and turning, I was still deeply worried about the hurt I would inflict on my mum Betty if she ever found out.

Jane was very reassuring. Amazingly, she had done this before with four other friends, so was now a seasoned sleuth. In all four cases, Jane had found the missing parent and each case had produced a happy outcome. She saw no reason why my experience shouldn't be the same. So, taking charge of the search, Jane told me that my initial task was to get hold of 'The File' – which must exist somewhere – recording my time at the orphanage and the history of my adoption.

So far, so good. But where to start…?

I wrote to the Sisters of Nazareth, the religious order that had run the orphanages. I knew the orphanage no longer existed, the same being true of the Catholic Children's Society, which had organised my adoption. I eventually discovered that I had to apply for my file through my local social services department in Camden. The area, in north London, is a typical London metropolitan borough. While it is home to many celebrity residents, such as Jude Law, Daniel Craig and Gwen Stefani, all living in their multi-million-pound Regency properties, the borough also houses large tranches of inner-city estates where many live in abject poverty.

I knew my plea for help with my adoption file would be way down the social services department's list of priorities: and quite right too. But I wrote and asked them if they could help. My letter was acknowledged – and then it all went quiet. Four months or so later, I was sorting through my post at home and saw a brown envelope marked 'Camden Council'. I naturally assumed it was another dreary circular about recycling. But, no. In one brusquely typed paragraph, the letter said, 'We have obtained your adoption file. Please make an appointment to come and see it.'

The letter slid out of my hand onto the kitchen floor. At last, it was really happening. I bent down, picked up the letter, placed it on the kitchen counter and went to work. I was an assistant editor on

CHAPTER FOUR

the *Daily Telegraph* at the time, dividing my day between their office in Parliament and the paper's HQ in Victoria. Not surprisingly, I was highly distracted all day and came home early. Picking up the letter, I read it again – at least half a dozen times – before phoning Jane and my friend Amanda Platell, saying, 'Let's do it.' And so, about a week later, there I was, walking into the council's office block and about to delve deep into my past.

The experts I had consulted advised me to bring a friend, as they knew how bewildering and upsetting this process could be – advice for which I was very grateful after we were shown into a plain, faceless meeting room in the modern and nondescript building. It was unbearably hot and I could feel the sweat rolling down my back. Was it really the airless room that felt so suffocating? Or was I suffering from a mixture of guilt, fear and hope? Guilt, because my family – my real family – knew nothing about this. Fear of what I might discover. And hope… hope that a woman who had given me up forty-five years ago would even want to meet me. If, of course, she was still alive.

As we waited for what seemed like for ever, Amanda smiled and squeezed my hand reassuringly. Yet she looked about as terrified as I was. A kind-looking, middle-aged social worker finally walked in and stood opposite us. I noticed that she never sat down. Wearing a grey trouser suit and no make-up, she radiated tension. She placed a thick blue file on the Formica desk in front of me. I noticed that on the front cover, my name was spelt out in capital letters underneath the words, 'Copy of information held on file at the Catholic Children's Society (Diocese of Clifton) in respect of Andrew Pierce.'

It was an extraordinary moment. My heart almost stood still. I knew that the file contained the complete history of my life in Nazareth House Orphanage, the children's home where I had lived from the age of five weeks until I was almost three years old in the early 1960s. It would also reveal the story of just how I was rescued from it, so no one was keener than me to read its contents.

In the room there was some small talk between the three of us and, strange as it might seem, I sensed that the social worker was hesitant about opening my file. Finally, with a slight sigh, she placed her palm on the file and said, 'Could I just say a few words?' I nodded, assuming that I was about to be given the standard warning that birth parents don't always welcome an approach from a child they'd given up for adoption decades earlier. But I was wrong. Very wrong.

'I've been doing this job for more than twenty-five years,' she said. There was a long pause, before she added, 'I have to say that this is one of the most complicated files that I've read. Ever.' My heart sank, only to sink even further when she continued: 'Your birth mother went to quite extraordinary lengths to cover her tracks. To ensure she would never be found.'

I was astonished. I could hardly believe what she was saying and was even a little irritable. 'Oh, for heaven's sake! I was adopted in the early 1960s,' I pointed out. 'More than a decade before the law changed, enabling children to trace their birth parents. She could never have known or feared that the law would be changed, so why would she have employed any subterfuge?'

Caroline, the social worker, looked genuinely pained. There were hints of warmth and concern in her voice as she said, 'I'm really sorry. But even then, I can assure you that your birth mother was taking no chances that anyone would ever find her. The only addresses to be found in this file showing where she lived are nursing homes.'

That was yet another shock, even before I had opened the file.

CHAPTER FOUR

It appeared that my birth mother was a nurse or, I assumed, at least a trainee one. Apparently, Margaret had lived in the heavily state-subsidised nursing accommodation near the hospital. Even then the recruitment of nurses was a problem. The homes were long gone and, with them, any chance of getting a forwarding address. But Caroline hadn't finished. Unfortunately.

'Your birth mother, I'm afraid, also crucially omitted her middle name from the birth certificate in order to make finding her even more problematic. The absence of a middle name speaks volumes. It suggests she was trying to be vague or evasive, even then. Because your surname is also a very common Irish name,' the social worker added. 'So is her Christian name of "Margaret". She has also excluded her date of birth from everything. I am telling you this,' Caroline continued, 'to try to prepare you for the fact that your birth mother might prove to be impossible to track down. I'm so very sorry. I wanted you to know the worst before you start reading the file, as I'm sure you've been thinking about finding her for a very long time.'

The words 'a long time' kept going round and round in my head. *'A long time'?* I thought. *How about a lifetime?* But then Caroline smiled and, with a flourish, produced from the file a transparent plastic folder containing a little handwritten note. Apparently, it was written by Margaret when she decided to give me up for adoption. 'It shows that she loved you very much and wanted to do the right thing by you.'

But I wasn't listening. My heart was racing. My palms were sweaty. All I could think about was that I had come this far, only to discover that the woman who gave me up for adoption had clearly done so with two main objectives in mind. Not only had she made every effort to ensure that no one would ever know about her illegitimate son. But she had also, quite deliberately, gone out of her way to make certain that neither I – nor anyone else – would be able to find her.

CHAPTER FIVE

The plain and nondescript box-like room in Camden Council's main office block was rapidly becoming unbearably stuffy. My vision was blurred and my temples were beginning to throb with the stirrings of a tension headache.

At some point, I registered that the two files were slowly being pushed across the table towards us: one for Amanda and one for me. But I just couldn't bring myself to open the file. All I could think about was that matters appeared to be going badly awry, because this interview was definitely not following the script that I'd been writing for so long. I felt physically sick, even a bit faint and increasingly dizzy, muttering my thanks to Caroline, the social worker, as she opened a small window to let in some fresh air.

My mind drifted away again, even though I was conscious that Caroline was still speaking, a look of concern etched on her face. How many times? I was asking myself. How many years had I made excuses, or found reasons to put off applying for my adoption file? A file which, it now turned out, the Camden social services department had so easily obtained from the Nazareth House head office in Hammersmith, west London. So *why* had I always been far too busy? *Why* had I repeatedly found some pretext for not obtaining the file?

Moreover, why had I finally changed my mind and decided to go through this torture when I had procrastinated for so many years? Especially as I really loved my mother Betty, who'd adopted me and who was at home in Swindon this very minute – totally oblivious to where I was and what I was doing. I dreaded her ever finding out, because I knew that she would be completely devastated. Even thinking about it brought tears to my eyes.

On the other hand, I could just walk away. I could do so easily, since there was nothing to stop me, certainly no law I'd ever heard of that would compel me to open the file. Besides, what *was* the point if I was never going to be able to find Margaret? Did it really matter that I would never know anything about her? What she might have done over the years since my birth? Did it really matter that I would never be able to discover if I looked like her, or had any of her characteristics? I felt utterly crushed and emotionally exhausted by the choice confronting me. But suddenly, logic and common sense came to my rescue.

Flooding back into my mind were the basic, very important reasons *why* I was sitting in this virtually airless and stiflingly hot room. Because, of course, my main impetus had always been that my birth mother needed to know the truth. To know that the baby whom she'd placed in the orphanage in 1961 – when he was just five weeks old – was now a healthy, happy and successful middle-aged man. I truly believed that a brief meeting, even a phone call or card, would not only lift her heart but also remove any anxiety she might have suffered over the years. Having read so many desperately sad stories of mothers who'd given their children away for adoption, I felt certain that she must have worried about her son Patrick James,

CHAPTER FIVE

wondering where he was and if he'd been actively looking for her. For my part, I very much hoped that she had managed to find happiness in a loving marriage with more children of her own to care for, I also thought that she would want to know all about the couple, my mum and dad, who'd not only adopted me but had given me so much love over the years. I remembered what my wonderful, kind, gentle dad had said to me on more than one occasion: 'Son, find that birth mother. She visited you all the time. She deserves to know you're OK. But whatever you do, don't tell your mother I told you to find her.'

I recalled Dad's words as the social worker continued in her reassuring tones. I gripped the desk and squeezed Amanda's hand. 'I have to do this,' I muttered urgently. 'I must make sure Margaret knows that I'm OK.' So, my heart racing, I opened the file. On page one, there was a brief summary. In total silence, I turned to page two and read, 'Birth Mother: Margaret Connolly. She was approximately 29 years of age at the time of your birth.'

'*What...?*' I exclaimed out loud, Amanda turning to gaze at me in concern. 'Twenty-nine! Twenty-nine! Twenty-nine... Twenty-nine... Twenty-nine!' I couldn't seem to stop myself from repeating the same words, over and over again, before turning to Amanda. 'She wasn't an ignorant young girl. She was a 29-year-old nurse, for heaven's sake! She *must* have known all about birth control.' This shocking discovery was quickly followed by the thought of Margaret's true age now. If she was twenty-nine when I was born, and hopefully still alive, then she was now approaching eighty years of age.

I took a deep breath and tried to concentrate on the file in front of me. But I was still shocked and confused by the discovery that my birth mother had been a fully grown, mature woman. Definitely not, as I'd originally assumed, a possibly empty-headed, ignorant teenager who was tempted into losing her virginity by a lustful classmate.

So how on earth had she become pregnant at twenty-nine? According to the summary I'd just read, she was not only a fully trained nurse but an experienced one, so she must have known all about the need for contraception, especially if she was embarking on an affair. She must have known – who better than a well-qualified nurse – the many risks an unwanted pregnancy would incur, not just for her health but also her employment. Moreover, if Margaret was then a strong and practising Catholic who took her religion seriously, she must have known that she would have to carry her baby to full term. Because I was pretty sure that in 1961, the Roman Catholic Church would have considered abortion a 'mortal sin', which meant that anyone who totally embraced their faith would never have ignored such an edict, involving as it did a possible excommunication from the Church.

My stomach felt as though it contained a heavy, leaden weight. Now I was finally beginning to understand why the kind social worker had tried to prepare me for the worst-case scenario. 'If Margaret was twenty-nine when she had me,' I said slowly, trying to marshal my thoughts into some kind of logical order, 'I can only think that she must have been involved in an affair. And she must have also known the risks she was running,' I added, looking up at Caroline, who was still contemplating me with concern. 'So, is she engaged in all this secrecy and subterfuge because she's trying to protect the man who fathered me? Could that be the reason she went to such lengths to ensure that she would never be found?'

But, of course, the social worker – however much she might have wanted to – was in no position to help me. It was nearly fifty years

CHAPTER FIVE

since my birth mother had first discovered that she was pregnant, so there was no way the three of us in that stuffy room could possibly answer that, or any of the other questions prompted by the files in front of us. Even in my dazed and confused state, I already knew that it was going to take a lot of time, a great deal of research and frankly a miracle or two if I was going to have any hope of discovering the truth.

In the meantime, I swiftly skimmed over some basic, salient points in the file, while Amanda was doing the same with her copy as the social worker paced the room. I was still confused and mentally exhausted by having to completely readjust my original impressions of Margaret. So, I decided to leave the bulk of the file until later, when I could take the time to absorb every bit of relevant information before formulating a plan for my research.

After thanking Caroline for helping us as much as she could, and being reassured by her that I was welcome to ring her for help and advice any time, Amanda and I left the town hall in search of a restaurant and a stiff drink. Alas! The restaurant and stiff drink would have to wait. Because, although it seemed like we'd spent a lifetime in that little room, it was only 10.30 a.m. However, we did manage to find a small café selling hot, strong coffee, which slowly helped to expel the thick miasma of shock and incredulity from our minds.

Neither of us had expected Margaret to be twenty-nine when she had me, and we wondered just how difficult it was going to be to find her. I was still puzzled as to why she had apparently gone to such great lengths to disappear. Especially as there wasn't even a hint back then, in 1961, that adopted children would one day be able to try to find their blood relatives.

'I'll tell you one thing,' I said, as the coffee did its work and I began to feel halfway human. 'I've obviously been a bit hesitant and dragged my heels about trying to contact Margaret in the past, mainly because I feared upsetting Mum and Dad. But that's definitely not going to happen again. Because now I'm absolutely determined – however long it may take – to find out exactly *who* and *what* lay behind all Margaret's lies, half-truths and highly misleading, evasive behaviour.' Although I didn't blame Margaret herself. It was becoming as clear as daylight that she must have been under extreme pressure, from an as yet unknown person, or embroiled in a disastrous situation to have acted as she did.

Amanda and I both continued to scan our respective copies of the Nazareth House report – all fifty-five pages of it – and then another mystery occurred to me. Margaret was a nurse in Birmingham, so why did she give birth to me 100 miles away in a Bristol hospital? I had worked in Birmingham for almost two years, oblivious to the fact that my birth mother had been living a fifteen-minute bus ride from the *Post & Mail* offices. I then called a courier company, handing one copy of the report to the motorcycle rider to deliver to Jane Moore's home in south London, before calling her to say the file was on its way. As I'd hoped, she was ready and itching to get to work on it, quietly confident that she'd be able to find Margaret within days, or a few weeks at the most. But although the file contained Margaret's last known address in Birmingham, I suspected that it would turn out to be the local nurses' home, while the building itself – as I'd already encountered with the Nazareth House Orphanage in Cheltenham – would very likely have been demolished years ago.

I phoned my editor at the *Daily Telegraph*, saying I was out meeting contacts, profusely thanked Amanda for 'holding my hand' that day, then returned home to study the report again. Reading slowly through the file was a strange experience, particularly as very

CHAPTER FIVE

few of us are ever able to read a running commentary on our birth and general welfare from five weeks old up to the age of three. I started making a few notes, which I stored with the report in a drawer of my antique roll-top desk – which I kept carefully locked at all times. This was to ensure that my mum, Betty, who frequently came up from Swindon to stay with me after Dad's death, as she loved going to parties and the theatre, would never discover the file by accident. Happily, to her dying day, Betty remained blissfully ignorant of anything to do with the search for my birth mother.

As a busy journalist, I didn't have as much time as I'd have liked to carefully check the large amount of material in the report or conduct the necessary research. It was over dinner at Andrew Marr's house in north London that the idea of writing a book about the search for my birth mother slowly became a reality. Andrew and his wife Jackie, a fellow journalist, are close friends, they knew the story of my adoption and thought it could be turned into a book. I had already worked on one book in 1995, *Great Parliamentary Scandals*. I was one of the main researchers for its author, Matthew Parris, who was then a colleague at *The Times*, so a book about my adoption would be my first solo effort.

I finally decided to take the plunge when having lunch with Vicki Field, a leading agent married to the former MP and Foreign Office Minister Mark Field. She was certain that there would be a market for the book, and when I sketched out some of the details of my life, she became even more convinced. So, I returned to the file and my sheets of notes, slowly realising that perhaps taking my future readers with me as I sought to track down my birth mother might be the way forward.

But, as I continued to read through the report and carry out more research, I came across more and more extraordinary revelations about life in the early 1960s that now seem almost antediluvian. In particular, how many young girls and women about to give birth to illegitimate babies were sent, like my birth mother, to a specific place for six weeks to await their labour. And this did not just apply to Roman Catholic women. Indeed, the Anglican Church had just as many, if not more, homes for pregnant women, where they were kept in seclusion until they had their babies, most of whom were already marked for adoption.

In my birth mother's case, it was the St Raphael's Home for Mothers and Babies in Henbury, Bristol, which was part of the Convent of the Good Shepherd, a French order of nuns. All the expectant mothers were expected to sing for their supper by performing household chores, cleaning, preparing meals and doing the washing. On average, it seems there were around fifteen women in the house at any one time.

Quite how Margaret ended up at St Raphael's Home in Bristol when she'd been a nurse in Birmingham some 100 miles away is totally unexplained. Nor is there any explanation in the report I'd received of exactly how she had arranged for her baby to be born in the nearby Southmead Hospital. These were, in fact, the first two major conundrums I'd come across when reading through the report.

However, when carrying out some in-depth research on various mother and baby homes around the time of Margaret's pregnancy, I uncovered a desperately sad account of one woman's experience. After having spent her last six weeks before the birth in very much the same kind of mother and baby home as Margaret – albeit on the other side of the country in East Anglia – the anonymous woman was sweeping a stairway when her waters broke.

CHAPTER FIVE

> I was sent off alone to hospital. There, I was put in a windowless room and after the nurse had checked I was in labour, she left me alone. I was very scared and had no idea of what lay ahead. I had no one to talk to and encourage me or to help me through labour.
>
> The hours wore on and a nurse looked in a couple of times, but I was offered no pain relief and no help or support. Finally, at about midnight I realised I was starting to push. I called out and a nurse came in and told me to keep quiet as the other mothers were sleeping. She then made me get up off the bed and walked with me to the delivery room where I gave birth to my beautiful son. I couldn't believe he was mine and I loved him intensely from the first moment I saw him. I couldn't imagine losing him.

But lose him she would. Apparently, her baby had already been earmarked for a married Catholic couple who were on the adoption register. The unnamed mother's account continued after she left the home. To read it is heartbreaking.

> I returned home that day and it took me some months to come to terms with what had happened. I went through a period of depression and although I returned to my previous job, I wasn't able to 'get on with my life' as I had been told to do. I eventually met and married a good man (I told him about my baby). I had two more wonderful sons and have now been happily married for more than 40 years. But, I have never forgotten my first son and have wept many secret tears for him. I have carried my burden of guilt and shame over the years and have never been able to speak to anyone about my experience.

Was it the same for Margaret? The adoption report says that after six days in Southmead Hospital she was sent back to St Raphael's Mother and Baby Home with me. During the day I stayed in a nursery with the other babies. Mothers were only allowed in to feed and bathe their children. All the mothers bottle-fed their babies. The nuns believed that breastfeeding enhanced the physical bond between mother and child, which was, it seems, not to be encouraged under any circumstances.

As I mentioned earlier, further research revealed that the homes were run by various religious orders – Protestant, Catholic and many other denominations – but most of them received financial help from the government. They were established in the 1920s and it appears their main function was to 'hide' the women who had fallen pregnant out of wedlock. The homes were known as places for 'fallen women', a shelter where they could 'hide their shame'. 'Shame' was very much a Victorian word – and remained common currency in the early 1960s. But perhaps the most 'shameful' aspect of the homes was the need for them in a society which – unbelievably, only sixty years ago – witnessed young girls and women being thrown out of their family homes because of the perceived 'crime' and the 'shame' of having an illegitimate baby.

The turnover at St Raphael's seems to have been fairly rapid. Margaret's stay was limited to six weeks before the birth and a maximum of six weeks afterwards. The timing was calculated to determine that the babies were developing healthily. Adoptive couples did not want disabled children.

Following my birth, I only had one public outing with Margaret while I was at St Raphael's. It was my baptism. Normally, this was a proud affair in a Roman Catholic household, but obviously, mine had to be low-key to protect my mother's identity. So, it took place

CHAPTER FIVE

on 1 March 1961, two weeks after I left the hospital where I was born, at St Anthony's RC church in Henbury, near to St Raphael's. Details of the ceremony are sparse. A priest conducted the ceremony and there was a godmother, who was called Margaret McGuire. Who was she? Did the mother and baby home wheel her out for every christening when there was no father? She certainly didn't appear to be a friend of Margaret's, so I don't think anyone is likely to know the answers. Following the ceremony, Margaret and I went straight back to St Raphael's.

Margaret's file containing the report made it clear that her family still resided in Ireland. But there was a small note attached to one of the papers, to the effect that she apparently had three brothers, one of whom lived in Birmingham. This fact may have explained why she gave birth to me 100 miles away in Bristol, so he would not know about her shameful predicament. But, once again, there was no information about that particular brother in the file. Another dead end – as so accurately predicted by Caroline the social worker.

However, I noted that the day after the christening, Margaret had signed an agreement with Clifton Catholic Rescue Society, the adoption charity that would care for me after I left St Raphael's. The agreement form was headed by a strong, black, bold message: 'It is very important that this form be accurately completed.'

There was, first of all, the basic issue of who should pay for my keep and how much. Margaret, who was paid £8.10 shillings a week as a nurse in Birmingham, agreed to provide my £2 weekly board and lodging costs. In the agreement, she was required to answer a series of questions about my health and where and with whom I was living.

Another question assumed that I had been recommended to the Rescue Society by the 'parish priest' and a space was left for his name.

It was one of the sixteen questions that Margaret declined to answer. There was another question: 'Is the baby legitimate?' The answer was succinct: 'No'. And also, 'Is the baby offered for adoption?' 'No'.

Looking back, I have found myself wondering how Margaret was able to give birth in relative anonymity in Bristol. Was she given help? On balance, I think she must have had some assistance, from someone in a position to help her. How else would she have been able to arrange leaving her nursing job in Birmingham, for a minimum of six weeks, in order to have her baby? And, of course, there was the problem of how she managed, until six weeks before my birth, to conceal her pregnancy. She was, it seems, a slightly built woman. The file stated that she was 5ft 4in. tall in her stockinged feet so concealing a baby bump wouldn't have been easy. Did a doctor she worked with in Birmingham help her? Or was she one of those lucky mothers-to-be who managed to hide her pregnancy until almost the last minute? But since I weighed 8lb 11oz at birth, I didn't think that was likely.

In the course of investigating Margaret's past, I tried to research St Raphael's records. After all, that was my first home – albeit for only a few weeks before I was transferred to Nazareth House Orphanage in Cheltenham. I was taken aback by the response my enquiries received. There was a 2014 Freedom of Information request on St Raphael's file with a blunt, curt message in reply to every query: 'The file is to remain closed for 84 years.' Why? 'The file contains sensitive personal information which would substantially distress or endanger a living person or his or her descendants.' Hmm... So who was that, I wonder?

The more I thought about Margaret, in St Raphael's with girls young enough to be her daughters, the more I became convinced I wasn't the product of a one-night stand. I was beginning to form

CHAPTER FIVE

a picture of a devout Roman Catholic who'd thrown herself on the mercies of the Church when she fell pregnant and entrusted her first-born son to a Roman Catholic orphanage. So, who was my birth father? Was he still alive? Was he Irish too? Possibly a Catholic? Did he come and see me in the orphanage? And why, above all, was he leaving Margaret to pay all the necessary expenses, making absolutely no contribution? After all, each week she handed over a quarter of her gross salary to the nuns of Nazareth House. How could she possibly afford my board and lodging fee? Was someone helping her financially?

In the adoption file there was another bombshell to come. Scrawled in spidery black handwriting was a devastating sentence in the agreement with Clifton Catholic Rescue Society: '[The] mother is an SRN nurse who has a three months' work contract to finish. She is getting married in July – and will then withdraw the child (we hope!).'

Marriage? *To whom*? I don't know why, but I'd never expected this. And once again, there were so many questions. For instance, why was the father not on my birth certificate? If Margaret did get married, what happened to her husband? I arrived at Nazareth House on 5 March 1961 and Margaret told the nuns I would be reclaimed in four months when she got married. But she never came to get me, and I didn't leave the home until November 1963, a full thirty-two months later, with a new set of parents. So, what changed? Was her lover married and had he subsequently refused to leave his wife? Was he a doctor who had made her pregnant and who'd promised he would do the honourable thing and marry her, then gone back on his word? Or was it a priest who was pulling all the strings behind the scenes and was much closer to Margaret than he should have been?

Then there was a letter that must have dumbfounded the nuns. Its contents were confined to a single scrap of paper. They must have been the most difficult two sentences Margaret had ever written. Dated 16 November 1962, the letter said, 'After all this time, I have decided to have my little boy adopted. Unfortunately I have no OTHER choice.'

When I read this, my heart ached for Margaret. She had tried and failed, it seems, to give me the start in life she wanted me to have. But why had it taken her so long to reach this decision? For two long years, Margaret seemed to have nursed the forlorn hope that one day, she would be able to take me home and bring me up herself. But with whom? Certainly not on her own as a single mother. The stigma of illegitimacy was still far too great for social acceptance, especially in an Irish Roman Catholic family in the early 1960s. She also could not have afforded to do so on a meagre nurse's salary. So, was there someone she was hoping to marry and who was willing to bring me up as his own son? My real birth father, for instance?

One possible answer was in the very last paragraph of the agreement with the Rescue Society. It was a paragraph that caused me to cry out in disbelief as I stared down at the piece of paper in my hand.

There was an innocuous reference to Margaret, whose occupation was listed as a State Registered Nurse (SRN), and after that was a space for 'Father's name'. I'd automatically assumed it would be blank or say 'Unknown', like my birth certificate, issued only days before. But I was quite wrong. Because there were the words, 'James Coffey, 227 Slade Road, Birmingham'. And under 'occupation' was written, 'Engineer, Standard Motor Company'. So, I had a named father after all – despite my birth certificate stating the opposite.

So who was James Coffey – and what had become of him?

CHAPTER FIVE

There is a description of James Coffey in the report, but no photograph. 'James Coffey was approximately thirty-four years old at the time of your birth.' *That's odd*, I thought when I first read those words, surprised to find that they didn't have a precise age for the guy. 'James attended a state school and later qualified as an engineer. He was Irish, single and a Roman Catholic.' Then came the final shock: 'James Coffey died from a road accident on April 15, 1961.'

I could hear myself shouting, once again, '*What on earth's going on here?*' How could this be? If the information was correct, James Coffey (whoever he was, and whatever his relationship to Margaret may or may not have been) had died barely four weeks *after* I was placed in Nazareth House Orphanage. If, indeed, James Coffey really *was* my father – and not a figment of Margaret's fertile imagination?

My mind was in a complete whirl. If James was real, if he had ever really existed, I wondered if he'd ever met or seen me. Had he even known anything about me at all? His death – if he really was dead – must have been devastating for Margaret, of course. But, as I read more of the file, I discovered that Margaret had only told the Nazareth House Orphanage about James Coffey's death in March 1963. When he had been dead and buried for nearly two years! And four months after she'd written to Nazareth House saying she was giving up her fight to keep me.

After she'd written to the nuns, Margaret had also written to Father Hall, who was based in Bristol and who reported to the Bishop of Clifton, who was Chairman of the Society. Once again, these words must have been so difficult to write: 'I have decided to have Patrick adopted. I trust in God that I have made the right decision.'

A reply came the next day and it was brusque and to the point:

Dear Margaret,

Thank you for your letter.

We would like to arrange a meeting with you at Nazareth House, Cheltenham, as soon as possible but this seems to be unlikely before the New Year.

Yours sincerely,

Administrator

The letter was unsigned and there was no word from Father Hall or any explanation of why she was giving up on me. Margaret couldn't attend the next meeting at the home, which she postponed to March. Here, they discussed the details of my adoption and James Coffey's name re-emerged as she signed the papers agreeing to my adoption.

At this point, Margaret was informed in writing that the process of introducing me to potential adoptive parents had begun. In a letter dated 24 April 1963, she was told, 'In the circumstances I think it would be better if you did not visit.' The letter clearly came as a shock to her and two weeks later, she wrote to Father Hall:

Dear Rev Father,

Will Patrick be visited by adopters soon? If not, may I visit a little nearer the time when he goes for adoption? I am worried lest he should not be visited.

Yours respectfully,

Margaret Connolly

The reply was terse to the point of brutal. The unsigned letter from the Administrator, written on 6 May 1963, said:

CHAPTER FIVE

We are arranging for people to visit Patrick regularly and I must repeat I think it would be better for you not to visit Patrick now that you wish to have him adopted.

Yours sincerely,
The Administrator

If the penny hadn't dropped before, it would have then. Margaret had seen her son for the last time. The orphanage would not facilitate any more visits. She never had a chance to say goodbye.

It was as if I were somehow trapped in one of these country house mazes, where whichever way you turned or whatever questions you asked, you always seemed to come back to the same place, with no obvious answer or reasonable exit in sight. It's no wonder that I spent many days exclaiming aloud, in acute frustration, 'What the heck's going on here?'

While Jane Moore was facing great difficulties in locating Margaret, I made it my mission to do all I could to solve the 'James Coffey problem' once and for all. And since he was thought to have died in March 1963, I knew the first thing I had to do was obtain his death certificate.

CHAPTER SIX

Before beginning this last, ongoing search for my birth mother, I'd taken very little interest in my birth father's identity. I'm still not entirely sure why I hadn't seriously thought about him before now. But it might have been more to do with how imperative it was to track down my birth mother rather than any lack of interest in who her lover may have been. Besides which, I had been wrapped in such a happy, warm and loving relationship with my adoptive parents that I'd no need to spend time wondering about, or searching for, a totally unknown man. Especially when I knew that if I did, they would find it incredibly upsetting.

But now, as I stared at Margaret's contract with the Clifton Catholic Rescue Society, the question of exactly *who* my father might be suddenly became important. Especially as the agreement clearly stated that they agreed to care for me in Nazareth House Orphanage until Margaret's planned marriage in July – some five months after my birth. Following which, she also agreed to withdraw me from the orphanage, presumably to join her in her new married life.

I found it hard to believe what I was reading.

Frankly, I was suspicious, mainly because the timings made no sense. The report added that James Coffey was from Galway in west Ireland, that he had blue eyes (like mine), was 5ft 6in. tall (I'm 5ft 9in.) and had the same black hair as Margaret. My hair was black too, until the dreaded grey flecks took over. The report added, 'James's parents were living at the time of your birth, but there is no record of any brothers or sisters.' There was, moreover, a telling sentence at the end of the section on James Coffey. 'The person providing this information is Margaret Connolly. There is no written confirmation by James that he is your birth father.'

My mind spinning, I called Amanda Platell and Jane Moore. They too voiced some doubts because of the timings. Then, I telephoned Caroline, the social worker who'd first showed me my adoption file, to ask her opinion on James Coffey. I reminded Caroline of her warning to me, that Margaret had seemingly gone to extraordinary lengths to make absolutely sure that she would never be found.

'I'm not convinced that James Coffey is my father,' I told her. My blunt statement hung in the air and there was a long silence at the other end of the telephone. 'It just appears to be all far too convenient,' I added. 'For instance, James Coffey seems to have died only a few weeks after I arrived in the orphanage. Yet Margaret never told the nuns for another two years. Frankly, it simply doesn't make any sense. Do you think that he's my father?' At last, the social worker said, 'I would advise you to treat the claim with scepticism.' Her low, quiet voice sounded concerned as she added, 'If you do manage to locate your birth mother, you might find that she will be evasive on the issue.'

Putting down the phone, I leaned back in my comfortable armchair and thought long and hard about the matter. So, was my birth father the love of her life? Did she have such strong feelings for him

CHAPTER SIX

that she was prepared to move heaven and earth to prevent anyone finding out about their love affair?

My questions seemed endless, which is why I decided, while Jane Moore was still hard at work trying to overcome the many 'roadblocks' and 'red herrings' that Margaret had put up so long ago – and which were still proving to be remarkably difficult to overcome – that I would do my best to try to track down James Coffey. This wouldn't be an easy task, considering that the man was meant to have died nearly fifty years ago. But I was determined to uncover who he was, what had happened to him and if he had any living family. Above all, I wanted to discover if he really could be my birth father.

Having applied for James Coffey's death certificate, which I knew would take some time to arrive, I looked up the Standard Motor Company. As I leafed through a reference book, I couldn't help thinking how odd it was that James had worked in a car factory, just as my own adopted dad had done for almost forty years. I discovered that the Standard Motor Company was formed in Coventry in 1903, while in 1945 Triumph was added to the production line, and it wasn't until 1959 that the company became Standard Triumph.

All of this brought back memories of when I was sixteen and rebelling against my parents by deciding not to stay on and do A-levels – which I needed if I was to pursue my dream of becoming a journalist. So, I decided to apply for various jobs and was eventually offered an engineering apprenticeship at British Leyland, the factory where my father, George, worked on the assembly line. Needless to say, I was aghast at the thought of eventually becoming an engineer. Especially as I couldn't have been less interested in the job. In fact, I'd been hoping for a marketing apprenticeship, which would have been far more what I was looking for. But unfortunately, in a sign of the many difficulties that Leyland were then undergoing, I learned that the company had recently abolished the marketing apprenticeships. Luckily, I had by then come to my senses, returning to school a slightly older and much wiser lad, intent on obtaining the necessary qualifications required to become a newspaper reporter.

However, not wanting to waste any time while waiting for the death certificate, and impatient to track down James Coffey, I decided to take a shortcut. As a journalist and member of the British Newspaper Archive, I knew it wouldn't take long to find a press cutting of his death in a road accident in April 1961. And indeed, I found it within a matter of minutes. The article reporting James Coffey's death had appeared in the *Birmingham Post*, bizarrely the very same newspaper I'd worked for at the beginning of my career.

The report from Monday 17 April 1961 was headlined, 'Girl of four died' and it began with: 'A four year old girl and an Irishman died in road accidents in Birmingham during the weekend.' First describing the death of the little girl, the report continued, 'The other death occurred on Saturday, when a van in collision with a lorry, swerved across High Street, Erdington and crashed into a shop front. One of the three men standing by the shop was a Mr James Coffey, aged 37, of Hunton Road, Erdington. He was killed instantly.'

It was the sort of report I had written time and again when I worked for local newspapers. I would often have to go to the dead person's home to try to borrow a photograph. We used to call it the 'death knock', which often proved highly disturbing for both reporters and the grieving families. In this case, there were no photos of the four-year-old girl or James Coffey.

CHAPTER SIX

The report continued, 'A second man, Mr Michael Kilmartin, aged 30, received a broken leg. The third man, Mr Brian Mahoney, aged 27, of Cecil Road, Erdington, was unhurt. The van driver, Mr Charlie Keith Lewis, aged 21, of Pilkington Avenue, Sutton Coldfield, and his sister Miss Margaret Lewis, a passenger, were taken to hospital.' This was obviously yet another extraordinary twist in the tale of Patrick Connolly's first few years. As I read the report again, I wondered if any of the other people involved in the road accident might still be alive. And if so, would they be prepared to talk to me?

By now I was keenly on the hunt and additional research revealed that according to both the telephone directory and a local electoral register, there were a number of Kilmartins still living in Birmingham. So, this would be the obvious place to begin my enquires. I decided to call the first name on the list, who, according to telephone records, was a Mr M. Kilmartin, the same initial as the man who'd sustained the leg injury in the accident. However, just to make sure I was along the right lines, I cross-referenced his address in the electoral register. As I'd hoped, he was named as a Michael Kilmartin, exactly the same name as the man in the crash. It was almost too much to hope that after fifty years, Mr Kilmartin was still alive – he might well have had a son or grandson bearing the same name.

With all my fingers crossed, I called the number.

'Hallo,' said a male voice.

'Hallo,' I responded. 'My name is Andrew Pierce. I'm sorry to disturb you, but I'm researching my family tree. So, I wonder if you can help me? I'm trying to locate a Mr Michael Kilmartin who was involved in a road traffic accident in Birmingham, during which a man called James Coffey was killed. It all took place a very long time ago. In 1961.' There was a long silence at the other end of the phone. 'Mr Kilmartin?' I said. 'Are you still there? Can you possibly help me?'

After another long pause, the man replied slowly and deliberately. 'Yes. I can help you… I can help you. I was standing next to Jimmy when he was killed.'

I was utterly flabbergasted. Not only to find that Michael Kilmartin was a well-preserved 87-year-old but also that he had immediately recalled the name of James Coffey, although it was now almost sixty years since his death. But would you ever really be able to forget the name of the man who had died when he was mown down by a van while standing next to you? Especially if you'd known him? However, as I was about to discover, it seemed that Mr Kilmartin knew James Coffey very well. In fact, he was happy to explain the circumstances that led up to the accident.

'First of all, everyone knew him as "Jimmy" – not James,' he told me, after which he explained that the building in Erdington high street which he, Jimmy and the other man were standing near when the accident happened was a popular baker's shop. 'Luckily, as it turned out, they hadn't yet opened their doors to the public. So, we were standing in the high street early that Saturday morning and waiting, as usual, for the van to pick us up. To take us to work,' he added. 'We were working on a housing site.'

I was confused. 'Hang on a moment,' I said, thinking I must have got it wrong, after all. 'I thought that James Coffey was working as an engineer for the Standard Motor Car Company at the time of his death?' Which was what Margaret had told Nazareth House, when providing them with the name of her future husband and his occupation.

'Oh, no. No. He was a building labourer, just like me,' Mr Kilmartin

CHAPTER SIX

said firmly. 'We'd worked together for two or three years. Jimmy was a nice enough bloke. He came from Galway, the same part of Ireland as me. We both came over to England in the 1950s, looking for work.'

He explained that the three men were on Erdington high street, waiting at their usual pick-up point for that particular job. It was the same spot they'd used for the other jobs they'd carried out over the past two or three years.

'I looked up when I heard the crash, as the van and lorry collided,' Mr Kilmartin continued. 'The van then swerved across the road. Straight at us. It all happened so fast. Jimmy went down. I knew it was bad. The van ended up going through the shop's window,' he added, his words spilling out rapidly as he recalled the details of that cataclysmic day.

'I had a serious arm injury. Not a "broken leg" as the newspaper said. But the other lad, standing with Jimmy and myself, wasn't hurt at all,' he said. 'People came running across to see if they could help. I thought it might be serious for Jimmy as he wasn't saying anything. He was totally silent. I didn't know it at the time, of course, but I remember being told later, by a nurse at the hospital, that Jimmy was already dead.' Mr Kilmartin told me that he himself was taken to the local hospital and kept there for two weeks. Interestingly, it was the same hospital where Margaret had worked as a nurse.

That first, bombshell telephone conversation with Mr Kilmartin stiffened my resolve to uncover all I could about Jimmy Coffey's death: the man who may – or may not – have been my father. I felt like I needed to find out if the van driver and passenger might also still be alive. Of course I knew that I was unlikely to get lucky twice. Yet, once again, I decided to use the basic journalistic techniques I'd learned so long ago, especially as, in this case – where so many years had passed since the tragic incident – it made sense to approach the youngest and most likely survivor first.

So, I decided to start with Margaret Lewis, who was listed as the 21-year-old passenger in the van's front seat. I combed through marriage records, searching for a girl with the same name and who was approximately the same age in the Sutton Coldfield area. Eventually, I came across a Margaret Lewis, who was now a Mrs Margaret Rawlings. It seemed that she still lived in the area and her age appeared to be about right, so I decided she might fit the bill.

Taking a deep breath, I called her number. The phone was answered quickly and I can recall giving thanks to my guardian angel for the person I was calling having a landline phone, particularly when so many of my friends, with the advent of mobile phones, were busy throwing their old, bulky telephones away. I explained to the voice on the other end of the line that I was looking for the sister of a Charlie Lewis, who had lived in Sutton Coldfield many years ago.

'No', said the female voice at the other end of the line. 'No. I'm sorry, but I can't help you.'

I was crushed. I'd had a really strong feeling that this was the right woman. Quickly, I decided to explain exactly why I was calling, specifically outlining to Mrs Rawlings that I was trying to locate either the driver or passenger who'd been in the van that was involved in a collision in 1961, in Erdington high street. A dreadful accident, which had resulted in a pedestrian being killed.

I hadn't expected what came next. After a short silence – by now I was getting used to them – the woman exclaimed, 'But that's me! I was in the front seat with my brother.' I was confused. She'd just told me that her brother wasn't Charlie Lewis. As if reading my

CHAPTER SIX

mind, Mrs Rawlings's voice interrupted my thoughts. 'I'm sorry, but what did you say the driver was called?'

'Charlie,' I answered quickly. 'Charlie Keith Lewis.'

'Oh, well – there you are!' she said. 'That explains it. You see, no one ever called my brother "Charlie". He was always known as "Keith". He was driving the van. I was sitting next to him. It was really awful.'

What were the odds of this? The first two people I had called on my list were exactly the people I was looking for from that horrific accident. Both of them, as it turned out, with vivid memories of what had happened. I asked Mrs Rawlings if she would mind if I questioned her about the accident, as I was conscious it might bring back some uncomfortable, perhaps horrific, memories.

'No,' she said. 'I don't mind at all. It was a very long time ago.' So I asked her to describe what had happened.

'Well… we were travelling up Erdington high street. My brother was taking me to work. I do remember that I was smartly dressed,' she added. 'Because after work I was going to the shops to choose an outfit for his twenty-first birthday party. Knowing me, I was probably chatting away to my brother when I suddenly saw the lorry coming straight at us from the left. I can remember yelling, "Keith! He's not stopping. Keith! Keith… He's not stopping!"'

Her voice rose instinctively as she relived the old memories. 'Seconds later, there was a loud "Bang!" as the lorry collided with our van, which immediately caused us to swerve across the road.'

Mrs Rawlings said that the van had ended up lodged in the Wimbush bakery, a popular local store. Mercifully, as she pointed out, it wasn't yet open, because otherwise the death toll could have been much higher.

'I didn't see them. But the police told me afterwards that there were three men sheltering from the rain in the doorway of the shop,' she added, before explaining that as the van had smashed into the shop, she'd been catapulted through the front windscreen. 'It was, of course, long before the advent of seat belts. Although, I learned later that if I hadn't gone through the windscreen, I might have lost my legs. I'm told that I ended up lying on the pavement. But I must have been knocked out. Because the next thing I knew, I was waking up in Birmingham General Hospital. Luckily, Keith wasn't injured at all.'

Remarkably, as it turned out, she escaped with just cuts and bruises and was discharged from hospital five days later. A week after my conversation with Mrs Rawlings, she returned to Erdington high street to familiarise herself with the scene of the accident. Afterwards she told me, 'It was quite extraordinary how little the high street and the shops had changed. Also how, even after all these years, everything about the accident suddenly came flashing back into my mind. I remembered, almost vividly, how we were driving past the big church on the high street when I first saw the lorry. And yelling a warning out to Keith, when I suddenly realised the lorry wasn't stopping. Then, so swiftly – and it's the last thing I can recall – it felt like we were spinning at top speed towards the bakery. Which, by the way, is long gone and has been replaced by a pharmacy.'

I told her that the man who had been killed, Jimmy Coffey, had never suffered. Having just received his death certificate and the coroner's report, I was able to reassure her that the coroner had recorded that he had died instantly. So, poor Jimmy was clearly dead on arrival at the hospital.

'Thank you so much for telling me that. It really is a huge comfort,'

CHAPTER SIX

she said, before explaining that her brother Keith was now living in Scotland and suffering from early-onset Alzheimer's. 'I know that he will take great comfort in knowing that the poor man never suffered any pain too. Because it truly was a genuine accident.'

Since that conversation with Mrs Rawlings, I've also been back to Birmingham and retraced Jimmy Coffey's steps on Erdington high street. I stood by the church where the lorry emerged, before suddenly colliding with the white van driven by Keith Lewis, with his sister by his side, who was excitedly making plans for his twenty-first birthday. I gazed across the road at the pharmacy, which was once the bakery, and tried to picture Jimmy Coffey on that bleak early Saturday morning. One moment he was sheltering from the rain and chatting to his mates, the next, his life was suddenly over.

Did he know anything about it before he hit the ground, his body shattered by horrendous injuries? What were his last thoughts? I like to think that an image of Margaret flashed through his mind, or maybe his parents and his home in Ireland.

My conversations with Mr Kilmartin and Mrs Rawlings were important. I now wanted to know far more about James Coffey – even though, when I started this journey, I'd only been interested in finding my birth mother and telling her she had no need to worry about the son she'd given up for adoption. But now, after listening to two witnesses to his death, I felt a strong obligation to discover exactly what sort of man Jimmy Coffey had been.

When his death certificate arrived from the General Register Office, the certificate itself (which cost £25) made for grim reading. The cause of death was described as 'shock and haemorrhage due to multiple injuries including fractured pelvis, ribs and legs, with ruptured spleen and kidney'. At the inquest, held on 12 May 1961, the coroner for Birmingham, George Billingham, said, 'He was dead on arrival at Birmingham General Hospital,' and recorded a verdict of 'Death by Misadventure'.

The death certificate also threw up two interesting items. Facts which directly contradicted what Margaret had told Nazareth House all those years ago. It said, 'James Coffey, of 57 Hunton Road, Erdington, was a pipe layer.' While Margaret, in her submission to the Clifton Catholic Rescue Society – written just five weeks *before* James Coffey's death – said that he was an engineer with the Standard Motor Company and lived in Slade Road.

I went online and Googled Slade Road. It is a third of a mile from Hunton Road, the address given in the death certificate as his home. Both addresses skirted Erdington high street, where he died. Today, both houses are private homes. So why the discrepancy? Did Jimmy Coffey really move from Slade Road to Hunton Road in the five weeks after Margaret took me to Nazareth House? While it is possible that he did so, I do wonder if she was trying to avoid any mail being sent from Nazareth House to Jimmy's correct lodgings in Hunton Road. And why the fib about his occupation? Was she a bit of a snob at heart? Or was Jimmy the one who'd lied about his job? Maybe trying to impress his girlfriend…? On the other hand, maybe both his wrong address and false occupation would prove to be yet more inventions or possible 'red herrings', designed by Margaret to deter anyone from discovering the truth about my real birth father? Whatever the truth, the death certificate spurred me on to keep digging and, hopefully, to discover as much as I could about James Coffey.

I have decided to leave one of the final and most interesting parts of my many conversations with Mr Kilmartin until the end of this chapter. On one occasion he was telling me how he'd been kept in hospital due to his severe and painful injuries for over two

CHAPTER SIX

weeks. He was adamant that he'd suffered a compound fracture of the arm. Definitely not a mere broken leg as the *Birmingham Post* had reported. He also told me that when he eventually came out of hospital, he was upset to discover that he couldn't attend the funeral of his good friend, Jimmy Coffey, because it had already taken place.

When I wondered aloud if he knew how Margaret Connolly had coped in the aftermath of Jimmy's death, he immediately replied, 'I'm sorry. I don't know who you are talking about. Who is Margaret Connolly?'

'She was Jimmy Coffey's girlfriend,' I replied. He was going to marry her in July.' There was another long pause at the other end of the telephone.

'Well! It's news to me that he had a serious girlfriend,' Mr Kilmartin said firmly. 'I worked with him for the best part of three years. He definitely never mentioned anyone by that name.'

I took a deep breath and asked, 'Did he ever mention the fact he was going to be a dad? And that he now had a baby – a newborn son – with his girlfriend, Margaret Connolly?'

Mr Kilmartin chuckled out loud. 'A baby...? A son...? A girlfriend...?' He gave another short bark of laughter. 'He never mentioned any of that. Believe me, I worked closely with Jimmy for three years, so I think he'd have told me if he was going to be a dad. And, of course, I reckon that he'd also have told me all about it, when he really *was* the father of a newborn son. Don't you?'

CHAPTER SEVEN

Maybe it wasn't only Jimmy Coffey's work mates who knew nothing about his private life? Possibly, even his family were unaware of the fact that only four weeks before he was killed, he'd become a father for the first time? Mr Kilmartin's views on his good friend Jimmy Coffey had been very convincing, especially when it came to Jimmy's romantic life and whether he had become a father to a baby boy.

But perhaps Jimmy was just shy and retiring? A man who didn't like talking about his private life? Although, on the whole, I tended to think that was unlikely. As for becoming a father for the first time…? Surely, he would have wanted to go to the local pub, to wet the baby's head with his work colleagues? Or to at least celebrate the news with his family and friends?

Of course, there was still a huge stigma attached to illegitimacy in Britain in 1961, and even more so in the deeply rural communities of southern Ireland. In general, the blame, and most certainly the shame, seemed to be mainly borne by the girls. But it never quite seemed to stick to the men who'd got the girls into trouble in the first place. And, of course, there was the possibility that in Jimmy's case, he might have been giving his parents their first grandchild.

If so, there was only one way to find out. I would have to track down Jimmy Coffey's family. This was not likely to be an easy task. Primarily because the only information I possessed was that he'd originally come to Britain from Galway. Mr Kilmartin had also told me that he and Jimmy had both been part of the exodus of almost half a million people who'd left their homes in Ireland in the 1950s, seeking a new life in Britain or the United States.

I did, however, have one or two clues to help me with my search. Starting with the address on Jimmy Coffey's death certificate: 57 Hunton Road, Erdington. But, just to complicate matters, it was a completely different address to the one Margaret had supplied when she'd signed the adoption agreement with the Clifton Rescue Society, allowing Nazareth House to take me from her. The address she'd given then was 227 Slade Road, which, I discovered, was only about ten minutes' walk from Hunton Road.

I looked up both properties on a map and also the electoral register, to see if there were any members of the Coffey family living at either home. It was a long shot, but I was thinking of my own mother. She had lived in the same house in Swindon for fifty-nine years. It was her first home with my dad and also her last. But, all these years later, there was no one with the right surname living in either Hunton Road or Slade Road. Although, after the passage of so many years, I was not surprised.

So, it was back to the telephone directory. And almost straight away – bingo! I found there were about a dozen or so people by the name of Coffey listed in the directory, so I cross-referenced them again with the electoral register at the reference library in Birmingham. This all meant going back many years. It was painstaking work, but it did produce some rich dividends, as I managed to make

CHAPTER SEVEN

a list of three or four families – all of whom appeared to have been living in the same house for at least twenty years.

At this stage of my research, I didn't know how many brothers and sisters Jimmy might have had. But I hoped that if he came from a typical Irish Catholic family of that time, there was a good chance he was unlikely to have been an only child. And, if he did have siblings, it was possible that some or all of them might also have crossed the Irish Sea to England in the hope of gaining employment.

Before I tried the first Coffey on the list in my trusty reporter's notepad, I tried to put myself in Jimmy's shoes. If he really *was* my birth father, might he have been a somewhat reluctant father? Which might explain his reticence with his fellow labourers? Moreover, did he *really* plan to marry Margaret in July 1961? Or was he reluctant to give up his bachelor lifestyle? Because, even with absolutely no evidence, I somehow felt that Jimmy wasn't exactly the marrying kind. But, even so, he would surely have felt a moral responsibility to support Margaret financially? Yet, if he'd felt any responsibility for my birth, why was his name so conspicuously absent from the agreement that Margaret had signed with the Clifton Catholic Rescue Society? Especially the part where she stated, quite clearly, that she would be the only one contributing to the cost of my board and lodgings. It was all very strange.

There seemed to be no easy answer as to exactly why Jimmy Coffey hadn't agreed to pay the minimal sums required to support his child. Maybe he was paying Margaret privately? Possibly with cash? And if so, maybe that was how she'd managed to make ends meet on her small nurse's salary?

I also couldn't exclude the possibility of my birth being the product of a brief fling, even a one-night stand with some unknown man. Maybe Margaret had found herself embroiled with a married man, who had no intention of leaving his wife? But, overall, I found those possibilities highly unlikely. I honestly couldn't imagine that Margaret — a qualified nurse when she fell pregnant with me — would have got into trouble after a boozy night at a pub or ended up in the bed of a relative stranger.

Of course, I could have been entirely wrong. But I was beginning to form an image of my mother, that of a devout Roman Catholic and God-fearing woman. Obviously there were times when Margaret had been somewhat 'economical with the truth'. But despite being responsible for several misleading, carefully constructed and highly evasive statements, so far, I hadn't encountered her deliberately committing herself to any outright lies.

I reminded myself that my friend Jane Moore was still hard at work on my behalf. And I held on to the fact that the main focus of her current efforts was to untangle the many 'dead ends' and copious evasive tactics all employed years ago by my birth mother. Because there could now be no doubt that, for whatever reason, Margaret Connolly had set out all those years ago with just one aim in mind: preventing anyone from ever finding her.

But, when trying to decipher Margaret's motives, I couldn't see how a one-night stand fitted in with her decisive statement to the nuns at Nazareth House, whereby she promised that within a few months, she was going to be married to her new son's father. I also saw, from the report given to me by Caroline, the social worker, that when I was first placed in Nazareth House, in March 1961, Margaret even told the nuns the proposed date of my departure. It was intended to be four months later, in July 1961.

Rereading the passage in the report which was written at the

CHAPTER SEVEN

time of my arrival in the orphanage, a member of staff had written, '[The] mother is an SRN nurse who has a three months' work contract to finish. She is getting married in July – and will then withdraw the child (we hope!).' And I found myself believing that when she made that statement to the nuns, Margaret truly meant what she was saying.

However, I did have one other nagging doubt. If she was in a loving relationship with Jimmy Coffey, why on earth would she want to put me in an orphanage? Would it have been far too scandalous for her and her new baby to move in with him? And if so, how was she planning to explain the presence of a baby boy who would be nearly six months old on the date she planned to marry Jimmy Coffey in July 1961? Perhaps she was going to say that she'd adopted me? Although I really can't see the nuns agreeing to such a ridiculous story.

Yet, speculating about Margaret and Jimmy's relationship – whether it had really existed or not – wasn't going to get me anywhere. What I really needed were some hard facts, which, in turn, meant contacting members of the large Coffey family, as there were quite a few in the phone book. Primarily, of course, to see if by any remote chance they were related to Jimmy. Or, as was more likely, if they knew of someone who was.

The first person I called was a Philomena Coffey. A wonderful name, which reminded me of the film *Philomena*, starring Dame Judi Dench. Portraying the real-life story of a woman's heartbreaking search for the son she'd given up while living in a mother and baby home in southern Ireland, Dame Judi had been nominated for a well-deserved Oscar. When I watched the film in the cinema, I thought I'd have to leave because I was crying so much, particularly when her son is taken away by wealthy adopters while Philomena is in the chapel, oblivious to what is happening to her little boy and given no chance to say goodbye to him. It was so cruel.

I took a deep breath as I dialled the number. The telephone was answered quickly and I explained why I was calling. The usual long pause followed, but I was used to those now. And then a female voice called out, 'Quick, quick!' But, as I was about to repeat my question, it became obvious that she wasn't speaking to me. 'Quick! Come over here. Come to the telephone.'

A much younger voice came on the line. I explained again that I was researching my family tree and, while doing so, I'd come across a James or Jimmy Coffey – who was killed in a road accident in April 1961, which was why I was trying to track down his living relatives. I was stunned when the unknown voice replied, 'Oh, yes. He's my uncle.'

Before I responded, a thought flashed across my brain: *Well! If Jimmy turns out to be my father, this woman must be my first cousin, which would mean that she's the very first blood relative I've ever spoken to.*

Then I told her my name and she happily chatted about her family, imparting important information, such as the fact that the family were indeed from Galway – just as Mr Kilmartin had told me. She also revealed that James Coffey was the eldest of six children. He had a twin brother, Eddie, but they were definitely not identical twins, Jimmy being 5ft 6in. while Eddie was 5ft 9in. The other four children were: Patrick; Robert, known as Bob; a sister, Kathleen, and the youngest son, Tommy, who was still alive and living in Ireland. Moreover, it seemed that all the children had moved to England for work in the 1950s, leaving their parents back in Ireland. Their parents were Edward Coffey, always known as Eddie or Big Ned, who was seventy-seven when he died, and his wife, Agnes, who'd been the matriarch and had died before her husband, aged seventy-two.

I plucked up enough courage to say that James, or, as the family called him, Jimmy, had been named in official papers as my father, principally by my birth mother, who had given me up for adoption. I realised that I'd taken a chance, wondering if the telephone might be slammed down in anger at that point. But not a bit of it. In fact, she couldn't have been more helpful.

'I'm Rhona. Patrick's daughter. So, if Uncle Jimmy really is your dad, I want to do everything I can to help you.' *Another Patrick*, I thought to myself as Rhona continued: 'After all, you have a right to know. I mean... I would definitely want to know if I was in your shoes,' she said firmly. 'But to be honest, I have to say I've never heard that Uncle Jimmy had a son. Or that he was going to get married. But, on the other hand, it's not surprising that I don't know very much about him, since he died before I was born. However, I'll talk to my family in Ireland. Jimmy was my dad's brother. So, you've definitely got the right part of the Coffey family. Because I've always known all about my uncle being killed outside a shop, here in Birmingham. It seems that he was run over by a van.'

Rhona was as good as her word. Within twenty-four hours I was on the telephone and speaking to Elaine, who was also potentially a first cousin and living in Ireland. Her father, Tommy, was the youngest of the six Coffey children; still very much alive and living in Limerick. Like Rhona, Elaine radiated a lovely, natural Irish charm and did everything she could to help. But having spoken to her father, she confirmed what I'd suspected. No one in the family knew that Jimmy was apparently about to get married. Moreover, they knew nothing about him fathering a little boy who was in a children's home. But, of course, as Elaine pointed out, in 1961 few people had telephones and it seemed that Jimmy wasn't the sort to write letters. More importantly, Elaine also told me that she'd mentioned Margaret Connolly to her father, Tommy. But the name had meant nothing to him.

From the Coffey cousins, I learned that the Coffey family had all been born and brought up in a little stone house with a galvanised roof. It was surrounded by a small farm, which contained some cattle and not much else, at Rockhill, Ballinamore, which is about forty-five minutes from Knock Airport. The farm would never have been able to generate enough income to sustain six fully grown adults, which is why all the children had moved to England. It also seemed that Jimmy's twin brother, Eddie, had eventually moved back to Ireland in the 1970s, as did his youngest brother, Tommy.

I thought that the name of Ballinamore sounded familiar, and I soon remembered why. It was because Ballinamore, the gateway to the spectacular scenery of northwest Ireland, has long been associated with the disappearance of Shergar, arguably the most famous racehorse ever to come out of Europe. The record-breaking Epsom Derby winner, who is still remembered because of his never-surpassed ten-length win in the 1981 race, was kidnapped by the IRA from his stable in County Kildare in 1983. A BBC documentary claimed that the horse was shot by the IRA after it broke a leg and is buried in a bog in a small rural area called Aughnasheelin, not far from Ballinamore.

While the family could shed no light on Jimmy Coffey's romantic liaisons, they certainly knew that he was a bit of a gambler. 'He was hugely into horses,' Rhona told me. 'He was in the bookies most days. My dad always said Jimmy had probably been in the bookies just before he died.'

So, did Jimmy Coffey have a gambling problem? And was that

CHAPTER SEVEN

the reason that Margaret was offered no financial help, particularly with the Nazareth House bill for my expenses? If so, and if Jimmy really was my father, I'd luckily not inherited his gambling trait. A wager on the Grand National, the Cheltenham Gold Cup or the size of a majority in a general election is about the limit of my largesse with the bookies. Even when I went to Las Vegas a couple of years ago I realised, as I was boarding the plane to return home, that I hadn't spent a dollar on a bet. Not even in the world's capital of casinos.

Both Elaine and Rhona promised to go through their family photo albums to see if they could find any snaps of Jimmy. I was excited by the idea that I might actually get to see the man who Margaret had claimed was my father. I didn't have to wait long for the pictures to arrive. My phone made regular pinging sounds as a series of black-and-white photos landed in it. Many of them were taken in Ireland and it was clear that the farm on which Jimmy grew up was very basic. There was a vague likeness between me and him, but I've never felt entirely sure, one way or the other.

I also showed the photos of Jimmy to some close friends. They, too, had their doubts. 'It could be that man was your birth dad,' one friend told me. 'But, to be honest, it could just as easily be a photograph of someone else.' Having studied the photographs, I could see similarities between me and some of the Coffey clan, even if I could find few with Jimmy. In return, I dispatched a couple of my own photographs to Rhona, to see if the family thought I might be part of their clan.

The response was a surprise. 'You must be joking!' Rhona texted back.

I was confused. 'Joking…? About what?'

'Oh, come on!' Rhona quickly replied. 'I watch you on television every morning. I can't believe you might be a member of our family. Haven't you done well?' So, that was my cover blown – good and proper!

Eventually, I decided I had to go back to Birmingham on a specific mission. As it happens, I visit the city fairly regularly, mainly to see old friends from when I worked on the *Birmingham Post & Mail*. And also to report on the Tory and Labour Party conferences, which have been taking place there over the past few years. But, just like when I was working there as a journalist, I never realised on my numerous trips to party conferences that many of my possible birth family might be living just a ten-minute cab ride from the conference centre. That I could, in fact, have been meeting them, while also making small talk with Prime Ministers David Cameron, Theresa May and Boris Johnson, as well as other senior members of the Cabinet. Likewise, when Labour was in town, I would have been busy chatting away to members of the shadow Cabinet. However, this journey was going to be different. I knew that I must return to Birmingham, specifically to track down the grave of the man who could be my father, Jimmy Coffey.

There is a website for almost everything these days, and I duly found Jimmy's headstone on findagrave.com. It appeared that he was buried in Oscott cemetery in the upmarket Sutton Coldfield district of Birmingham, as Roman Catholic tradition had dictated at the time – the Vatican had only permitted cremations to occur from 1968. So, it seems that this cemetery has been the final resting place for the city's Roman Catholics since 1939, the year Britain declared war on Nazi Germany. The actual cemetery itself is attached to St Mary's College, which is one of the last three working seminaries for the training and ordination of priests in England and Wales.

CHAPTER SEVEN

However, before going to the cemetery to find his grave, I decided to take a detour via the last two home addresses that had been listed for Jimmy Coffey. So, after arriving at New Street station, I first took a taxi to the Hunton Road address in Erdington, which sixty years ago would have been a much sought-after street in which to live.

Knocking on the door of number 57, I quickly checked my notes to make sure that this was, according to his death certificate, the place where Jimmy was living until his accident. Eventually, a man answered my knock and opened the door, but even though he was hard of hearing, it was obvious he had never heard of the name 'Coffey'. Likewise with the neighbours. I then walked the short distance to 227 Slade Road, which Margaret had clearly stated was Jimmy Coffey's final address. Yet again, the name meant nothing to the current occupiers or to their neighbours.

So, the next stop was the Roman Catholic Church of St Mary and St John in Gravelly Hill. It is the church where, traditionally, Jimmy's coffin would have been received the night before his funeral and was apparently the venue for various family members' funerals. After talking to her relatives, Rhona confirmed that it was almost certain that there would have been a full mass at the church for Jimmy's funeral. Back in 1961, the congregation was predominantly Irish. But on my visit, in a clear sign of how Britain's Catholic congregation has changed, the parish priest was Indian. Indeed, when I visited the church, a wedding for a young couple from Goa was taking place.

Following my detour to Jimmy's final address, it was only a short drive to Oscott cemetery to visit his grave. I'd been told that over the years family members occasionally visited the cemetery to put flowers on his grave. Rhona said that they had often found someone had been there before them as, frequently, there were fresh-cut flowers there. They had never discovered who put them there. Could it have been Margaret? Possibly. But that would mean she was still living in the area, which seemed unlikely. If she had eventually married another local man, she could have done so. If she *had* left the area, however, a regular journey to leave flowers on Jimmy Coffey's grave seemed very unlikely.

From talking to Rhona and Elaine, I learned that the headstone and plot were paid for by Jimmy's twin brother, Eddie, and Tommy, the youngest Coffey sibling. But it appeared that their parents, Agnes and Eddie, never travelled to England for the funeral, probably because they were both fairly elderly by then and they would not have been able to afford the fare.

If Margaret had attended the funeral, none of the remaining family I spoke to could recall any mention of her presence. So, why – if she was not just his girlfriend, but by then the mother of his child – wasn't she there? 'Frankly, we're all mystified and a bit shocked,' Rhona said. 'I don't think Jimmy told anyone he had a son. We obviously weren't a close family at times. After all, there was a seventeen-year age gap between Jimmy and his youngest brother, Tommy. But I'm told that Jimmy was best man at his twin Eddie's wedding in Erdington. So I just don't understand why no one knew about your birth mother.'

If Jimmy was close to his twin brother, then I wondered if he would have confided in him. 'Well… Eddie was very secretive, so, if he did know about you and your mother, he never told a soul,' Rhona said, adding that as far as she was aware, the first grandchild in the family was Alan, Jimmy's sister Kathleen's baby. She had two children out of wedlock in the 1950s that were both put up for adoption.

CHAPTER SEVEN

It's extraordinary that by 1961 a possible third Coffey child, then in Nazareth House, was also on the road to being adopted.

So, the answer to why Margaret Connolly attended neither the funeral nor the burial can be narrowed down to two possible explanations. The first is that, apart from claiming Jimmy Coffey as my birth father on an official document, she had virtually no contact with him and his family, either before or after his death. Unfortunately, I can think of no sensible reason or excuse to explain why Margaret would tell what appear to be blatant fibs, not only to the Clifton Rescue Society but also to the nuns at Nazareth House.

The second explanation is, I fear, mere speculation. It could have been that she was out of contact with Coffey, who had done a runner when he knew he was the father of her unborn child. The address on his death certificate, printed only weeks after I moved into the orphanage, was different to the one she gave the adoption society. If she had lost contact with him, she not only would never have known he was dead but would have known nothing about the funeral.

Until I was able to meet and talk to my birth mother in person, it was almost impossible to answer any of the numerous questions that kept flooding into my mind. To me, once the poor man was dead, it seemed almost cruel of her to have kept the birth of her child a total secret from Jimmy's family. They might not have been well-off, but she was clearly capable of earning her own living and I'm sure that they, plus his twin brother, would have done their best to provide even a small amount of extra financial support, especially as her child was all they'd have left to remind them of him.

After eventually finding Jimmy's grave, I immediately noticed that even after all these years, it was still very well looked after. The inscription on the headstone was a touching and very simple one:

PRAY FOR THE SOUL OF JAMES COFFEY WHO DIED 15TH APRIL 1961
RIP

I stood in front of his grave for some time, thinking about the unproductive day I'd just spent in his home town. I had thoroughly enjoyed my contact with the various members of the Coffey family, but however much I would welcome the discovery that I was indeed related to them, I still didn't feel any closer to Jimmy himself. Despite Rhona and Elaine's stories and other family recollections, I remained as firmly in the dark about my possible birth father as I was some weeks ago when first starting this quest to find him.

Immersed in my rather depressing thoughts, I was distracted by a rough gust of autumnal wind sweeping through the cemetery. Quickly glancing down at my watch, I realised that it was time I left to catch the train back home to London. And so, following the request on his headstone, I offered up a prayer for Jimmy's soul and placed a red rose on his grave.

CHAPTER EIGHT

After a long day visiting various people and places in Birmingham, I was feeling quite depressed at not having solved so many of the difficult and frustrating puzzles concerning Jimmy Coffey. So far, it looked like I'd totally failed to find any concrete evidence of his possible relationship with Margaret Connolly. Frankly, the chances of Jimmy turning out to be my birth father now seemed more unlikely than ever.

As the train began to slow down on its approach into Euston station, I decided to cast aside all my feelings of doom and gloom, concentrating instead on looking forward to getting back home to my flat and taking a reviving shower before having dinner with my friend Amanda Platell.

It would be good to see Amanda who, together with Jane Moore, had been such a staunch friend throughout my search for my birth mother. Maybe she might be able to make some sense of what I'd learned today in Birmingham? Or rather, why I had utterly failed to discover any solid evidence of a link between Margaret and Jimmy Coffey?

As I have already mentioned, the strong link between myself, Amanda and Jane has always been the world of journalism. Born in Australia, Amanda Platell followed her father into journalism, working on several newspapers before deciding to backpack around the world and ending up in London.

Originally, she freelanced for various papers, including *The Observer* and the *Sunday Express*, with the idea of earning enough money to return home. But she quickly made a name for herself, in both journalism and politics, and somehow never quite found the time or inclination to go back. Amanda and I first got to know each other when she was briefly editor of the *Sunday Express*. After the *Express* she moved into politics, becoming the Conservative Party's head of media and press secretary to the then leader, William Hague. I saw a lot of her in my role as a political journalist and we have remained the closest of friends ever since.

So, as I set off that evening to her home, I was not only looking forward to dinner (she's a really great cook) but also to telling her all about my disappointing day in Birmingham. Not to 'whinge' or let off steam, of course, but because Amanda has such a breadth of vision and a very keen, enquiring mind. So, if I'd missed anything important or failed to ask the 'right' questions during my search for Jimmy, she was likely to spot it straight away.

However, little did I know that Jane Moore was beginning to think that – as much as she would hate to give up the search for Margaret Connolly – she was running out of leads and further ideas about how to track my birth mother down. In fact, even as I closed my front door and was on my way to see Amanda, she received a call from Jane.

• • •

At this point in my narrative, I'm turning the story of that momentous

CHAPTER EIGHT

evening over to Jane. I know that I can trust her, as a renowned journalist, to relate the highly dramatic turn of events far better in her own words than any I can muster.

Over the years, I have helped various friends to find loved ones – be that a biological parent or, in one case, the child they gave up for adoption. But, finding someone's mother is always a far greater challenge than locating a father; simply because, more often than not, the woman goes on to marry and changes her surname. On top of that, as in Andrew's case, I was looking for someone called 'Connolly', which, as confirmed by Wikipedia, is a 'very common Irish surname'.

But perhaps the most challenging aspect of all was that close inspection of the scant documentation available made it abundantly clear that many difficult problems lay ahead. Because Margaret Connolly, for whatever reason, had been extremely economical with even the very smallest of details that are normally the starting point for any journalistic investigation. That was my initial reaction and it was based purely on gut instinct and experience. However, I also felt that Margaret's various deceptions and misleading statements had far more to do with her fear that someone in her family might discover her secret – rather than not wanting to hear from her son Patrick later on in life.

The address she gave to Patrick's carers at the Nazareth House Orphanage was actually an NHS building and so was probably used as nurses' accommodation at the time. These days, it's home to a mental health unit called 'Forward Thinking Birmingham'. Plus, it later transpired that she had lied about her age – and not for the first time, as Andrew can testify – which certainly made it hard for anyone to track her down. Particularly as I had no date of birth, no idea where she lived or whether her surname had changed.

After weeks of cross-checking the birth dates of multiple Margaret Connollys who would have been within the right age range, as well as searching the marriage registers, I came up with several potential candidates living in multiple and geographically distant locations. But there were none that I could definitively say was the right woman.

When you're searching for people, as I have done many times, there's a certain amount of gut instinct involved, so that when all the small threads start to point to one particular person, it's very exciting to think that you might be nearing the end of the search. But, unfortunately, that didn't happen with Margaret. In truth, I feared that it was getting to the point where I might have to consider the possibility I'd hit a wall; that I was never going to be able to find her.

Which is why, with a heavy heart, I eventually phoned Amanda Platell – one of my closest friends and a mutual friend of myself and Andrew – to chat through the problem. She explained that he was actually on his way over to her house for dinner at that very moment. 'Well, in that case,' I said, 'perhaps we should start the process of letting him down gently…? Maybe you could tell him that we've spoken and perhaps – however hard it might be – he should start to consider the possibility that we might never be able to find Margaret.'

Amanda was obviously as upset as I was, particularly at the idea of having to be the harbinger of such bad news. So, after putting the phone down, I sat in silence for around half an hour, feeling so sorry for Andrew, who'd had such high hopes of tracking down his birth mother.

As the moments ticked by, I continued just staring down at my notes and praying that inspiration would strike.

Aside from the NHS address which was too general to be of

CHAPTER EIGHT

any use, I turned to look again at some of the many scraps of paper, forms, documents and letters in the thick file from Nazareth House. Glancing through Margaret's letters to the orphanage, I came across one that had become detached from the others and which I hadn't noticed before. But, I had no problem in recognising that the brief letter, with its slightly faded, almost illegible ink, was nevertheless in Margaret's distinctive handwriting.

In the letter, she mentioned a small village in Ireland, where she'd once lived for a short time. It was called Carrigeen. Margaret had also, I noted, included a reference to something about farming. So, in one last-ditch attempt to find a connection to her, I began to delve deep into the Google search engine – way past the first few 'hits'. Eventually, I stumbled across an obscure list of sheep traders in Ireland. And there – in the Carrigeen area – was the name Connolly alongside a phone number. Well! It definitely had to be worth a try!

So, while dialling the number, I mentally rehearsed a scenario I'd used before when carrying out some other searches. Basically, I would tell the person I was calling that my mother had once worked with the person in question and I was trying to organise some sort of reunion. It was a harmless deception. Because, if the person on the end of the phone had no connection to them, it was no problem. It simply resulted in a quick chat and a 'so sorry to bother you…'. But, if it should be a relative – distant or otherwise – the story wasn't likely to arouse any suspicion.

The man who answered the phone was charming and very receptive to my story, about the fact that my mother had worked as a nurse in Birmingham many years ago, which was why I was trying to locate her former colleague Margaret Connolly. Did he happen to know her? 'Oh, yes,' he said. 'I think that you're talking about my

Aunt Margaret.' She wasn't called Connolly any more, of course. It seemed that she had married a man called Patrick Lennon and they lived in Selly Oak, a suburb of Birmingham. But unfortunately, he didn't have a phone number to hand. I quickly assured him, however, that that was definitely no problem. My mother would be delighted to hear that her old friend was still hale and hearty and I politely ended the phone call so he wouldn't ask any difficult, in-depth questions.

I then rapidly located Margaret and Patrick Lennon on an old electoral register. I also checked a modern register, whereby it seemed that Patrick had possibly died as she was living by herself at the same home address. All of which led, very easily, to tracking down a landline phone number. Thankfully, she wasn't ex-directory and, being elderly, had clearly not taken to using a mobile phone.

So, while Andrew was still at Amanda's house, I was able to call him and say that, far from hitting a dead end as I had suspected just a couple of hours earlier, I had in fact found his mother and she was still alive. I remember him being utterly speechless – which was, believe me, a *very* rare occurrence!

• • •

Well! I have to admit that on that latter point Jane Moore was, as usual, quite right! Because, when I had arrived at Amanda's house, totally ignorant of the true situation, as outlined in Jane's phone call, Amanda immediately poured me a large gin and tonic and cut straight to the point.

First she outlined some of the problems that Jane had experienced, such as Margaret's very common names, as well as there

CHAPTER EIGHT

being no certainty about her birth date, which in turn would make it hard to discover if and when Margaret might have married and changed her name. 'Jane thinks that you may have to go to Ireland to search through the records,' Amanda told me. 'But it could be like looking for a needle in a haystack.'

I was obviously deeply disappointed. I had considered that Margaret might have suffered from advanced dementia and would thus be unable to tell me anything. I'd also factored in that she might already be dead, especially as she was older than I had originally anticipated. But it hadn't occurred to me that we might never be able to find her.

So... taking that phone call from Jane, who was now telling me that, despite all her difficulties, she had finally managed to track down my birth mother, left me feeling absolutely flabbergasted. No wonder I was totally speechless! My mouth – according to Amanda, who was doubled up with laughter – was opening and closing without any sound. Just like a stranded fish out of water.

After that conversation with Jane, I was on 'cloud nine' for days. But now came the tricky part. How best to approach Margaret? I agonised over the problem and listened to endless advice. Writing a letter seemed the easiest way, but what if someone else opened her mail? A grandchild, or an adult son or daughter, for instance?

As a journalist, I've made some difficult telephone calls in my time: a death in the family, questions about a criminal conviction or an MP caught up in a scandal. It's all been part of my job over the years. But, it would obviously be a tremendous shock for Margaret to hear the voice of an unknown, middle-aged man claiming to be her long-lost son. Particularly when the last time she'd seen me, I'd been a mere toddler. Besides which, on a practical level, what if she happened to be hard of hearing? What if she hung up on me? Or, far worse, what if someone else answered the phone? Clearly, any attempt to phone Margaret would be fraught with difficulty.

I even consulted the ever-helpful Camden social worker Caroline, who told me that the best approach was to go to Margaret's home. But, this should be done by a neutral person and most definitely not me in the first instance. Moreover, it was Caroline's opinion that the first approach to an elderly lady should be made by a woman.

My first thought was of my sister Shirley, who had privately volunteered to help me find my birth mother before. But I was reluctant to complicate her relationship with our mother should Betty ever find out. By then, however, I had realised that Amanda Platell would be the perfect person. Unsurprisingly, Amanda was her usual kind and generous self and agreed to help me in any way she could. With Jane Moore's help we now had Margaret's address in Birmingham, so all we needed was advice on exactly how to approach my birth mother.

Caroline the social worker gave us very clear and concise advice. 'Go to the house – but not you, Andrew – in person. All the same, you will need to be somewhere close by, just in case Margaret wants to see you. But, you need to be prepared for the fact that your birth mother may deny that she's your mother. And also, I'm sorry to say, might express a wish to never see you, or certainly not straight away. But my strong advice is that your friend, who was with you when you first opened the file in our office in Camden, should make the first approach.'

Jane agreed with the advice – and added some of her own. So, Amanda and I arranged that she would also go armed with a large, white envelope. On the front in large, bold, capital letters would be written, 'Nazareth House; February 1961'; 'Southmead Hospital, Bristol'; and 'Patrick James Connolly'. She also brought a battered photograph of a chubby toddler dressed in a red duffel coat and Rupert Bear checked trousers, standing next to a flowerbed in the Nazareth House Orphanage garden.

Jane couldn't join us on the trip to Birmingham for that first, fateful meeting because of work commitments. So, we decided to leave London first thing in the morning, and on a weekday. This choice was dictated by the belief that if Margaret had any children or grandchildren living nearby, they would most likely be at work or school. And it was a fair bet that Margaret was retired and likely to be at home. I also had a strong feeling that she'd be very attached to her local Roman Catholic church. I had no evidence for this, but my own Catholicism ran deep and, when I look back, I suspect that I inherited it from Margaret rather than my adoptive parents.

A scan of the map of Selly Oak, the suburb of Birmingham where she lived, identified St Edward's Roman Catholic Church, which was only a few minutes' walk from her home. So, the plan was finalised. We were going to Birmingham on a Wednesday and Amanda and I would catch an early train from London's Euston Station.

It was a fast train. Amanda had been on an early morning filming session for ITV and looked as though she had come straight out of central casting for BBC *Question Time*. She was wearing a stylish black trouser suit with a grey overcoat and full TV make-up. Plus, what she called her lucky bright red and pink scarves. Not only were they lucky mascots, but they also enabled me to pick her out at the end of the street if she had to hang around for Margaret to show up. As she pointed out, the Queen always wore bright colours so people could see her on walkabout, and who better to copy?

There was no debate about what I was going to wear. It was my trademark navy blue suit, white shirt and a tie — as well as, unfortunately, a pained and nervous expression, which I couldn't seem to shift. In fact, I could almost feel my usual sallow complexion growing even paler and greyer as the train hurtled closer and closer to Birmingham.

I tried to read the newspapers, but images of my mum Betty, at home in Swindon, kept flashing before my eyes, which was distinctly unhelpful. I already felt sick with nerves and, when I thought of my mum, my stomach began to churn again. Like so many of those appearing on the TV programme *Long Lost Family* hoping to find their missing birth parents, I too felt a sensation of overpowering guilt as the thirty-year on/off quest to find my birth mother was reaching its climax. I knew that I wasn't really betraying my adoptive mother, to whom I was utterly devoted, but reason and logic had little to do with my emotions then.

As our train slid into Birmingham New Street Station, the sky was overcast and there was a persistent drizzle. We got into a black cab and were surprised that the cabbie knew the street where Margaret lived. 'Oh, yes. It's a well-known road. It's near St Edward's Church,' he said. I asked him to go via the church. It was an imposing and handsome building, obviously built at the turn of the last century. I was absolutely sure that Margaret would worship there. What I didn't know as we passed by was that she was actually inside the church at the time.

When we eventually arrived on Margaret's road, the taxi parked, as we had agreed, out of sight of her home, and Amanda walked quickly down the road to knock on the door. It must have felt like the longest walk of her life, but no one was in. The only sign of life was the sound of a dog barking. It was typical! You make all

CHAPTER EIGHT

these plans – and then travel miles – only to be thwarted at the last moment. Amanda came back to the taxi to confer with me and we agreed that we should wait around for a while. So, she returned to take up a spot on the opposite side of the road from Margaret's little house.

While all this had been going on, I'd noticed that the taxi driver was looking anxiously at me in his mirror. 'Are you feeling all right, mate?' he said, turning around in his seat to talk to me directly. 'You're looking very pale.' Catching a brief glimpse of myself in his mirror, I realised that he was right. My face was the colour of wax.

But, before I could reply, everything seemed to speed up. As I turned to clear the cab's back window with my folded-up newspaper, my stomach in a tight knot, I caught sight of a small figure approaching on the horizon. It was clearly an elderly woman. But, even though she was hundreds of yards away, I immediately knew who she was. For the first time in my life, or, more accurately, for the first time I could remember, I was looking at my birth mother.

As the woman began to come into view, my mobile phone rang. It was Jane Moore, calling to see how matters were progressing.

'She's about to walk past me,' I blurted out. 'I know that it's her. It's Margaret!'

Jane, as cool and calm as ever, said, 'I'm sure you're right. You will probably have an instinctive bond with her. Warn Amanda that she's on her way.'

As the elderly woman walked past the taxi, weighed down by two large plastic containers of milk, I stared at her face. I was even more convinced it was her.

Quickly, I phoned Amanda and shouted down the line, 'SHE'S COMING!'

'Who is?' Amanda sounded baffled.

'MARGARET!' I yelled, not even thinking about being heard. Luckily, the taxi's windows were all tightly shut against the cold drizzle outside the cab, and thus I couldn't be heard by any passers-by.

'But how do you know it's her?'

'Just trust me, OK? It's definitely her!'

I was aware that I wouldn't have too long to wait. Amanda knew that if the woman turned right at the top of the path it was going to be Margaret, but if she turned left towards the other house, it wouldn't be my birth mother. My throat was dry. My palms were sweaty. This time it was Amanda's turn to shout down the phone: 'Yes, you're right! It *is* her! She's turned right and gone into the house. It's definitely Margaret!'

The phone went dead. There was a long, long wait. It was agonising. *Dear God! What on earth was happening?* I asked myself in blind panic. Had Margaret invited Amanda into the house? Would she appear back here, at the taxi, with my birth mother? I don't know how long I waited. Whatever the amount, it was still far too long. Frankly, it seemed like an eternity. I was nervously aware of curtains twitching in some of the houses, on either side of the street, while the cab driver kept looking at me in his mirror. God knows what he or Margaret's neighbours must have been thinking.

Meanwhile, as I later learned from Amanda, back at the house, Margaret, a sprightly little lady with twinkling blue eyes, had opened the door. Apologising for being hard of hearing, she'd calmed down her yappy dog and smiled a big welcoming greeting at the stranger. Amanda knew she had seen that smile somewhere before, but it quickly faded when the elderly woman learned why this stranger was on her doorstep, especially when Amanda showed

CHAPTER EIGHT

her the envelope with the details of Nazareth House Orphanage and the hospital in Bristol where I'd been born. The warmth left her face in a heartbeat.

Sternly denying all knowledge of me, while firmly keeping Amanda at bay on the doorstep and not allowing her into the house, the woman protested that she had never heard of a child who might or might not have been put up for adoption. It had absolutely nothing to do with her, she forcefully repeated. Nothing at all!

'Why are you showing me this?' she demanded as Amanda held up the old, slightly battered photograph of the little boy in his red duffel coat.

To which Amanda said simply, 'You must know why. It's Patrick.'

The woman's face crumpled and she looked stricken. There was a tiny glimmer of tears in her eyes as she took the photograph and stared at it, standing frozen for what seemed like ages, before, as if in a trance, she began stroking the little boy's face. 'He's so sad. So sad...' she muttered. 'There are tears running down his face. He's crying and crying...' Although, in reality, the two-year-old wasn't crying. He was just gazing at the flower bed.

Amanda told her that I was up the road in a cab, and desperate to see my birth mother. 'We've come all the way from London,' she explained. But Margaret would not budge. 'I'm sorry you've come so far, but it's not me... it's not me. It's so cruel. So very cruel!' she repeated, before thrusting the photograph back into Amanda's hands and slamming the door shut in her face.

When Amanda returned to the cab, my heart sank. She looked dreadful. She was soaking wet and despite all the TV make-up, the colour had drained from her cheeks. I'd already guessed what she was going to say. 'Margaret says that it's not her,' Amanda said, confirming my worst fears. 'She says we've got the wrong woman. In fact, she's totally denying all knowledge of Nazareth House or the hospital in Bristol.'

I felt absolutely crushed. I had thought that she would deny any knowledge of me. From the adoption file and the social worker's warning, I already knew that Margaret had gone to great lengths never to be found, so it was unlikely that she would relent. Having been on an emotional high from watching her trudge past the taxi, I now felt shattered, as if someone had punched me in the solar plexus. It felt like a black yawning pit of despair had opened in the depths of my stomach.

On Jane's advice I had prepared a short letter for Margaret, telling her that my name was now Andrew, that I'd grown up in Swindon and had enjoyed a very happy childhood with my adoptive family. I also said that I had no wish to cause her any unhappiness, embarrassment or harm whatsoever. Principally, I said I thought that she must have been hurt enough when she had to walk away from me.

I jumped out of the cab, running through the rain to push the note through Margaret's letterbox, before returning to the car and telling the driver to take us to the nearest pub. It wasn't even 11 a.m. But we managed to find somewhere, keeping the cab waiting in the car park while we demolished a bottle of rosé – which tasted vile but was all we could find – in about thirty minutes flat. While we were tossing the alcohol down our throats, Jane called. When I related the full story of what had happened, Jane's advice was firm, succinct and blunt. 'She is definitely your birth mother. I am 100 per cent certain of that. So you know what you must do, Andrew,' she said firmly. 'You have to send Amanda back to see Margaret. Because it definitely is her. It is Margaret.' Emphatically, she added, 'I just know it is.'

CHAPTER EIGHT

When I told Amanda what Jane had just said to me, she let out a heavy sigh. And I didn't blame her. But clearly I couldn't go, as I knew there was no way that Margaret would ever open her door to me. Despite dreading the thought of being rebuffed again, Amanda took the phone from my hand. Telling Jane about her encounter with the elderly woman, she agreed that there was no alternative other than to go back and challenge Margaret.

It was a big ask and I felt awful about it, but, like Amanda, I couldn't think of what else to do. 'Yeah, I know. Jane's right,' she said, grimacing as she took a large gulp of the rough wine. 'I'll have to do it. After all, we've come this far and I'm damned if I'm going to give up now! Besides…' she added with a shrug, 'you and Jane are right. I've no doubt that it is Margaret. Frankly, Andrew, she looks just like you!'

The taxi took us back towards Margaret's house and I slunk down on the back seat, trying to keep well out of the neighbours' sight. Not very successfully, as it turned out, because I could see net curtains twitching all over the street again. However, Amanda, by now full of Dutch courage from the vile rosé, strode purposefully up the road again. If I'd still been a smoker – I'd packed up more than a decade earlier – I'd have gone through an entire packet of twenty as I waited for her to return. It felt like she was gone for an eternity.

As she appeared in the distance, however, I realised it had been no more than four minutes. As she came closer, I could see tears streaming down her face. Alarmed, I threw open the taxi door and rushed towards her.

'Whatever's wrong?' I asked anxiously. 'Are you OK?'

'It's her. It really is her!' Amanda blurted out, still sobbing and her voice cracking with emotion. 'Margaret has admitted that she's your mother and she wants to see you.'

After her first denial, Margaret had apparently completely changed on Amanda's return visit. 'She was smiling. Beaming. Her eyes were glistening,' Amanda said, adding that Margaret told her, 'From the moment you left, I have been praying to Our Lord. Praying for you to come back. Praying for forgiveness. It *is* me! He was my child. Tell him that I'll see him,' she told Amanda as her little dog, Bobby, continued to yap incessantly.

In retrospect, we realised that when Amanda had first turned up on her doorstep, Margaret had become so gripped by blind panic that she totally denied all knowledge of Patrick's existence. But, having been given time to think, and read the note I'd pushed through her front door, she'd realised she couldn't keep denying what was patently true. So, as Jane put it, 'When Amanda returned, Margaret did the right thing and owned up!'

Amanda recounted that as Margaret was speaking, being a lot taller, she had looked over the older woman's shoulder. In doing so, she could see a statue of Our Lady and caught a glimpse of a framed photograph of a fair-haired man on the mantelpiece, whom she guessed was probably Margaret's late husband. I'd taken it for granted that she would have married and probably had more children. After all, according to the electoral register, she was now Margaret Lennon.

When the older woman stopped talking, Amanda took the plunge, saying, 'He's in a taxi only 300 yards away, Margaret. Why don't you walk to the car to see him or I'll call him and ask him to come here?' The conversation was still taking place on the doorstep, with Amanda not even being invited to cross the threshold. 'He could just come to say "Hi",' she added hopefully.

But Margaret was having none of it. 'No, not here,' she said firmly. 'I can't possibly see him here. Someone may see us. I have

CHAPTER EIGHT

grown-up children. I also have grandchildren. I really can't take any chances. They wouldn't understand. No one… No one…' she faltered as she anxiously clasped her hands together. 'No one knows about the baby. I will see him. But well away from the house,' she added emphatically. 'Ask him to write to me and we will arrange it. I promise you that I definitely will see him.'

Amanda's eyes were glinting with tears again. 'I can hardly believe it – but we've done it! We really have found Margaret. At last!' We hugged each other.

'Do you believe her?' I asked. 'Do you really think she will see me?'

'Oh, yes!' Amanda reassured me. 'You are so like Margaret. With the same high cheekbones and the same infectious smile.'

To say I was elated to hear the certainty in her voice was a complete understatement. My emotions were churning as I realised that finally I really *was* going to see and talk to the woman who had given birth to me, taken me to the orphanage and visited me as often as she could, until she decided – for some unknown reason – that she had to give me up.

So that was how, at the age of almost fifty, I finally found my birth mother.

CHAPTER NINE

Finally, my first meeting with Margaret was almost within my grasp. Where would it be? Or possibly, more to the point, what sort of place *should* it be? A swish restaurant? A café? Or, maybe, a church?

I decided that I should leave it up to Margaret to choose a venue, since it was obviously important to have it somewhere she would feel comfortable and relaxed. In the event, it was neither the location I had expected, nor the conversation I'd anticipated.

So, here I was on another Wednesday, one month later, on a fast train to Birmingham. Once I'd written to Margaret a couple of times to confirm a meeting and agree a date, she asked me in one of her letters to call her to fix a time and place. The telephone call – the first time I would speak to my birth mother – would be a momentous event. I was uncharacteristically nervous before I made the call. What would she sound like? Would she be friendly? Would she call me Andrew? And how should I react if she called me Patrick?

Luckily, I was a senior journalist on the *Daily Telegraph* at the time and could book myself into a private office to make the call on a landline. Margaret answered the phone quickly and I could hear her dog barking.

'Hello,' she said in an unmistakably Irish voice.

'It's Andrew,' I said. 'You were expecting me to call…?'

'Oh, yes,' she replied. 'How are you?'

That was it. Margaret's response on speaking to her first child, whom she hadn't seen for almost fifty years, was extraordinarily prosaic. But what was I really expecting her to say? Was she supposed to weep down the phone, wracked with emotion after finally being reunited with the son she thought she'd never see again? Of course not. That was a scenario for the story books. Margaret was friendly, matter of fact and businesslike.

After a bit of small talk about Bobby the dog and, of course, the weather, I asked her if she was still willing and happy to see me. And if so, where should we meet? Margaret had clearly given the matter some thought. 'Let's meet in the Home Store in Birmingham city centre. There's a very nice café,' she said. 'Everyone knows it.' I asked if she would like to make it lunch. She said that she couldn't be away from her house for too long because of the dog, so we agreed on a time and date. I was just about to put the phone down, when Margaret said: 'Oh, there is just one thing, Andrew. I do want to say…' She paused for a moment, shyly adding, 'I do think you have a lovely voice.' Her words were swiftly followed by a sharp 'click' as she terminated the call.

Having gone online to locate where we were going to meet, I was baffled. I couldn't find a 'Home Store' anywhere in Birmingham, let alone the city centre. Then the penny dropped. She obviously meant BHS or British Home Stores. Slap bang in the city centre. It was big, it would be busy – and there was a large café. It was a clever choice by Margaret, who would clearly feel far less conspicuous in a large, spacious building than in a more intimate restaurant. I suspected she wasn't the sort of person to visit chic little restaurants

CHAPTER NINE

or meet friends for lunch in pubs. In fact, I was almost certain that her life revolved around her family, especially as she'd already told Amanda that she had children and grandchildren – and the dog, of course.

BHS…? Right! Well, if that's what she wanted, that was what she would get. While I thought that I might be able to take her somewhere a bit more upmarket, I belatedly realised that the venue would give us something to talk about. When I was at sixth form in Swindon, I had a Saturday job in the town's large BHS. First, I'd worked in the café, clearing tables and cleaning up after customers, before reaching the dizzy heights of working on the enormous dish-washing machine. The commercial dishwasher operated on a conveyor belt, as there were literally thousands of dishes to wash every Saturday. It was hard work, but also great fun. In fact, I hoped it would prove to Margaret that I came from an ordinary and down-to-earth family background.

On the train, accompanied again by Amanda, my excitement was tinged with distinct feelings of nervousness and unease. What if she didn't like me? What if she resented my totally unexpected appearance in her life? Would she be genuinely pleased to see me? Or was she meeting me out of a sense of duty? But above all, I was worried that she might not keep her word and would fail to turn up.

I also hoped, but wasn't entirely convinced, that the prospect of meeting me would bring her some closure. However, I had a nagging doubt that this might not be the case. So, I resolved to tell my birth mother that I wasn't looking for a deep and meaningful relationship, because I already had that with my mum Betty. Basically, my plan was to reassure her that I was happy in both my private and public life. I also needed, as much as for my own sake as hers, to establish that she was well and healthy. Undoubtedly, her family was looking after her. But, if she had any health or financial problems, I wanted her to know that I would happily give her any help she needed. And of course, I wanted to reassure her that I was not planning to interfere in her life, in any way.

As we neared Birmingham, I made a mental list of the many questions to which I needed answers: Why had Margaret thought that she would, somehow, be able to bring me up on her own? What had led her to keep me in Nazareth House Orphanage for more than two years after the death of Jimmy Coffey, the man she had claimed was my father? Because if that was the original plan, something went horribly wrong. Was Jimmy Coffey dragging his feet about marriage even before he was killed in the car crash? The address Margaret had given Nazareth House for him was different to the one on his death certificate, one month after I was put into the orphanage. So, had he already done 'a runner'? If so, and he'd tried to wriggle out of his obligations to Margaret and his unborn child, would she ever have admitted it? Maybe it was his untimely death that had put paid to Margaret's talk of marriage?

I also wanted to ask her about paying for me to stay in the orphanage – while she was working hard as a nurse back in Birmingham – with the intention of giving me a home when the time was right. But when would that have been? Was there another man in the wings? If so, who was he? And was he still alive? I was bursting to ask Margaret these questions, but I had no plans to bombard an elderly lady. I certainly didn't want to overwhelm her or put her under any pressure. So, I planned to ask only one or two general questions at our first meeting. Hopefully, there would be more time together. Apart from wanting to know what sort of man my birth father was, I also wanted to be reassured that after settling down with Patrick Lennon, she'd had a happy and fulfilled life.

CHAPTER NINE

The train was on time. We walked to the large BHS building and I was relieved to spot Margaret waiting for us, easily identifiable with her distinctive head of thick, white hair. She was wearing a colourful scarf, sensible shoes and a warm coat that ended below her knees, and she was smiling broadly as we approached. She obviously recognised Amanda, but what was I supposed to do when I met her? Kiss her? Shake her hand? Or maybe kiss her on both cheeks? I obviously didn't have a clue about the correct protocol when meeting one's birth mother for the first time, and certainly not when it was at the advanced age of forty-eight.

Amanda did the formalities, saying simply, 'Margaret, this is your son Patrick James. He's now known as Andrew Pierce.'

I gazed at her. I felt uncharacteristically shy and reticent and was not at all sure of what to do or say to her, before I at last managed to pull myself together.

'Margaret, it's so lovely to see you and to meet you. Thank you for agreeing to see me because I've been wanting to meet you for a long time. Well, a lifetime, in fact!' I gave myself a swift, mental kick in the shins, because this was clearly neither the time nor the place for the slightly ironic tone of my last remark. Quickly, I added, 'I hope my sudden appearance in your life hasn't been too much of a shock? Because, I want you to know that I'm OK. That I'm happy and have had a wonderful life. I do hope you have too?'

She quietly replied, 'Thank you for coming,' and extended her arms towards me. I hugged her, realising how bird-like her frame was, and then we went downstairs to the café. While I ordered cups of tea for us both – she did not want any food – Amanda chit-chatted with her and then made a strategic exit.

I asked Margaret about her family. Her husband was Patrick Lennon. Her eldest son was called Sean and she had a second son named Patrick, as well as a daughter, Anne. When she said she had a son called Patrick, I briefly wondered whether he was named after me or his father. The dark irony of Margaret living with two 'Patricks', having already given up her first child with that name, appeared to be entirely lost on her. As the time passed, it became apparent where I'd inherited my reputation as a chatterbox. Margaret was now busily talking away about her family: her late husband, her three children and six grandchildren and, of course, Bobby (the yappy dog) – all in considerable detail.

Initially, I wondered if it was because she was nervous about the situation she found herself in, but then I realised it was clearly a diversion. Because, Margaret was conspicuously asking me nothing about my life. Absolutely nothing at all. Not where I was brought up, not what my adoptive parents George and Betty were like, not whether I'd been happy at home and school and not whether I had any brothers or sisters. I did tell her a few details about my own very happy family background, but that was primarily to keep the conversation going, rather than satisfying any curiosity on her part.

I have to confess that I was puzzled. Why wasn't she interested? Was it too difficult for her, even after all this time, to hear about the adoptive parents who'd brought me up? Or had she repressed all the memories of that time in her life? Had she buried, deep in her psyche, all remembrances of my conception, birth, Nazareth House and the deepest and darkest secret of all – the identity of my father? The only question Margaret asked me was whether I was married to Amanda or planning to marry her. Adroitly, as it turned out, I fibbed and told her that we would probably be getting married at some point in the future. She nodded her approval and said she hoped it would be in a Catholic church.

We talked about Ireland and how she had left the country for

CHAPTER NINE

Birmingham in the 1950s to train as a nurse. She said life on the family farm in County Mayo was hard, and how much she had loved nursing. I told her I was going to Belfast in a few weeks' time. For a moment she stopped her incessant chatter and said sternly, 'I don't like the people from the north of Ireland. The ones who aren't Catholic.' I asked her why she disliked them. 'They have funny views,' she replied firmly. 'They believe in abortion and gays. Which are both mortal sins.' (I would later discover that her husband, Patrick, was from Northern Ireland.) Well, that decided it. This was hardly the time, and maybe there would never be a time, to confide in Margaret that her first-born son was gay.

Looking at my watch, I saw that thirty minutes had already elapsed and I was none the wiser about the real reason why, in comparison to so many other illegitimate children, I hadn't been taken away for adoption as soon as I was born. And also, why she had decided to place me, and then subsequently left me, in Nazareth House Orphanage for over two years. But she was still rattling away, continuing to tell me all about her life with Patrick Lennon. Her husband had died in the 1990s and he sounded like a fine and decent partner, as well as a good father. But obviously, he was nothing to do with me. As if she could read my mind, Margaret suddenly said, 'My husband never knew anything about you. I didn't tell him. I didn't tell anyone. My family in Ireland never knew. No one knew.'

Now was clearly the time to ask about my birth father. Very gently, or so I thought, I ventured, 'Margaret, can you tell me about my birth father? Starting with the most important question: *who* was my father? Is he still alive? And if so, are you still in contact with him?' I certainly didn't expect the response she gave me.

'I don't remember. I don't remember anything about him,' she said.

'Really?' I said, barely able to disguise the note of scepticism in my voice. 'But you told the nuns at the orphanage that you intended to marry in the summer of 1961, which was three months after you put me in the orphanage. It's in my Nazareth House report.'

She stared at me blankly. 'Is that what I told the nuns? I don't remember.'

'Well, is it true, Margaret? Were you planning to marry my birth father?'

She stonewalled me again. 'I don't remember. I can't remember. Because, you see, it was a sin.'

'I don't understand. *What* precisely was a sin?' I asked, floundering around and feeling like I'd suddenly found myself on stage in the middle of some avant-garde, totally incomprehensible play.

'What I did. Getting pregnant when I wasn't married. Sex outside of marriage is a sin,' she explained slowly, as if to a particularly dim child. 'I knew that. I have had to pay for that sin all my life. *That's* why I can't remember anything.'

I repressed an urge to exclaim, 'Wow! What an utterly brilliant idea. "I can't remember because it's a sin" could cover just about anything in life, from petty theft to murder!' But these were uncharitable thoughts. Mocking an old lady probably *was* a sin and I should be thoroughly ashamed of myself.

My watch now told me that forty minutes had passed and Margaret had hardly touched her tea, had declined a second cup and refused any food. So, I tried again. 'Do you remember if you were in a long relationship, or a short relationship with my birth father? Were you engaged to him? Had he bought you a ring?' I asked. 'Surely you must recall what he did for a job?' I hoped that she wasn't feeling pressurised, but she could hardly have been surprised by the questions.

CHAPTER NINE

'No,' she said. 'I can't tell you anything, because I have absolutely no recollection of any of it.'

Then, when I asked if she remembered visiting me at the orphanage, it was the same story.

'I've put it out of my mind for good,' she insisted. 'I don't know how I got there.'

Gently, I reminded her that she'd left me in Nazareth House Orphanage for two years before she decided to give me up for adoption.

'Do you have any recollection of why you put me in Nazareth House? And *why* you left me there for two and a half long years? And then why you finally decided to give me up for adoption?'

She fell silent, staring down at her cup, before she repeated her mantra. 'I don't remember,' she muttered. 'I don't know why you were in the home for that amount of time.' The conversation, such as it was, had clearly stumbled to a halt. So, I decided to try the direct approach.

Staring straight into her eyes, I said slowly, 'Margaret, who is James Coffey?'

Her eyes narrowed as she stared back at me and slowly replied, 'Who? Who did you say?'

I repeated the name slowly. 'James Coffey. Who is he, Margaret?'

There was another long pause before she shook her head and said emphatically, 'I don't know who he is.' And again, when I asked her whether the name was even vaguely familiar, she shook her head and reiterated, 'No. I don't know who he is.'

Refusing to give up, I then pointed out, as gently as I could, that in the papers lodged with Nazareth House, and in her own handwriting, she had described Jimmy Coffey as my father.

But I instinctively knew what was coming next…

'Oh. Did I?' Margaret mumbled, carefully avoiding my gaze as she stared down at her now cold cup of tea. 'I don't remember.'

I took a deep breath and tried not to show my increasing exasperation. Was it really possible that she had forgotten? Had she actually managed to bury all recollection of the two long years she had visited me in Nazareth House? And conceal from herself not only her memories of her child but also the man she'd told the nuns was my father?

I already knew a great deal about the horrible effects of Alzheimer's disease from my own adoptive father's experience of it. I had personally witnessed the fact that, more often than not, distant memories are the last to fade. George retained vivid memories of growing up in London's Isle of Dogs to the very end of his life, but he was unable to remember a conversation he'd had with me five minutes earlier.

So, James Coffey might well have been her lover when she fell pregnant with me in 1960, almost half a century previously, but Margaret was resolutely sticking to her guns. She knew nothing about James Coffey and so couldn't say if he was my birth father, nor could she recall why I'd been left in the orphanage for so long. I quickly realised that it would be senselessly cruel to point out the many and obvious inconsistencies in what Margaret could and could not remember, especially the blatantly overlapping events of summer 1963. Because, while she was able to recall her nursing career, plus her engagement, and her marriage to Patrick Lennon, she was simultaneously unable to remember anything about Nazareth House, the nuns or visiting her young son. Well, there was clearly no point in prolonging this particular conversation. Not today, anyway.

Amanda returned when we had just five minutes left, as Margaret hadn't wanted to leave her dog for too long. Smiling, Amanda asked her, 'Did Andrew tell you that he's a very successful journalist?'

Margaret looked at me and said, 'Is that so? I didn't know that.'

Amanda looked puzzled. I gave a slight shrug and whispered to her as Margaret bent down to retrieve her handbag, 'She never asked. She never asked anything about me at all.' By now, Margaret was arranging her scarf – her best one, she told us, which she was wearing in my honour – as she was ready to go home.

I felt ashamed of my momentary irritation at her total lack of interest in, or curiosity about, my life. She was, after all, an elderly lady who must have found meeting me, for the first time in forty-eight years, both tiring and emotionally draining. Walking with her to the front of the shop, I offered to pay for a taxi, but she has having none of it. 'I'll go on the bus. If I arrived home in a taxi and people saw me, they would know that's not something I'd ever do,' she said adamantly. 'I don't want to be seen doing anything out of the ordinary.'

I found myself thinking, 'Hmm... still covering your tracks, Margaret, even after all these years!' And then, cross with myself for being so cynical, I asked her if she'd been pleased to meet me.

'Oh, yes! I'm so happy to have met you today, Andrew,' she said, with a big smile. And when I mentioned that I really hoped we could meet again, when she might be more relaxed in my company, Margaret gave me another beaming smile. 'I've felt really relaxed. I was a little bit nervous before I met you, of course. But you're a really charming fellow,' she added. At which point she reached up and kissed me directly on the lips. 'Thank you,' she continued, 'for making my day. Making my week. And in fact, thank you for making my life. I'm a happy woman, and I'll see you again soon, Andrew,' she promised, before delivering another one of her knockout smiles and turning to walk swiftly away.

She never looked back. I watched her until she disappeared from view and then, weirdly, I started worrying about her bus journey home. Amanda and I made our usual trip to the pub and in Margaret's honour we bought a very nice bottle of rosé – quite unlike the terrible bottle we'd downed in record time the day Amanda first knocked on Margaret's door. But, still worrying about her, I called Margaret at home.

'I'm just checking that you got back OK,' I told her. 'And that you've no regrets about meeting me?'

Margaret sounded happy and cheerful. 'It's nice of you to call, Andrew. I'm fine and I've no regrets about seeing you. I don't know if I said it to you – but you're a fine-looking man.'

I couldn't resist. 'Do I look more like you or my birth father?'

Quick as a flash, she replied, 'Ah – if only I could remember.'

Both in the pub and on the way back to London, I endlessly replayed to Amanda what had happened between Margaret and myself. She was struck by the fact that Margaret had asked me nothing at all about my life. Absolutely nothing. She had shown no interest in what had happened to me since the last time she'd seen me when I was only two and a half years old. In fact, she hadn't seen me for months before I finally moved to Swindon.

We both believed that Margaret would have found it far too upsetting to hear endless stories about how happy I had been with my adopted mum and dad. The only mum and dad I had ever known or wanted. We also thought it might be her way of protecting her own feelings, because my reappearance in her life must have stirred up some very painful memories of her pregnancy – about which, of course, no one must know anything. Not to mention going through the birth on her own, the misery of the mother and baby home and then visiting me in Nazareth House. Although, she was now

CHAPTER NINE

claiming to have no memory of anything, let alone of who my father might have been, which I found simply impossible to believe.

Margaret had told me she had become more absent-minded as she had got older, but her memory seemed good. She knew all about her marriage in Birmingham to her husband Patrick and told me about her three children, six grandchildren and her church, working as a nurse and all about her husband. So, I was quite confident that when we next met, the answers to some of my questions would come tumbling out. I thought that perhaps she needed more time to really feel at ease with me. The experience in BHS must have been daunting, especially being asked to open up and recount painful memories to her first-born child – someone who was, in fact, a complete stranger to her.

I was already looking forward to the next time I would see her. Maybe I could persuade her to meet me in a restaurant or smarter café, where she might find it easier to talk over lunch. When she said goodbye, Margaret had pledged that she would see me again and had repeated the promise when I telephoned her to check that she'd got home safely. But, as I was to discover, with painful consequences, it seemed that she had no intention of keeping her word.

CHAPTER TEN

After our first meeting, I kept in touch with Margaret by writing the occasional cheery letter. I also telephoned, but not often, because she was hard of hearing so it wasn't the best way to communicate with her. Margaret was always friendly on the telephone, but she seemed to have an unspoken rule: she would never ask me about anything personal. Nothing about what I was doing or anything concerning my early life in Swindon, nor did she ever make any reference to my family.

It was exactly the same approach she'd taken when we first met at the BHS café. She was always happy to chat about her family, her little dog and her daily trips to church. I told her that my parents had stuck to their agreement with the Catholic Children's Rescue Society and that I had been brought up as a Roman Catholic. I thought she would be thrilled and fire endless questions at me, but far from it. She never asked me a single thing. No questions about what kind of school I went to or if I still saw anything of my older brothers and sisters. Nor, rather strangely, did she ask whether I still regularly attended church. This was especially odd since her faith was clearly so important to her.

Most of our telephone conversations were fairly short and much more prosaic than if she had taken any interest in my upbringing. For instance, she would talk at length about Bobby, her small yappy dog, and particularly the fear that if anything happened to her there would be no one willing to look after him. This was understandable, since I imagine it's a fear that haunts many ageing dog owners.

Then, quite out of the blue, she wrote that she would prefer it if I restricted any contact to the telephone. Her short note said, 'I worry that if the good Lord takes me in the night, my children might find one of your letters. They might suspect something. I hope you don't mind?' I was surprised, but I also understood her fear.

History was clearly repeating itself. Just as she had done when she'd placed me in the orphanage, Margaret was once again taking no chances and covering her tracks. Christmas came and went, but there was no card from Margaret, nor a telephone call. I never sent a card as that would obviously have set off alarm bells. What if any of her Connolly children saw it in her home and asked, 'Who are Andrew and Amanda?' And fair enough, I suppose, since I always looked at my mum's Christmas cards to see who they were from. I assumed that Margaret's children and grandchildren would be no different.

At that time, my birthday was approaching and I thought this would be a litmus test. Once, way back on my thirty-fourth birthday, my mum had surprised me when she revealed that she'd thought about my birth mother on all my birthdays until I was about thirty. What I didn't tell her then, was that on all my birthdays from my late teens onwards, I'd thought, however fleetingly, about the woman who had brought me into the world. Was the day difficult for her? Did she think about me? Rather vainly on my part, I'd assumed that she always did. After all, how could she forget the horror of giving birth to me, quite alone in that soulless hospital

CHAPTER TEN

in Bristol, in February 1961? Not to mention the weeks she'd spent under the harsh and unforgiving regime of St Raphael's mother and baby home.

I was almost certain that it would be a day she'd never forget. I had read about adopted children and the agony their birth parents faced on birthdays and at Christmas, so I knew that the adopted child's birthday could be a day of dread; a painful time when birth mothers would be constantly thinking and worrying about what had become of their child. Usually, then, as I opened birthday cards or joined friends or family in having a drink, I uttered a silent prayer to my birth mother in the hope that if she was still alive, she was happy and not tortured by what had happened decades earlier.

My forty-ninth birthday, in February 2010, fell on a Wednesday and Amanda was planning a small supper for me at her home in north London, just a fifteen-minute walk from my flat. I had joined the *Daily Mail* from the *Daily Telegraph* only a few weeks earlier. On my way to Amanda's I decided to make a call. A significant one. I was going to telephone Margaret. I had wondered if she would call to wish me a happy birthday. There had been no birthday card from her, but that hadn't surprised me. Maybe she had assumed that I would call her.

'Hallo, Margaret,' I said. 'It's Andrew. I'm sorry to disturb you.' She was, as usual, pleasant, polite and asked if I was well, and she asked after Amanda too. I got straight to the point. 'Margaret,' I said. 'It's a special date today. Do you recall what it is?'

There was a long pause before she said, 'No, I'm afraid I don't. Tell me.'

I was disappointed that she neither knew nor even hazarded a guess that it might be my birthday. Surely she must remember that I was born in February?

'It's my birthday,' I said. 'I'm forty-nine today. Surely you must remember that I was born in February 1961?'

There was another pause and then she exclaimed, 'Is that so? Well, happy birthday, Andrew.'

Briefly, I actually wondered whether she'd made any connection between my birthday and herself. I was flustered. 'Margaret,' I said softly. 'Don't you remember? You gave birth to me on that day in Bristol and then I went to the Nazareth House children's home. You then had me adopted a couple of years later.'

She halted again before replying, 'Oh yes, I know. It was me. But I had forgotten when it happened.'

Forgotten? Or had she somehow contrived to obliterate all her memories of me as a coping mechanism?

Margaret seemed touched when I told her that for many years I had thought about her on my birthday, always hoping that she was well, healthy and happy. 'Well, that's a nice thing to know,' she said. 'To think that you were thinking about me – especially when neither of us knew anything about each other.'

I ploughed on. 'I always thought my birthday might be a difficult day for you. But it now seems that you forgot when it was.' Margaret remained silent, so I tried to get through to her yet again. 'I imagine the first birthdays, after you put me up for adoption, must have been very painful for you.'

But, as usual, she was giving nothing away. 'I don't remember,' she persisted. 'The main thing is you're happy.'

'Well, no, Margaret,' I countered quickly. 'The main thing is that *you* are happy, that you've had a good life, with a nice husband and family. Remember, the reason I tracked you down was to let you know that I was OK. Just in case you might have been worrying about me.'

CHAPTER TEN

But, if she had worried about me after she'd started her new life with her husband and children, she was not prepared to say. So, I ended the conversation, saying, 'I'm planning another trip to Birmingham in the next month or so. It would be lovely if you're willing to see me again. And at the same place, if you would prefer to meet up there?'

'Oh, yes,' she said. And there was no pause this time. 'Yes, you deserve that.'

As it happened, I was going to Bromsgrove, where I used to work for the *Birmingham Post & Mail* in the 1980s, to see my friend Tony who lived in Feckenham, a glorious Worcestershire village. I planned to take my usual trip down memory lane. I would go to Bromsgrove high street and seek out the stylish clothes store I used to frequent whenever I visited Tony. But first of all, I would go to Birmingham and see Margaret.

On the telephone we had agreed that I would see her at 11 a.m. in her favourite 'Home Store', aka BHS. Before I left London, I chose a bunch of spring flowers while I wondered whether Margaret would prefer dark or milk chocolate. My mum Betty, in Swindon, had always hated dark chocolate. Cadbury's Milk Tray was her favourite, so they were out! So were Roses, because Mum loved them too. I wasn't going to buy Margaret something my mum in Swindon loved. So I bought a box of Maltesers, mainly because I thought most people like them – and they aren't fussy or flash. I knew that 'flash' would not be Margaret's style.

As the train moved closer to Birmingham, I was beset with nerves about whether she would actually show up. I was on my own this time. Amanda's reassuring shoulder wasn't there to lean on, or cry on, if necessary. Because I was so jittery, I called Margaret from the train to double-check she would be there. At first, I'd thought everything would be OK, because when I called her on my mobile just as the train was leaving London she said, 'Oh, yes. I'll be there at 11 a.m.' So why was I no longer convinced that she would turn up, despite her cheery assurances? Was it a journalistic hunch? Or had there been, perhaps, a slight lack of enthusiasm in her voice? Or could that merely have been nerves? After all, it was only the second time she was going to meet the son she must have thought she'd never see again.

On the train, I rehearsed over and over again the conversation I wanted to have with Margaret. I would tell her that I was going to Bromsgrove later in the day. I wondered if she knew the area? I would talk about Amanda. I would show her the photos of two-year-old Patrick in his checked trousers when I was still living in Nazareth House and being visited by my future mum and dad. The image of me in the Rupert Bear trousers, and a little red duffel coat, would have been the last memory she had of me, because it seemed as if all contact with me was forbidden after Betty and George became serious candidates to adopt me. If this conversation went well, hopefully I could raise my questions about James Coffey again.

Arriving early, I went to a coffee shop with my flowers and chocolates and talked to Amanda on the telephone. As ever, she was a tower of strength and support. After the call, I set off for BHS with a spring in my step, enjoying the fresh April morning. I hoped that Margaret might be less restrained and might actually reveal what life was really like in Nazareth House and explain why she had held on to me for so long.

I also longed to know whether James Coffey was just a fleeting acquaintance or the man she'd really loved. Or even, possibly, someone she'd used as a decoy to divert attention away from the identity of my real birth father? I really hoped that she would be

CHAPTER TEN

more relaxed, especially as we'd got on so well at our last meeting. I didn't think that I'd overwhelmed her with questions the first time we'd met. And, she should at least realise that I was a successful, middle-aged man who'd had the good fortune to enjoy a very happy family life, which is obviously what she would have wanted for me when she'd agreed to my adoption.

As I drew closer to BHS, it suddenly felt as if someone had punched me in the stomach. I had an awful, all-too-familiar feeling – a ghastly mixture of terror and scorched nerve ends – which I always associate with impending doom, or when I just know that something is about to go horribly, *horribly* wrong. 'She's not going to be there!' I exclaimed out loud, doing my best to ignore the strange glances of the pedestrians close to me. I stopped in my tracks to gaze down at my watch. It was 10.55 a.m., so I was five minutes early. Maybe it wasn't the end of the world, after all…?

The first time we'd met, Margaret admitted she'd been like a cat on a hot tin roof. She confessed to having kept popping her head out of the entrance foyer to see if Amanda and I were on our way. She even mentioned that she'd arrived at the store well over thirty minutes early. But, ominously, this time there was no sign of a little old lady with a smart grey coat and distinctive shock of white hair, peering nervously up and down the street. I looked at my watch again. It was still only four minutes to eleven. Plenty of time for Margaret to make it. But, nevertheless, I knew. I just *knew* she wasn't going to turn up. What I didn't know was why.

Pacing up and down in front of the store, I kept gazing at my watch, looking into the store and then up and down the street. I cursed myself for not bringing a newspaper to read. But to be honest, the print would have been a blur. My stomach was churning. I thought, *Surely she's not going to fail to show up?* Then I had the chilling thought that something terrible might have happened to her.

So, after fifteen minutes, I quickly nipped downstairs to the cafeteria where we'd first talked, in the hope that she might have gone straight there. I walked round and round the café staring intently at any woman who appeared to be over the age of sixty-five. Nothing. Not a sign of her. I went back up to the entrance, but she was still nowhere to be seen. There was still no one I could see who looked even vaguely similar to Margaret. Now, I was panicking. I charged around the shop floor, even walking directly up to any older woman with grey hair. I actually spoke to one or two, apologising profusely for mistaking them for someone else.

And then, my mobile rang. Was it Margaret calling to explain her delay? Or a reason for not being able to come after all? But no. It was Amanda, who was just checking in to see if all was well. But she didn't need to ask if Margaret had shown up. As she told me later, she could almost feel the pain and confusion in my voice. Amanda suggested there could be a perfectly reasonable explanation for the delay. She could be stuck in traffic on the bus. Because, needless to say, Margaret had rejected my offer that very morning to pay for a taxi to bring her in and out of the city centre, and if she was delayed, she didn't carry a mobile to call and alert me to any problems. But I wasn't convinced about the traffic. And I could hear in Amanda's voice that she wasn't persuaded either.

I hung up and, after another ten minutes, I walked into the cafeteria again. But still no sign. I had already called Margaret's home in Selly Oak, several times. The phone rang, but no one answered. So was she on her way? Had she been delayed? Or had she received an urgent call or a better offer in the hour or so between me calling

CHAPTER TEN

her and our appointed time to meet? Or was she at home, ignoring the telephone? It would be some time before I found out.

I waited at the large store for a soul-destroying eighty minutes before I finally decided to give up. My spirits crushed, I felt cold and bewildered. Why would she suddenly decide not to see me, when she had quite clearly told me, barely an hour before we were due to meet, that she would be there? I phoned Amanda and Jane, who both said I must give her the benefit of the doubt. Which of course, I would do. I kept thinking she would call me to explain. Or send me a note. But there was nothing from Margaret. No call. No letter. I began to fear, all over again, that something terrible had happened to her.

I caught the train to Bromsgrove and nipped into the smart fashion store on the town's high street, which I'd just discovered, to my amazement, was actually owned by Margaret's eldest son Sean. I don't remember much about who served me that day. Was it Margaret's son? My half-brother? It was all a bit of a blur. I went on to Feckenham and drowned my sorrows with Tony Flanagan, who could drink the Midlands dry, and returned to London the same night.

After a few days, and still no contact from Margaret, I plucked up the courage to call her. But I waited until mid-morning, as she'd told me she was generally at church early in the day and often helped out with the priest's domestic chores. She answered the phone and I said, 'It's Andrew. Is everything OK? I've been worried. You never showed up at the Home Store, Margaret. I waited for eighty minutes. It was cold and miserable – and I was very worried something untoward might have happened to you.'

I never expected the reply that came.

'Sorry,' she said. 'I had to help out with my little grandchild.'

I can still hear myself saying, 'Well, yes. Family is important, Margaret. I really do understand. But you could have called me. You could have let me know that you would be looking after your grandchild, especially when I called you, earlier that morning, to check you were coming to meet me.'

To which she responded, 'Yes, I should have called you. Sorry.'

After some small talk, I ended the conversation. Before putting the phone down, I asked, 'Margaret, I don't want to presume or to cause you any bother. But, are you still willing to see me again? Even if it is only for one more time.'

Her reply was reassuring. 'I said last time that I would see you – and I meant it.'

So that's all right, I thought. Perhaps Margaret had mislaid my telephone number? It was likely that she didn't like to leave it in a book or file – in case anyone in her family came across it. How many mobile telephone numbers was she calling at the time?

I knew I had a forthcoming date in Birmingham in the summer, as I was chairing the judges' panel for the Midlands Media Awards. I thought I could see Margaret either on my way to the awards, which were judged in central Birmingham, or afterwards. I decided to try to make it in the morning. Less time, I thought rather cynically, for Margaret to change her mind. So, the time was finalised. Yes, she would be at the 'Home Store' as she quaintly called it, 'at 11 o'clock in the morning'. This time, I took the precaution of calling her the evening before and she confirmed that she was very much going to be there. I also called her again from the train when I was only an hour away from Birmingham, and I reminded her of my telephone number – just in case there were any last-minute hitches.

When I got off the train, I deliberately left no time for a cup

CHAPTER TEN

of coffee – mainly because I thought that would prevent me from spending too much time worrying about whether Margaret was going to show up. So, I made my way straight to BHS and, yet again, as I edged closer to the store, I became aware of that horribly familiar, cold, dank sense of dread. Despite the two encouraging telephone calls I'd had with Margaret, I just knew that she was going to let me down for a second time. Badly. And when I entered the store, all my instinctive fears were confirmed. There was absolutely no sign of her.

It was just before 11 a.m., so I went straight down to the cafeteria. Nothing. I went to the back of the shop and drew another blank. I approached every woman who might have been her, just in case I had forgotten what she looked like, which was ridiculous of course because even as I was approaching them, I knew that I was clutching at straws. How could I possibly forget what my birth mother looked like? I had wondered for decades if I looked like her and I had discovered that we bore a very close resemblance to one another. Moreover, I had seen her from the back of a black cab in her street and known instantly who she was, and not long after, I had sat opposite her in BHS for over fifty minutes. I would never be able to forget that shock of thick white hair, the pronounced jaw and those sparkling blue eyes.

After twenty minutes and another 'no show', my phone rang. This time, I never even suspected it might be Margaret. I knew it would be Amanda.

'She's not here,' I shouted into the phone.

'Oh, dear God!' Amanda sighed. 'What on earth is it this time?'

I explained that I'd telephoned her at home and there had been no answer, so I was going to wait again, at the front of BHS, for about another hour, just in case she had been delayed for any reason.

Amanda called a couple more times. So did Jane Moore, who'd thought that Margaret was genuine about her reasons for not seeing me the last time. Now, though, I was not so sure. 'To leave you standing for an hour would be cruel. Margaret isn't cruel,' Jane said. 'There must be a reasonable explanation.'

I never thought she was cruel, either. At the time, I thought Margaret had lost her nerve. Yet again. Perhaps it was too painful for her to talk about the past? Even though she had freely conceded that I had a right to ask and was fully entitled to answers. But did I have to face up to yet another uncomfortable truth that Margaret was rejecting her birth son all over again? A second 'no show' was hard to put down to unforeseen circumstances, especially as I had telephoned her barely an hour before we were due to meet.

This time, I abandoned ship after an hour. I was miserable. Yet again there was no telephone call, or letter, to explain her last-minute change of heart. So, after a few days, I telephoned again. Her reason this time? Her son Patrick (my birth name!), who was apparently employed as a taxi driver, had unexpectedly turned up for a cup of tea and she had no way, she said, of explaining to him that she had an engagement elsewhere, so by the time he had gone, Margaret had decided that I would have already left. When I asked why she hadn't telephoned me, Margaret said she had mislaid my number. But if she really was with her son, as she said, why hadn't she answered when I called to see where she was?

With a heavy heart, I asked her one more time, 'Margaret, are you still happy to see me again? Even if it would be for just one more time?' As I waited for her reply, I reminded myself that I'd never anticipated forging a deep and close relationship with her, mainly because I already had such loving care and support from my mum and dad, Betty and George. And again, I reminded myself

CHAPTER TEN

that all I had intended to do when I found my birth mother was to make sure she knew that I'd had a very happy upbringing with my adoptive parents. However, it was becoming increasingly likely that I wasn't going to have a relationship with Margaret at all. But she surprised me once again.

'Yes,' she said. 'I will see you, Andrew. I will be there the next time. I'm sorry that I've messed you about again.'

Having discussed the situation with Amanda and Jane, we decided that the third attempt should be at the end of September, when I was due to be in Birmingham for a party conference. It was the annual Conservative Party conference, so Amanda would be there too. It also meant that I would already be in Birmingham and not travelling to the Midlands with the specific purpose of seeing Margaret, together with all the associated stress and anxiety I'd suffered in the past.

The night before we were due to meet, I was at a reception talking to David Cameron, who wanted to know all 'the latest political gossip'. He was now the Prime Minister after forming a coalition government with the Liberal Democrats. I had known Cameron ever since he was a young special adviser to Norman Lamont, when Lamont was Chancellor of the Exchequer in John Major's government. We used to go to lunch together at Joe Allen's in Covent Garden. Even then, David Cameron was clearly destined for great things. He oozed the self-confidence that comes from being an Old Etonian and having studied at Oxford.

I'd been attending Tory conferences ever since joining *The Times* in 1988 as a reporter in the gallery of the Houses of Parliament. I was on good form that evening and thoroughly enjoyed myself. A couple of nights earlier, I had met a really nice man at a reception. He worked for the party, appeared to have a similar outlook on life, and he was single. He was at the same reception where I spoke to Cameron. We had a light breakfast the next day but I told him nothing about where I was going straight afterwards. Little did I know this man would go on to become my civil partner.

In fact, I was going to Amanda's room, where she telephoned Margaret. They had a nice chat and she reminded Margaret that we were due to meet at BHS that morning.

'Oh, yes,' she told Amanda. 'I will be there this time. I promise I will.'

Amanda told her that we were leaving for the store in thirty minutes and offered to get her a taxi. As usual, the offer was gently rebuffed.

'I'll be getting the bus,' she said.

We walked the short distance to the store from our hotel, which was by the conference centre. As ever, the time agreed was 11 a.m. And, as ever, we were five minutes early. On the way we chatted about the conference, about the man I had met at the reception and then, about Margaret. Amanda was certain that she would be there to meet us. But for my part, I couldn't shake off an awful sense of impending catastrophe: the strong feeling that Margaret was going to repeat the same trick of not showing up.

How right I proved to be.

The same swarm of butterflies was flying around my stomach when, on our arrival at the BHS store, we saw she wasn't there. Amanda stayed outside, chain-smoking her little cigarillos. I went straight to the cafeteria and then raced around the store before establishing that there was no trace of Margaret. We waited outside for twenty minutes. I bought some tea from the cafeteria, which we drank standing outside the store.

Amanda kept ringing Margaret's number. Should we be encouraged

CHAPTER TEN

that there was no answer? Was it a sign she was on her way? Could she have gone out somewhere else? Or was she, as I suspected, completely ignoring the telephone? Amanda and I went back inside the store and I told her that I was going for another walkabout. She caught a glimpse of me in one of the many full-length mirrors on the shop floor and told me afterwards that she was shocked. 'Your face was twisted in pain and distress. It was heartbreaking to see.'

After ninety minutes we decided it was time to go. But, as we did so, Amanda telephoned Margaret one more time. And to our total surprise, she answered.

'My little dog, Bobby, got sick after you called me. And I had to take him to the vet,' she said. 'So, I didn't have time to call because I was worried about Bobby.'

Amanda is a fine journalist who, unlike me, has edited national newspapers, but I must say that she's an even finer friend, who was both angry and upset on my behalf.

'Margaret,' I heard her saying. 'You have left your birth son – *your eldest son* – waiting in the cold for nearly two hours. This is the third time you've done so. Why do you keep doing this to Andrew? He is your flesh and blood. He just wanted a few answers to some questions. Questions which you agreed he was fully entitled to ask. I don't understand it, Margaret. I really don't!' There followed another mumbled apology from Margaret. Amanda said, 'Look, Margaret, Andrew is right here. Won't you at least talk to him?' But she declined to do so.

Even though I felt quite numb at that point, I decided I had to try to find out why Margaret was behaving like this. I could have understood her failing to show up once, maybe even twice, but not three times. So, when I got back to London, I had a long phone conversation with a very old friend, Father Dermot Power. He was not merely a Roman Catholic priest of more than thirty-five years' standing and a former chaplain of St Mary's School, Ascot, but a distinguished scholar. He made a surprising suggestion.

'You, Andrew, are going back to Birmingham. I'm going to go with you and so will Amanda, who will talk to Margaret. As a devout Catholic, I think she will be happy to talk to a priest. What's more, I'm sure that she will undoubtedly *listen* to what a priest has to say.'

A month later, the three of us were on the train to Birmingham. This time there was no prior arrangement. Father Dermot had decided that a cold call was the best way. He'd suggested a time of around 10.15 a.m., which was usually when I'd call Margaret to check if she was coming to our ill-fated meetings at BHS. As we all chatted happily on the train, I filled Father Dermot in on the limited conversation between Margaret and myself, the first time I'd met her. He listened in silence, then said, 'I have come across some women, normally Irish and of Margaret's generation, who found the only way they could deal with the trauma of giving up their child was to try and bury every memory of what happened. It's like burying toxic waste, though,' he added. 'Because if it comes to the surface, the material is potentially very harmful. Margaret made a new life for herself, somehow contriving to put you out of her mind completely. Which is the reason why, if she was really telling the truth, the date of your birthday meant nothing to her. It would also explain why she never asked you anything about your life with your adoptive parents in Swindon.'

Father Dermot continued: 'She didn't want to be reminded of anything that happened from the moment she discovered that she was pregnant. Not the distress of giving birth to you on her own,

CHAPTER TEN

nor the miserable mother and baby hostel with no friends or family by her side. She would have also been grappling with an enormous amount of Catholic guilt and shame. It must have cut her in two to visit you in the orphanage and then leave you behind. Knowing all the time there would be no other visitors. Knowing she could never talk to anyone about her little boy; nothing about wanting him to be with her, and then the sheer misery of visiting you in a bleak orphanage. So…' Father Dermot added thoughtfully, 'it's possibly understandable that when Margaret finally agreed to the adoption, she also somehow managed to bury every memory of you. In my opinion, she must have been given advice on having the baby in Bristol, miles from where she lived and worked.

'In fact, getting you into the orphanage on her own was a considerable achievement, especially when it would usually have been organised by the parish priest. Frankly,' Father Dermot gave a slight shrug of his shoulders, 'I would be very sceptical of the suggestion that James Coffey is your father. It's a tragedy that he died only just after you were born,' he added, sighing heavily. 'But it's also a very convenient story and could be a distraction from your real birth father. Also, if Coffey was your father, why wasn't he making a financial contribution to your stay in Nazareth House? Considering that Margaret had announced she was getting married only a few months after you entered the orphanage.'

It was definitely food for thought as I settled in to wait at a small café near Margaret's home, while Father Dermot and Amanda set off for her little semi-detached house. They weren't gone long, however. Margaret had been in and was very friendly, even greeting Amanda like a long-lost friend. But at the same time, she pointedly never invited either of them into her home. She also continued to insist that her failure to turn up to the previous three meetings was for genuine reasons. When Father Dermot told her that I was in a café nearby, she said, 'Oh, yes. I know it well. I'm going out in a few minutes so I'll walk that way and say "Hello" to him. I'll definitely be there in about ten minutes.'

Father Dermot sat down with Amanda as they ordered and then drank their coffee while they waited. And waited. And waited. Margaret never showed up.

Jane Moore, who had travelled down on a later train, arrived. She was astonished to find Amanda and Father Dermot there with me and not at Margaret's house. After waiting with us, she suddenly took charge of the slightly stunned company and made a swift decision. 'Come on, Andrew!' she pronounced. 'We are going to Margaret's house to say "Hello".'

We made our way to the house and Jane knocked loudly on the door. But, as I'd expected, Margaret wasn't in. A neighbour told us that they'd seen her leaving about ten minutes earlier. When the neighbour pointed out the route Margaret had taken, it was obvious that she'd left in the opposite direction to the café. A route that she knew meant we wouldn't be able to catch sight of her.

This time I wasn't upset or disappointed. Nor, to be frank, was I even surprised. Mainly because it had by now become abundantly clear that after our first meeting, Margaret had no real intention of ever seeing me again. She obviously found it difficult to say on the phone, or in a letter, that she didn't want to meet in person again – it was simply much easier for her not to show up.

I now understood that Margaret was totally focused on the danger I represented to her previously safe and predictable way of life, and above all else she was utterly determined to hide my presence from her family. So much so that I don't believe it ever

CHAPTER TEN

occurred to her to even consider how hurtful it was to leave me, literally, out in the cold.

On our return to the small café, Father Dermot was remarkably sanguine about what happened, firmly stating that it was now important that I moved on. He then turned to me, speaking slowly and carefully. His words almost took my breath away.

'Let us, for the moment, put aside the problem of Margaret. What we now have to do, is to find that little lost boy.'

I stared at him in astonishment. 'What little lost boy?'

'Why, Patrick, of course.'

'Patrick…?' I said, staring at him in confusion. 'Patrick, who?'

'Patrick Connolly,' Father Dermot said quietly but resolutely.

'But…but…' I protested. 'I haven't been Patrick for forty-six years.'

Father Dermot grabbed hold of my hand, squeezing it tightly as he said, 'When your adopted parents told you that "Patrick's in the cupboard", they were wrong. He wasn't actually in the cupboard. Because at that time, you were still Patrick. But then you retreated further and further inside yourself, which means that Patrick is still locked away, somewhere deep inside you. And it's now become clear that we have to find him,' he added firmly. 'It's obvious that Margaret has rejected you all over again, Andrew, so Patrick will be badly hurt. Very badly hurt. Which means that we need to get inside your head and your heart to see how much it's upset Patrick. Trust me. Patrick is upset all over again – and you need help to deal with it.'

So it was that, at the age of almost fifty, that I found myself agreeing to go into counselling for the very first time in my life. I'd always been sceptical of shrinks and psychologists. But, if some sort of therapy could help to solve my present confusion, dismay and heartbreak at Margaret's decision to totally avoid me, then surely it would be worth following Father Dermot's advice?

Although, as I discovered, travelling back to Nazareth House meant I would rediscover some shocking and deeply disturbing memories of my time in the orphanage.

CHAPTER ELEVEN

The faceless woman is like a ghost and appears to be pushing a pram. A spectral figure, it's not just her features that are unclear; I can't see her hands or her legs either. But somehow, I know for certain that she is pushing a pram in which there is a young child tucked up under blankets. It's impossible to discern the child's age or sex. It's night time.

There are lights twinkling in the background. Stars? Street lights? The woman seems to be walking past endless rows of grey, nondescript houses which form a homogeneous blob, their lights shining out of downstairs windows. There is no one else in the street, which appears to be deserted. No cars drive past. In fact, there are no sounds at all. Just silence, which combines with a very strong impression of the woman's overwhelming sadness. Maybe even her desperation? Because I can sense it. Because I am the child in the pram.

It is, of course, a dream. A bad dream or a nightmare that I was first aware of growing up in Swindon with my adopted family, even though I was very happily settled in the first family home I'd ever known. Despite my new and very loving parents, the nightmare persisted for many years before fading away as most bad dreams eventually do. But now, all these years later, this particular nightmare is back. And it's not the only one. I have a vivid image of a goat or a ram with menacing horns glaring down from its position high up above me in what I now know is a highly ornate stained-glass window. It's an image I haven't seen for decades. It was the dream that used to wake me, usually shouting and screaming, when I was a young child. Back then, I'm told that I used to cry out loudly, 'It's the nanny goat. The nanny goat!' So why had the nightmares returned with a vengeance?

It was in my first therapy session that I slowly realised they were, somehow, directly linked to Margaret. Principally, it seemed, because my birth mother was repeating her pattern of behaviour from so long ago. But this time, it wasn't that she'd failed to turn up to see her first-born son on just one occasion. Now, she was cruelly turning the screw by breaking all her promises and failing to appear on at least four separate occasions.

After Father Dermot Power, despite his best efforts, had failed to persuade Margaret to meet me at the café near her home, he decided to put me in the capable hands of Father Peter Burrows. A highly academic Roman Catholic priest with a string of degrees to his name, Father Peter was a well-known American psychotherapist who'd studied at the University of Southern California. He had extensive and varied experience of working with people from broken families. Not only adopted men and women themselves, but also many birth mothers, who had often spent a lifetime grieving for a child they'd been forced to give away, usually only weeks after that child was born.

By this time a retired parish priest, Father Peter used to see me in his room in a large 'religious' house he shared with other priests in north London. Some of the priests were retired, while others

CHAPTER ELEVEN

were missionaries back from Africa, usually to convalesce after long periods of illness. As I talked to him in his room it felt like a refuge where I experienced complete safety. But why did I need this protection? And why was I feeling so insecure?

However, I quickly realised that Father Dermot was quite right when he'd raised the subject of 'Patrick' with me. He was also responsible for my decision to try to find 'Patrick', who was apparently buried deep in my unconscious self. Father Dermot believed that it wasn't Andrew who was feeling insecure; it was Patrick, the little orphan boy I'd once been. The little boy I thought I'd seen for the last time when, at the age of just three, he'd been sent away for ever, into the large cupboard in my new family's kitchen.

I hadn't told anyone that, since my reconnection with Margaret, the frightening dreams had returned to haunt me. Nor, even when I was first adopted, had I ever told my family about the dream about the woman and the pram. Possibly because it was all so nebulous? But also, I suspect, because I was so young that I didn't have the necessary language skills to accurately describe that particular nightmare. Although, eventually, my new mum and dad did get to know about the dreaded 'Nanny Goat'.

Father Peter managed to coax the details of these dreams out of me over the first two or three weeks of our sessions, which could sometimes last for up to two hours at a time. The dream about me in the pram was, according to the priest, based on Margaret's time with me in Nazareth House. When I was a small baby, did she take me out for walks in a pram? If so, how could I possibly remember it? Especially as I must have been just months old at the time. But Father Peter thought the dream was about more than just me. He seemed certain that it was about Patrick, dreaming of the mother who'd left him, possibly while looking high and low for a home for both of them. In the dream, the faceless woman is continuously walking up and down the same street. Was she looking for a place for both of us to live: the proverbial 'room at the inn'? If so, how or why did that dream plant itself in my mind? Father Peter was convinced that it was also a sign that when I went to Swindon to live with my new family, I had taken some of the orphanage with me.

'I suspect the dream began when your adopted mum, Betty, began visiting you at Nazareth House,' he told me. 'Was Margaret allowed to tuck you into bed at night? She will probably have kissed you goodnight, or goodbye. So, did she encourage you to call her Mummy? The part of you that was still Patrick must have become very confused in your new home. Going off to sleep in your cot in Swindon but still bewildered and confused when thinking about Margaret. It must have been very upsetting for a small child.'

Father Peter also thought that the dream would probably have surfaced at night when living with my new parents, especially if I'd been thinking about Margaret and worrying about what had become of her. We both realised that the frightening, so-called 'Nanny Goat' dream in a stained-glass window must have begun in Nazareth House. After all, it was Catholic, run by nuns whose chapel would have undoubtedly had many large, Victorian stained-glass windows, so it wasn't too difficult to work out that maybe a goat-like image in one of the chapel's windows had spooked me as a toddler; and that, too, had followed me to Swindon.

Father Peter wanted to know all about how often, and when, my new mum and dad had told me that 'Patrick is now in the cupboard'. As I talked, he listened intently. He said nothing, but gently shook his head from side to side. After a long period of silence, he finally said, 'It was clearly a noble and loving idea to tell you that Patrick

CHAPTER ELEVEN

was now in the cupboard. They obviously loved you, wanted you to get used to being called Andrew and also to the strange experience of living in a family for the first time. But unfortunately, it was a mistake. A really bad mistake. Because it will have reinforced the view, in Patrick's young and vulnerable head, that he – Patrick – was "unwanted and unloved", which was why he had to be replaced by another child, called Andrew. It was done by your loving adoptive parents with the very best of intentions, but it meant that the feelings of rejection and hurt you felt when your birth mother suddenly disappeared from your life were exacerbated all over again.'

So, if we fast-forward from the time when, as a little boy, I was struggling to come to terms with my new identity, According to Father Peter, the three times Margaret had failed to show up at BHS had caused the feelings of rejection, which had been buried deep in my inner soul for decades, to suddenly come crashing back up to the surface. I had had no idea about that, of course. I just thought that I was bitterly disappointed and sad about Margaret's behaviour.

It had never occurred to me that Margaret's rejection, including Father Dermot Power's idea of surprising her with an unexpected visit from himself and Amanda, was likely to revive the hurt and misery I had experienced as a toddler. From Father Dermot's perspective, it might have seemed a good idea, that Margaret would meet up with us all in a little local café. But in retrospect, it was always doomed to fail. Maybe I should have warned my friends. I had enough of my birth mother's blood in my veins to know, without a shadow of doubt, that Margaret would be far too sharp and canny to allow herself to be cornered like that, especially if it meant facing questions from a distinguished priest – questions she clearly had no intention of answering. So, promising to be there in ten minutes, she'd speedily taken off in the opposite direction, never to be seen again.

I'd always prided myself on being confident, assertive and emotionally resilient. But here I was, in the run-up to my fiftieth birthday, having therapy about the distress I'd suffered nearly five decades earlier. This took some getting used to, but, as Father Peter pointed out, it seems that I had lived with the problem my entire life. He gently explained that Margaret's failure to turn up, or even to warn me that she wasn't coming – and not calling afterwards to explain herself – had reawakened dormant feelings of total rejection. In his view, the young, almost two-year-old Patrick would have been deeply hurt, confused and utterly miserable when the only visitor who came to see him at Nazareth House abruptly stopped coming, and he never, ever, saw her again. There would have been no chance for her to say goodbye or to try to explain why she wasn't coming to see me again. Although, to be fair to her, she wasn't given the opportunity. From the Nazareth House files, it's clear that she was surprised and hurt, and then highly distressed, to be told – once she'd made the final decision to put me up for adoption – that she would never, ever, see her little boy again.

At nearly two, Patrick wouldn't have ever heard the word 'rejection'. 'He couldn't have known or been capable of understanding either the word or the concept,' Father Peter explained. 'But I can assure you that Patrick will have been very upset. Also, very possibly, he could have been extremely angry when Margaret stopped seeing him. You may have regarded her as your mother. You may have even called her Mummy. It's not clear. But we do know that Margaret was the only visitor you'd ever had.'

As Father Peter pointed out, 'You would probably have also looked forward to the treats which your birth mother would have

CHAPTER ELEVEN

undoubtedly brought you. And then, everything was immediately cut off, very suddenly and abruptly. Patrick will have absorbed all that hurt but he obviously had no one to talk to. And, even if he had, the poor little boy was far too young to be able to explain his deep feelings of rejection, all of which were bound up with the inexplicable and unexplained loss of the only mother he'd ever known.'

Everything that Father Peter said made perfect sense to me. Because, even if the orphanage's nuns might have been sympathetic, they had many other children to care for. In 1963, the year I first met my adopted parents, there were thirty-nine children in the home. So, the plight of one nearly two-year-old toddler grizzling about his missing mother definitely wouldn't have been high on the Sisters of Nazareth's list of priorities.

In November 1962, Margaret had written to the nuns, saying that she had reluctantly reached the painful decision that she could not offer me a home and that I should, therefore, be put up for adoption. But sadly, there wasn't a queue of would-be parents for a monosyllabic toddler who wouldn't reach his second birthday for another three months. Particularly as, according to the file, I was shy, introverted and spoke very rarely. Moreover, the first potential parents only began visiting Nazareth House in spring 1963, which meant that I was virtually on my own for well over four months. 'Four months is a long time to a young child. Especially long if, as we can now see, you seem to have found yourself locked into a lonely little world of your own,' Father Peter said, with a sad shake of his head.

Even though I'd read my file many times, it now appeared that I hadn't really done the maths. It had never occurred to me that I'd been left – totally alone – for all that time. And of course, it could have been for much longer. Margaret was told to stay away in November 1962, when she had been informed that if I was to be adopted, her visits must cease.

'The sense of rejection, which you would have probably sensed right from birth, would be driven even more deeply into you,' Father Peter continued. 'So that when potential adopters came to see you, it would be understandable if you held back or were unwilling to trust even some nice, smiling visitors, just in case they never came back. As you may already know,' he added, 'this is a key time in a child's mental and emotional development. But you were suffering from deprivation syndrome and, I'm sorry to say, it's with you for life.'

'Deprivation syndrome?' Before my sessions with Father Peter, I had never heard anything about the condition, but it's apparently a state of 'retardation' caused by early parental rejection.

It had never occurred to me that therapists would ever find a place in *my* life. Many years ago, I read *The Severed Head* by Dame Iris Murdoch. A highly successful book, it concerned various middle-class couples indulging in extra-marital affairs and featured, among other characters, a psychoanalyst called Palmer Anderson. To tell the truth, it completely put me off the idea of ever confiding my innermost thoughts to total strangers, or so I thought! Coincidentally, the book was published in 1961, the year I was born.

I began to dive into textbooks and medical dictionaries, looking for anything I could find about deprivation syndrome. Usually, it is triggered when a child is given up for adoption very early on in his or her life or is brought up by a single parent and a father figure is absent. Well, as far as I could see, I straddled rather than ticked the boxes. Apparently, it's also known as 'maternal deprivation syndrome' and was first identified in 1951, in research published by a British psychiatrist and psychoanalyst, John Bowlby. His research on the effects of separation from their mothers on infants and young children was published in a book called *Maternal Care and Mental Health*.

Other psychologists have identified that such separation can lead children to 'feel lonely, dejected, or have masked depression, where they project externally that everything is fine, but internally they might feel lonely. It depends on the age group. In very young children, there could be biological symptoms like excessive or less crying. It usually affects children aged between zero and five years old.'

Armed with more information about the condition, I saw Father Peter Burrows once a week for months. We had a lot to talk about. Over endless, strongly brewed mugs of tea and digestive biscuits, he helped me to trawl through my brain for long-forgotten memories. Sometimes it was very painful, but it was astonishing how easily Father Peter unlocked the secrets which I hadn't just stored away but had never even realised that I had done so. Was I more like my birth mother than I thought?

Margaret had clung to the highly unlikely story that she recalled absolutely nothing of me in the home in Cheltenham or anything to do with my adoption. She even insisted that she knew nothing about a James Coffey, whom she'd declared to be my father on two official adoption forms and who was, presumably, the man she was referring to when she told the nuns that she was intending to get married in July 1961.

Maybe Margaret really had managed to bury all the evidence and her memories without trace, as a protection mechanism. Was it possible that I had done something similar?

As I discussed it with Father Peter, he dislodged from somewhere deep in my psyche a long-forgotten memory. I used to wonder what was so irretrievably broken about me that my birth mother had decided to give me away. I also used to wonder if she was ever going to come back. But, was I willing for her to come back? Did I really want to see her again? Maybe I just wanted to ask her why she had walked away. To be entirely honest, I'm not sure. I dearly loved my adopted family, so could it just be the idea, or the possibility of her returning, which had caused me such huge anxiety and feelings of guilt in the past?

And still the secrets came tumbling out. I found myself telling Father Peter that I often used to wander around a crowded room – or sometimes a church or a shop, or it could even be a beach during our family summer holiday – surreptitiously looking for a face that I thought was similar to mine. I used to think a lot about what my birth mother might look like. Did we resemble each other at all? Or was I a daddy's boy? At this point, Father Peter's face lit up.

This was our fourth session and he explained that what I was describing was called 'living in the ghost kingdom'. Apparently, this is the place adopted children often go to try to imagine a life where they haven't been adopted. 'You were looking for someone who was your blood family,' he added. 'On the surface, you are happy. But deep down, you are struggling with your emotions.'

With a start, I suddenly recalled my tenth birthday: a milestone in a child's life, the first birthday in double figures. As a precocious young boy, I thought, 'Hey, I'm ten now. I'm a young man. But my birth mother probably wouldn't recognise me – not even if I walked into a room. I'm sorry about that, because it means that if she does bump into me, she won't know it's me. And I won't know her.'

Father Peter thought that my deprivation syndrome had started way back, from when Margaret had given birth to me. 'Margaret knew that she was putting you into care. You had an abnormal first

CHAPTER ELEVEN

few weeks in the mother and baby home, no breastfeeding and limited contact between mother and child. And then, two or three weeks after you were born, you were taken to Nazareth House. Whereupon you were left there, quite alone. Baby Patrick needed to be with his mother. But she was miles away, living her own life, harbouring her secrets and visiting you only when her job, her family and her financial commitments allowed.'

The priest paused to let his words sink in. 'There is much written evidence that a baby is capable of sensing the dislocation and the rejection,' he continued. 'A baby feels very keenly the absence of warmth, love and affection from their mother, especially in the first few days and weeks of their lives. In Patrick's case, this went on for almost three years. It appears to me as an absolutely classic case of deprivation syndrome.'

Sometimes I became overwhelmed by the therapy sessions, almost choking with a large lump in my throat. Father Peter always urged me to let the tears come, but somehow, I felt compelled to fight against showing too much emotion. He would gently prod me: 'Stop protecting Patrick. He needs to cry. He needs to let out those pent-up feelings. They have been locked away for far too long.'

Between the various therapy sessions, I was reading articles about emotional and maternal deprivation and was reassured to learn that even the best and most loving of adoptive parents could never completely eliminate the pain and insecurity of their child's past, and my parents were absolutely the best. If my mum and dad had known that I was regularly plagued by feelings of deep insecurity, not only would they have been very sad and concerned, but they would have gone out of their way to make me feel even more at home. Yet I cannot envisage what more they could have done. They lavished so much love on me that I knew, without a shadow of a doubt, that I was incredibly lucky to have been chosen by such a loving couple who were determined to treat their adopted child in exactly the same way as their other three children. And they definitely succeeded in doing so.

Although, to tell the truth, I had always secretly believed that in their heart of hearts, I was my mum and dad's favourite child. Of course, I now know that wasn't true, as they really did treat us all alike, but the really magical thing was that I totally believed I was 'the chosen one', which was a great source of comfort and a stabilising factor throughout my early years. My research uncovered another study that suggested children brought up in an orphanage can lose one month's worth of development for every three they spend in that facility, but that on moving to a foster home or to an adopted family, many experience astounding developmental spurts. Apparently, the first studies into deprivation syndrome attracted instant criticism, as they were exploited by some people to claim that they supported the argument for why women should not leave their young children at home to go to work. The reports also highlighted that in the 1960s, some of the children who were suffering from deprivation syndrome had also experienced poor hygiene, poor nutrition and an absence of love and affection, with some children having virtually no educational stimulation at all.

With the benefit of hindsight, as well as Father Peter's psychology sessions, I now see that the emotions I often battled, and which had the effect of making me feel guilty and anxious, were born out of something over which I had absolutely no control. Although I never knew it at the time and would probably have dismissed the old adage 'blood is thicker than water' as utter nonsense, I now see that I was probably wrong. The process of adoption can often cause a split, creating a division between a child's biology and their

CHAPTER ELEVEN

biography, because part of knowing who you are is knowing where you came from. In the world of the adopted child, this frequently culminates in a 'search' for his or her original family background and history, and all histories have a starting point. So, for many or most adoptees, their beginning started well before they joined their adoptive family.

Many adoptees will deny their desire to search for their origins, and often believe that they will somehow hurt their parents' feelings. This is a common sentiment, even among those who have their adoptive parents' support. It definitely affected me; the dread of upsetting my much-loved parents was the chief reason I left the search for my past until it was almost too late. And, even now, there are some important gaps in my family history, such as my father's real identity, which I realise I may never know, or at least not for certain, although the use of DNA testing is now a huge advantage for those looking to establish their paternity.

Over the months I saw Father Peter, he returned repeatedly to my physical health in the orphanage. What could I remember? Was I ever sick or had I ever been, at any time, really ill? Was I small or tall for my age? Overweight or underweight? I really couldn't understand why he kept on about it, especially as I hadn't a clue and was thus unable to answer any of his questions. Eventually, however, Father Peter became more specific. 'When you arrived at your new home in Swindon, can you recall any health issues?'

Even as he was speaking and before he'd even completed his sentence, I was transported back to the family kitchen in Frobisher Drive. It was a Friday bath night and my mum had sat me down on top of the washing machine. Wielding pieces of tissue paper, she was attacking the large boils on my neck. The pain was excruciating. I was in floods of tears during what had become a dreaded, weekly routine. The boils that kept breaking out on my neck were livid red lumps that oozed a deeply unpleasant pus. My mum's job was to squeeze them until they were empty. I can still recall her saying, 'I'm so sorry. I'm doing my best to be quick but the doctor says I've got to get the core out of the boil.' I knew when the mission was accomplished. The 'core' would literally fly out, causing an even sharper cry of pain, and my mum would triumphantly parade the congealed mess of blood and pus on the tissue paper in front of me. Eugh! It was absolutely disgusting.

None of my siblings had to endure this weekly ordeal. And now, looking back, I wonder if the boils were caused by the diet in Nazareth House. Or possibly, the stress and confusion at the abrupt change in my surroundings? Seeing my reaction, Father Peter sensed that he was on to something and kept pushing me about my health, which suddenly led to me remembering, with blinding clarity, a visit to the dentist. I wasn't entirely sure, but I think that it was just after my fourth birthday. It was definitely the first time I can remember going to the dentist. And it's no wonder that the memories of that first visit came flooding back, because the dentist extracted ten milk teeth in one go. Luckily, I was given gas, so I was knocked out during the procedure. Yet I still have vivid memories of waking up and finding myself tucked under a blanket on a couch in the surgery – and with a mouth full of blood.

I now suspect that my siblings were secretly thrilled at my discomfort because it meant that we went – the whole family – on a very rare and exciting trip to a café, in search of an early lunch. The outing was certainly a 'first' for me and would have smashed a big hole in my parents' budget, as money was always desperately tight. I can clearly recall having tomato soup and ice cream as a very special treat because I wasn't allowed to chew. And the café venue?

CHAPTER ELEVEN

It was British Home Stores in Swindon town centre. The very same BHS where I would get a Saturday job, aged seventeen. And also, albeit in Birmingham, the same BHS where I met my birth mother, Margaret Lennon, for the first time since she'd left me, almost fifty years before, at Nazareth House Orphanage.

The stories about the boils, tooth extractions and my limited vocabulary when I first arrived at my new home encouraged Father Peter to press for ever more information about my time in Nazareth House. But, as I'd left before I was even three, I simply couldn't remember anything, although I did tell him about the problem with my legs, which my mum had told a friend only a few years before. It seemed that after I arrived in Swindon, every night before I went to bed, my mum gently smoothed an antiseptic moisturiser on my legs to try to soothe the red weals and sores I made worse by my constant scratching. This went on for months. Naturally, Father Peter wanted to know more, but I genuinely had no idea why my mum had done that, and absolutely no other recollection about my legs to offer him.

It was then that he told me there was one way to unlock what he needed to know: regressive therapy. This meant that, under hypnosis, he would attempt to take me back to Nazareth House, to see if there were any experiences or memories that needed to be confronted. I wasn't at all sure I wanted to do that. What deadly demons might the therapy expose? But by that point, I had full trust in Father Peter and, reluctantly, I agreed. In his room, I'd noticed the photographs of him, posing with his daughter, taken when he was both an academic and a married Anglican priest – who had then defected to Rome in the 1990s. I found it very reassuring to know that he was a real father: a dad. I felt that gave him a clearer insight into 'Patrick' and his problems.

After dithering about the regressive therapy for two weeks, I was in my usual chair in Father Peter's room when he began talking to me about how he was going to try to release any 'buried memories'. He explained that hypnotic regression is the process by which you enter a trance, thus enabling you to recall material from deep inside, past memories that are normally not available to the conscious mind. He told me he'd helped many people to release details of events they'd found difficult to cope with, events which had been pushed into the hidden recesses of the mind – the unconscious. So, as he counted down and encouraged me to breathe slowly while gazing at a crystal, I drifted into a deep sleep.

It seemed as though my head was filled by a large, dark building. Was I back in Nazareth House, demolished well over fifty years ago and which I had never seen, except for a brief look at a photo, taken when it was in the throes of demolition? As I spoke, Father Peter took rough notes. I was describing the building. It seemed enormous. Colossal! Was it a building for giants? Or was I looking at a building solely from the perspective of a two-year-old? A small child, to whom an orphanage – home to dozens of children and staff – would probably seem more akin to a skyscraper? I could also see a park. I knew there was one close to where the old Nazareth House had stood, because I had been there as an adult when I worked on the local newspaper. The park itself could have been anywhere, of course. But Father Peter, the deep and unearthly tones of his voice now sounding as if he were speaking through a long, underground pipe, kept on urging me to describe not just what I could see – but also what I could feel.

But then, I suddenly found myself back home at Frobisher Drive, our family home in Swindon. Once again, it was a Friday bath night, the only day that the expensive immersion heater was

Nazareth House, Bath Road, Cheltenham. Courtesy of the Sisters of Nazareth

Margaret as a young woman. Author's collection

The photographs uncovered by Philomena Olver of children at Nazareth House, Cheltenham, the first photos Andrew has ever seen of himself below the age of two. They show: Andrew and Ann in a playpen in the garden; (*from left to right*) Ann, Adrian, Nigel and Andrew playing in the garden with the old-fashioned prams in the background; and three boys, possibly including Andrew and Nigel, gazing at a nativity scene inside the orphanage.

Andrew as a young boy, wearing his duffel coat in the garden behind Nazareth House, 1963.
Author's collection

Coming third in the 'Happiest Family' competition at Butlin's, Minehead, 1967.
Author's collection

PUBLIC OPINION

WHY I'VE ADOPTED MY MUM!

I WAS pleased to read Marje Proops's article, "Haunted by the past." I am fifteen-years-old and was adopted when I was two. I have two loving, generous parents.

For me my mother is my real mum. The woman who gave birth to me does not exist in my mind at all and I don't expect I do to her now. My mum has cared for me, fed me, clothed me and loved me and I would not swap my parents for anything.

Forget the myth that blood is thicker than water. It is not. If you publish my letter, please give my name. I am not ashamed of being adopted. — Andrew Pierce, Swindon, Wilts.

● ONE of the most heartbreaking stories I have ever read was that of the Quantock Staghunts. It is a pity the local residents couldn't drive Mrs. Ruth Thrower into the sea and watch her drown after a three-hour fight for her life. — Mrs. J. E. B. Dartford, Kent.

■ BRITAIN is still an island of startling contrasts in regard to wealth and the quality of life. Tory MP Sally Oppenheim receives £600,000 for a house and has an estate worth a million. According to Dr. Geoffrey Taylor thousands of old people will die this winter through hypothermia due to inadequate heating.

I do wish that those who keep on shouting about the plight of the once-wealthy would pipe down.—R. Bovett, Bristol Avon.

I SEE that when Princess Anne was asked about the possibility of motherhood, her reply was: "What an impertinent question." I recall that a few weeks ago her brother Prince Charles asked a young girl: "Are you on the Pill?" Are the Royal Family really as arrogant as they sometimes appear to be?—J. Palmer, London, E1.

Andrew's letter to Marje Proops under the heading 'Public Opinion', 1 November 1976. © *Daily Mirror*

Andrew with his parents as a small child, 1963. This was his first picture with them. Author's collection

ABOVE Andrew with his parents in Hackney, London, 1988.
Author's collection

LEFT Andrew with his siblings – Shirley, Sue and Chris – at a family wedding.
Author's collection

Andrew and Jane Moore in Hove, 2021. Courtesy of Jane Moore

Andrew and Amanda Platell in Athens, 2009.
Author's collection

James Coffey. Courtesy of the Coffey family

Andrew at Margaret's house in County Mayo. Author's collection

Andrew in County Mayo. Author's collection

ABOVE Andrew with Margaret in her care home. This is the first photograph of him with his birth mother.
Author's collection

Requiem Mass for

Margaret Lennon

25th May 1926 - 2nd February 2021

Friday 5th March 2021 at 10.00 am
St Edward's Roman Catholic Church,
Raddlebarn Road, Selly Park
thereafter to
Lodge Hill Cemetery
Weoley Park Road B29 5AA
Celebrant: Father Denis McGillycuddy

LEFT The order of service for Margaret's funeral, 5 March 2021.
Author's collection

CHAPTER ELEVEN

used. I always had my bath after Dad and the water was still piping hot, even after he had soaked for twenty minutes or so after another hard week at the car factory. I enjoyed the bath but I could never put my face in the water, because it was a bit grimy by the time I got in. I never minded that, but having my hair washed – before or after the bath depending on the queue at the kitchen sink – was an entirely different matter. Because, kneeling on a chair, my head over the kitchen sink, was an absolute ordeal. I used to scream blue murder. The shouting, hollering and protesting continued for several years. Why did I hate the sensation of jugs of cold water being sloshed over my head to rinse off the shampoo? I never knew why, but I hated having my hair washed from the first moment I arrived at the Pierce house.

Father Peter realised this detail was significant and continued to press me about my weekly hair wash. But, quite suddenly, I found myself transported back to what may well have been Nazareth House. Peter told me that he could hear a child crying. It was a boy, he was sure. But where was the child? Like the ghostly figure of the woman pushing the pram, I could not see the child. But Peter instinctively knew that it was me. I was the crying child. I appeared to be in some form of bath. The water was icy cold. I could not get out of the bath as a pair of strong hands held me down. Whose hands? And why was the water so chillingly cold? Before I got in the bath... or was it after... I felt my legs were tied up, impeded. I couldn't move them properly. And then I could hear Father Peter's voice and realised he wasn't talking to Andrew. He was calling out, 'Patrick! Patrick! Why are your legs trapped? Why is the water so cold? Where are you, Patrick...?'

Apparently, my words came out in a complete jumble. But, wrapped around my legs were what I can only surmise were sheets, or at least one sheet. And even in my trance I could smell it. And no wonder, because it stank. Very strongly. Of urine. My own urine. Had I wet the bed? I felt sure that I had because I've since been told that it was a problem from the time I first arrived at my new home in Swindon, where for the first few months I slept in a cot in my mum and dad's bedroom. This was mainly due to the dreadful nightmares that caused me to wake up screaming with fear. Both the nightmares and the bed-wetting gradually ceased, although I can still remember the blue rubber sheet on my bed 'just in case of an accident' after I moved into a bunk bed with my big brother. During this trance, I'd become uncomfortable and Father Peter gently brought me out. We talked about what had happened and what I remembered, which was blurred.

The next time we did regressive therapy, I went straight back to the cold bath. Father Peter asked me about it, gently prodding and encouraging. It seemed that the sheet was twisted around my legs all over again, making it virtually impossible to escape from the cold water. I had murky visions of being put in the bath by a firm pair of hands. The sheet by the side of the bath. Had I been wearing it? Or was I going to be made to wear it after the bath? After the therapy session, Father Peter said it seemed as if I was reliving a punishment. Probably a punishment for wetting the bed. Did that explain the red marks on my legs? The sores? It took my new mum months of applying cream to my legs before the redness faded and they stopped being so sore and painful and gradually returned to normal. At which point, Father Peter clearly decided that the regressive therapy had gone far enough. As a good Catholic priest, I think he began to worry what else might be exposed about Nazareth House. However, I kept the sessions going.

CHAPTER ELEVEN

I attended the counselling sessions for at least a year, sometimes weekly, or once a month. But as Father Peter and I were now very good friends, I found it helpful to discuss various problems in my life. He explained, for instance, that even when a child is taken into a new and loving family home, and even if the child is an infant, the lack of bonding with their birth mother can be a major disadvantage. 'It's a really crucial connection,' Father Peter told me. 'Because, as time passes and the child becomes fully aware of their adoption, the sense of loss can become a theme running through their subconscious. Adoption can be a joyous and wonderful thing,' he added. 'It gives the child a loving family and a completely new start in life. But there is usually not enough space for the child to grieve the loss of his or her past life, nor the absence of the birth mother.'

When it comes to adoption, there are some important practical issues. In my own case, for instance, there is very little medical history available. Was I predisposed to certain types of cancer, or heart disease? If I turned out to be Jimmy Coffey's son, there are plenty of the delightful and friendly Coffey family, as well as many members of the Connolly family in County Mayo, Ireland, who could tell me about what might lie ahead for me. Although, of course, the question of exactly *who* might prove to be my father is still not clear.

As a last word, and after having remained very good friends over the years, Father Peter reminded me, 'Being exposed to very severe conditions in childhood can be associated with lasting and deep-seated emotional problems, which are complex and vary over time. Even though you were brought up by a loving family, some of the damage was already done by the time you arrived in Swindon. On the other hand, such so-called "damage" can in fact have some surprising and beneficial results.' When I responded to his words with a slightly sceptical expression, Father Peter emitted a short bark of laughter.

'Well, let's see,' he said, his eyes twinkling with amusement. 'A well-known consequence of social deprivation can be the need to compensate for the loss of love and affection early on in childhood by becoming an almost unbearable show-off. It's known to be the classic behaviour of an adopted child, who may have deprivation syndrome, to want to be noticed and who will, in fact, do everything they can to be noticed.'

Father Peter grinned as he added, 'That's why I'm not a bit surprised that you're a well-known journalist and broadcaster, Andrew. It's a perfect choice for someone wanting to make their voice heard. And, subliminally, you may well have been hoping that your birth mother might see you on TV? And somehow make the connection between you both. Perhaps you look like the children she might have had after she gave you up? Or, you could have been hoping that she might catch sight of you on TV and suddenly see a family likeness, or maybe there's a strong resemblance to your birth father as well? Before long, the penny might drop, and she suddenly realises there's a good chance that you are connected to one another…?'

'Well, that's definitely not going to happen in my case!' I replied.

'No, of course not,' Father Peter agreed. 'But, it's a life that suits you admirably – and with your inheritance of both Celtic charm and the gift of the gab, you'll always make friends wherever you go. Also, you may well have hoped, when younger, that there was a chance of being recognised by a member of your lost family. Hmm?'

'Well, maybe…' I muttered. Because, of course, I'd have to agree that Father Peter wasn't entirely wrong about my secret teenage hopes and desires. 'Oh, all right…' I laughed, giving up the struggle to keep a straight face. 'You win! Because I'll admit that I was a bit of a show-off when I was younger.'

Deprivation syndrome…? So was that why I was always in trouble at school for being a chatterbox, which helped to make me popular with the other kids? Was that why I'd entered all the speech competitions and often had a plum role in the school drama productions? Was it why, as an altar boy, I had often delivered the reading at some of the big masses in the church year – Easter or Christmas – and would often sing a solo too? Not to mention on our summer holidays, when I would make a tidy sum from singing at the end of the pier or entering talent shows? I had always assumed that I volunteered for just about every activity going because I thought there might be a prize to win. But was Father Peter right? Did I participate in everything I could, simply because I wanted to be noticed? Did I owe my success in seaside talent shows solely to Patrick's need to be remembered? And was I really hoping to be discovered by someone from my unknown birth family?

'You were born with many talents, Andrew.' Father Peter's voice cut through my somewhat disordered thoughts. 'And, as far as I can see, you've made the very best of each and every one of them. So, as I don't think you're going to need my help much longer,' he added, handing me a glass of malt whiskey, 'here's to your future success – in journalism and, hopefully, in discovering exactly who your real birth father is!'

CHAPTER TWELVE

While I was in the therapist's chair there was effectively no contact with Margaret. Father Peter, my counsellor, and the handful of friends who knew about her were unanimous. There were to be no attempts to meet Margaret at the BHS café in Birmingham. Ever. They simply didn't believe Margaret's numerous reasons for not turning up: the grandchild, whom she'd suddenly been asked to look after; the son – a taxi driver – who'd called at her house without any warning in the middle of a busy morning; and her little dog who had suddenly needed to be taken to the vet.

One of these reasons could explain not attending a previously arranged meeting, they thought. But not three times in a row. Besides, if any of the 'excuses' were real emergencies, why did she never call me on my mobile phone – the number of which she'd been given time and time again – while I was waiting at BHS and put me out of my misery? The three-plus hours I'd waited for her outside that wretched store had been torture in slow motion. And in the late autumn and winter, I had felt chilled to my bones. Afterwards, once or twice, I actually found myself contemplating what seemed a far-fetched idea, that she perhaps wanted me to suffer, purely to try to deter me from ever coming to see her again. Was that possible? At the time, I'd quickly dismissed the thought as uncharitable, unkind and unfair. But with hindsight, maybe I was right? Because, adding insult to injury, she *never* phoned me to apologise afterwards. She let weeks go by until I was forced to ring her and listen to whatever excuse she'd decided upon.

I went through a mental list of reasons that could explain why Margaret hadn't shown up over and over again. I had talked exhaustively about it with Father Peter, who wanted to tackle my new feelings of rejection head-on. I think Margaret panicked as the hands of the clock moved closer to the 11 a.m. deadline. I'm also sure that she was haunted by the idea that her children might, somehow, discover her guilty secret and even possibly catch her in the act of talking to a half-brother they knew nothing about. At which point, I suspect she'd closed her eyes and said her prayers, fervently clutching a rosary and then, frozen with fright, decided to stay safely at home. And I'm quite sure that she prayed for forgiveness in church the next day. However, I am definitely not saying the above either ironically or as a harsh criticism of my birth mother. Nor am I intending to be judgemental in any way. After all, my arrival in Margaret's life must have been a seismic shock.

Even though she told me, when we said goodbye – the one and only time she did turn up to meet me – that in contacting her, I had 'made her day, her week and her life', I'm now quite certain that, in reality, Margaret would have been much happier if I'd never turned up at all. Because, while I believe that she hadn't been able to resist the sheer temptation of seeing me – just once – it obviously hadn't taken her long to realise that my sudden, totally unexpected appearance had all the potential to swiftly become a nightmare; one that was almost certain to wreck her previously safe, calm and orderly life.

CHAPTER TWELVE

I like to think that Margaret had drawn some comfort from the fact that her eldest son, whom she'd fought to keep but had eventually been forced to give away, had lived a happy and healthy life. But otherwise, I found Margaret herself to be a closed book. Was her reticence due to the fact she couldn't face, or was unwilling to risk, any emotional upheaval? Or did she fear the guilt and shame bound to be unleashed by even talking about, or looking back at, the past?

Given the chance, I would have liked to have got to know her a little better, albeit from a respectable distance. If we'd ever met again, I would have repeatedly assured Margaret that I had a very positive, happy and loving relationship with my adoptive mum. I did not want, and certainly wasn't looking for, a replacement for Betty. I merely wanted to be able to fill in what was currently a blank canvas concerning my two and a half years in a Catholic orphanage. I needed to know more about Nazareth House. And, specifically, why had it been shut down only one year after my adoption was finalised.

So, rather than plan any more visits, or send letters and postcards, I telephoned occasionally just to see if she was being well looked after, keeping healthy and, of course, if there was anything she needed. I knew it was highly unlikely that she would ask me for any help, but I wanted to try to sound accommodating and let her know that I was there if she should need me at any time. I never badgered her for another date for us to meet up. In fact, I never broached the subject, knowing in my heart that she was never going to suggest it.

A neighbour, whom I had talked to on that first, memorable trip to Margaret's home, had mentioned that Margaret's short-term memory was getting worse. So, in return, I'd lied to the neighbour that Margaret was a friend of the family through Amanda's Aunty

Dee. That the two women had worked together in the NHS in Birmingham for years until the 1980s when they had both retired. Whereupon, I explained, Aunty Dee had gone back to Australia and, as her own health declined, mostly due to old age, she had asked her niece, Amanda, to track Margaret down and say hello from Down Under. The neighbour didn't blink when I told her the story. Nor did I feel at all guilty about concocting this small white lie, particularly as it was merely a precautionary tactic in case we ran into any of my birth mother's family.

Pondering the fact that Margaret's short-term memory was poor, I wondered if it might, like my lovely dad, be a case of Alzheimer's. But, on the few occasions I telephoned her at home, she always seemed to know that my name was Andrew and she usually chatted about Bobby, her yappy little dog, and, of course, her local church. At some point in every call, she would always say the same thing to me: 'You have a lovely voice, Andrew. I would know your voice anywhere.' I wanted to ask if I sounded like James Coffey, who I'm sure would have had a strong Irish accent, or maybe another male figure in her life from the early 1960s, around the time of my birth. But, of course, tempting as it was, I always resisted the urge to do so.

One day, in 2013, when I was in the office at the *Daily Mail*, I decided to give her a quick call. My heart missed a beat when I dialled the number. It was unobtainable. I called it two or three more times, but all I heard was the same repetitive whirring noise. My heart was sinking fast. I thought she must have died or suddenly become very sick, so I called the telephone operator, who told me the number was no longer in use. A lifetime's instincts as a news reporter immediately kicked in as I swiftly Googled all death reports in Birmingham for Margaret Lennon. Luckily, there were none.

CHAPTER TWELVE

But while that was no guarantee she was still alive, I did wonder if my hunch about Alzheimer's was right. Knowing from my dad's case just how quickly it could progress, I realised that the loss of her short-term memory might have become more serious. Maybe she was no longer capable of living on her own? Had she moved in with a family member? Or gone into a home? Oddly, I found myself thinking about Bobby the dog. She had talked to me a lot about the dog and who would look after it if anything happened to her, so I swiftly decided to find out everything I could about where Margaret might be.

First, I went back to the neighbour, asking if she knew whether everything was OK with Margaret. And did they have a forwarding address? I chose those words with care. It would have been extremely tactless and insensitive to ask if Margaret had died. Moreover, as a so-called 'friend of the family', it would seem odd if I didn't already know if she was dangerously ill or had passed away. But the neighbour couldn't have been more helpful, immediately giving me the address of the care home where she was now being looked after. My suspicions were confirmed when the neighbour told me that Margaret's initial diagnosis of Alzheimer's had now become much worse. I called the home and was told that Margaret had been there for a few months. She had settled in well, was in very good spirits and was definitely happy to see visitors at any time.

So, on another pre-arranged trip to Birmingham, when Amanda could join me, we took a taxi from the railway station to the nursing home. It was set in lovely gardens, with a warm and happy welcoming atmosphere when the doors were opened. We introduced ourselves, filled in the visitors' book and were all ready, if we should be asked about our connection to Margaret, to trot out the Aunty Dee story. The staff, however, seemed very pleased to see us, hardly bothering to check our credentials and simply happy that one of their residents was having visitors.

When we were told that her children were regulars, I fought a wild impulse to say, 'Well, I'm her child too.' But of course I didn't. We were taken upstairs to what seemed like a common room. Margaret was in the thick of it: chatting, laughing and smiling at the other residents. Her face lit up and she was all smiles when she saw us. It gave me so much pleasure to know that she clearly remembered us and realised that we had come specifically to see her. The staff led us to a side room. As we walked there with Margaret, she instinctively linked arms with me and chatted away nineteen to the dozen. Not all of it made sense, but she was clearly comfortable in the home and seemed very happy and content. I did remind her of our names, although I'm not sure if she really understood exactly who we were. But, as we talked, she stared intently into my eyes, reaching up to stroke my face, time and again. It seemed to be a powerful connection, far more significant than anything I'd experienced with her at the BHS café.

It appeared then that Alzheimer's had one positive effect, for me at least. Because Margaret had obviously forgotten all her previous fear and caution. Totally at ease now, she no longer knew or cared about why she'd had to protect her secrets so fiercely or why she'd felt the need to be so reticent in my presence. For my part, I never sought to exploit the situation. Even though I had so many questions needing answers, I never asked her about James Coffey or Nazareth House. Nor how many times, before my adoption, she'd travelled to see me in Cheltenham. Neither did I ask why, or with whose help, she'd chosen Bristol as the place to give birth to me. But it seemed massively unfair to probe and also morally quite wrong to take advantage of a very confused old lady. So I just chatted away as

CHAPTER TWELVE

she held on tightly to my hand. She obviously knew that she had a strong connection to me and barely glanced at Amanda, who was sitting directly opposite her.

They brought us tea and biscuits and a senior member of staff came in to ask about our connection with Margaret. We trotted out the Aunty Dee story and no more questions were asked. In fact, the staff were all smiles, not least because they could see how happy Margaret was with us. Amanda took photographs of me with my birth mother – the first ever – and they are now among my most treasured possessions. Smiling broadly for the camera, she looked more than happy, once again, stroking my face and holding my hand.

Looking at Amanda, I said, 'Does she realise? Do you think she knows I'm her son?'

With tears stinging her eyes, Amanda responded, 'She is certainly very happy to be with you, and there's clearly a very strong bond between you. It's obvious that Margaret can feel it – even if she can't articulate it. She looks really content, and somehow she seems to instinctively know that you are her flesh and blood.'

After all the upset of the 'no-shows' – and I'm sure they deeply troubled Margaret too – I hoped that our meeting at the nursing home would bring her some happiness and peace – perhaps even some joy. History has taught us that the bond between a mother and child is a powerful one. So here we were at last, after more than fifty years apart, and it was evident to both Amanda and myself that the original bond was still there: not just there, but very strong as well.

As Margaret chatted away, we looked at the clock. Time was racing away with us. Although we were reluctant to tear ourselves away, neither of us wanted to outstay our welcome in the home.

What if one of Margaret's children arrived when we were there? We had deliberately chosen the morning, as we had with the abortive meetings at BHS, assuming that her family would be at work. So, we walked Margaret back into the common room, leaving her once again in the thick of the conversation with the other residents, her face wreathed in smiles, chatting to anyone who would listen and squeezing my hands as we left. I even got another kiss as we assured Margaret that we would be back to see her very soon.

Amanda and I restrained ourselves until we were in the cab, well out of sight of the nursing home, before we swapped notes. I asked Amanda again, 'Did Margaret realise that I was Patrick? That I was her son?' Because I'd felt a strong physical connection. And if I could feel it, was she able to as well? But there was no way of really knowing what she made of it. Her mind was more than likely engulfed in a thick, Alzheimer's-induced fog. But despite her confusion and uncertainty, her happiness seemed to shine through. It was Margaret's most positive affirmation of me.

Amanda and I reported back to Father Dermot, who had tried to persuade her to meet me in the café more than a year ago. I also contacted Father Peter Burrows, my therapist and counsellor. They were both delighted. Father Peter summed it up: 'The woman you met was no longer fraught with anxiety in case anyone worked out who you were. She was no longer burdened by her Catholic guilt about her unmarried pregnancy or leaving you in the home to be adopted by a couple she would never meet or know anything about. She probably could not pinpoint *exactly* who you were. But she obviously knew that you were part of her. She also demonstrated that the natural bond between a mother and her son, especially her first born, is normally very strong; capable of being able to withstand just about all the vicissitudes of life.'

CHAPTER TWELVE

He went on to suggest that I continued to visit Margaret in the nursing home, primarily because it would be the best quality time I'd ever be able to have with her. I took him at his word. Accompanied by Amanda again, we went back for a second visit, which followed very much the same routine as before: signing the visitors' book, telling the 'Aunty Dee' story, being shown into the common room and taking Margaret into the side room to chat. But we both noticed that her memory was getting worse. She talked less, but she still smiled, her eyes as bright and sparkling as ever. As on our first visit, she stroked my face and hands. And yet again, she virtually ignored Amanda, who understood and really didn't mind.

It was another successful visit. Margaret enjoyed the company and I remained aware of the strong connection between us. I felt as though I had finally bonded with her, although there was no way she could put what she felt into words. Moreover, she wouldn't have understood me even if I had tried to articulate my own feelings. Unfortunately, it was all too evident that her powers of comprehension and concentration were fading fast.

Once a month or so, I telephoned the home in Selly Oak to check on her. One day, there was another heart-stopping moment when I called.

'I'm sorry. Margaret's not with us any more,' said a calm female voice.

'WHAT...?' I thought that could only mean one thing. Had she passed away? I heard myself blustering down the telephone, 'Whatever happened? Why isn't she with you?'

Very sweetly, the woman on the other end of the phone said, 'I'm so sorry. I meant to explain that Margaret's condition deteriorated and she now needs more intensive care, so she's been moved to a different nursing home.'

The relief was overwhelming. I asked for the address, but the nurse said that not only did she not know it but she wouldn't be able to give it out, even if she did. I quite understood her reluctance but, being a good hack and knowing how to get any information I needed, I simply rang round the nearest care homes, especially those whose websites stipulated that they specialised in caring for residents with dementia. It was only the second or third home I'd telephoned before I found Margaret.

'Yes, Mrs Lennon is here,' said the kindly male voice at the end of the telephone. 'She's settled in very well. She's a happy little soul.' And yes, it seemed the home was well equipped for visitors. 'The more the merrier!' he said.

A few months later and Amanda and I were able to visit the new nursing home. It was called Selly Wood House and was in the heart of Bournville, which was founded by the Quaker Cadbury family, primarily for its chocolate factory workforce. The home had a warm and welcoming atmosphere. It was bright, light and the staff were very friendly. They all said the same thing about Margaret: 'Oh, she's a delight. Very frail of course, but we all love her. She's absolutely no trouble.' The change in Margaret was dramatic, however.

We saw her in her bedroom, although I suspect that she spent little time outside it. I also realised that it was the first time I had been inside her room, which was clearly now her 'home'. At the previous nursing home, we'd seen Margaret in the common room. But on our first visit to her new accommodation, after signing the visitors' book, we were escorted to her room by a female member of staff. Margaret was in bed and appeared to have shrunk dramatically in size. She was asleep when we went in and I was pleased to note that she still had a good head of hair, while I was struggling with a thinning mane.

CHAPTER TWELVE

On the mantelpiece were some photographs. One was of a middle-aged woman with a healthy shock of white hair standing with a man who appeared to be her husband. She was wearing a pair of distinctive glasses and I wondered if she was Margaret's only daughter, Anne? But, if it was her daughter, there appeared to be no pictures of her two sons, Sean and Patrick. Perhaps Anne was Margaret's favourite? There were also small statues of Our Lady, which reminded me of my 'nanna', my mum Betty's mother, who'd died in 1970. She loved Our Lady and often said the rosary. Obviously Margaret did too.

As soon as I spoke, Margaret opened her eyes wide, held a hand up to me and smiled broadly. I clasped her hand. 'It's Andrew here to see you again,' I said. 'You used to know me as "Patrick". I hope you can remember me?' As I spoke, she stared intently at me, her eyes darting across my face, then her hand reached up to touch my cheek, and she sought my hand so I could hold hers. The conversation on her part was almost non-existent. I talked to her about the church. I mentioned her children by name and she tried to communicate in a form of babyish babble. I couldn't help thinking about George, my own much-loved dad, who was bedridden after having a stroke, when he'd already been diagnosed with Alzheimer's. Like Margaret, he'd been warm, comfortable, well fed, and well loved by my mum and his carers. When I was at home in Swindon, I used to talk to him constantly in the hope that he might understand some of my words and be able to tell from my tone of voice that I loved him very much.

Whenever I was in Birmingham, I would call in to see Margaret. I always telephoned the nursing home in advance to ensure it would be appropriate to visit. Her failure to show up at any of our scheduled meetings at BHS had been bruising and painful, but in the nursing home she was effectively a captive audience. When visiting her, I was invariably suited and booted, especially if I was in the area to conduct an interview or attend a party conference. I was often in Birmingham in my role as chairman of the judges' panel for the Midlands Media Awards, which always included a glamorous dinner. So, very often I'd call in to see Margaret before going off to hand out prizes at an event. This meant that I was slightly conspicuous, as few other visitors were wearing suits and ties.

There was always a risk that a member of Margaret's large extended family might already be in her comfortable little room when I got there, or that they might arrive while I was there, usually with Amanda. Margaret was bedridden, so there was no escape if any of her relatives turned up.

In fact, Amanda and I often discussed what would we say and do if the worst happened and we were actually challenged by one of Margaret's children. It could be very hard for them, especially when there was a very real danger of suddenly finding themselves face to face with a half-brother of whose existence they were totally unaware. So, if the worst did happen, we had originally resolved to firmly stick to the totally fictitious story that we were connecting with Margaret on behalf of Amanda's late Aunty Dee, who we claimed had worked with Margaret in Birmingham in the dim and distant past. It was the same nonsensical excuse we'd cooked up when we went to Margaret's first nursing home.

Over the years, we had found it necessary to slightly fine-tune the story. Aunty Dee, who'd originally died, had now, like Lazarus, risen from the grave. In her new incarnation, she was a hale, hearty and very rich 94-year-old, given to demanding regular reports on her old friend's progress in the nursing home. If anyone pushed us

CHAPTER TWELVE

really hard on the somewhat flimsy story, I'd planned that Amanda, blushing shyly with embarrassment (I'd have loved to have seen that!), would reluctantly confess that Aunty Dee was loaded and that she, Amanda, was hoping to inherit all her money, which is why she was so keen on carrying out her rich aunt's demands without demur. So, while it was total rubbish, it had the important effect of making Aunty Dee a real person. And luckily, it had served us well until that point and no one had challenged our story.

And then, completely out of the blue, it seemed that we had been rumbled, which meant that our alibi was very likely to be put to the test. Arriving at the nursing home with Amanda one day, we walked into the main hall in our usual characters, with Amanda muttering about how happy her Aunty Dee was to know that Margaret was being so well looked after in this nice home etc. etc. But, at the same time, I noticed that a middle-aged man in the nurses' office on the ground floor was staring hard at me. I sensed it might be a good idea to make our way, as quickly as possible, upstairs to Margaret's room.

As usual, she was fast asleep, and as I called her name gently, her hand slowly emerged from under the blankets in search of mine. She might have been trapped in the vicious claws of dementia, but she remembered enough to know that if she had a visitor, they would provide some comforting physical contact. I clasped her hand as I stood over her, while Amanda sat on a chair and watched the interaction between birth mother and son.

Seconds later, the man who had stared so hard at me when we'd arrived at the nursing home suddenly burst into the room and barked loudly, 'What are you doing here?' The colour drained from Amanda's cheeks. Was this one of Margaret's sons, my half-brother?

Once again, the man demanded roughly, 'Why are you here?' Very slowly, I lifted my head, all the while stroking Margaret's hand as I turned towards him.

Giving the man a big, friendly smile, I said, 'How can I help you?' While he was looking me up and down, I was staring intently at his features to see if there was any likeness to Margaret. But I couldn't see any at all.

The unknown man took no notice of what I'd just said, merely demanding aggressively again, 'Why are you here?'

I drew myself up to my full height, still holding one of Margaret's hands as I turned around to confront him. My journalistic training kicked in fast as I swiftly recalled the reporter's mantra: 'Always talk calmly, nicely and slowly when you want to extricate yourself from a difficult situation. Never panic, and only get the hell out of there if you think you're in physical danger.'

So, I embarked on the well-rehearsed story – speaking clearly and slowly – about Amanda's Aunty Dee and Margaret working together as nurses in Birmingham, in the 1960s. But he didn't seem to be listening. He continued to stare intently at me and was clearly not at all interested in my answer. Then, rather surprisingly, he said, 'I can't believe you're here!'

To which statement, and fearing the worst, I responded, 'Why?'

Then, in a complete *volte-face*, the unknown man proceeded to give me a broad and extraordinarily friendly smile. 'Because you're that bloke off the telly. I watch you every day. I mean… I really like you,' he added, with another friendly grin. 'It's just… well, I hadn't a clue that you had any connection with Birmingham. So, it's great to see you here. It really is!'

I didn't need to look at Amanda. I could almost physically sense the depth of her utter relief across Margaret's room, with its little

CHAPTER TWELVE

statues of Our Lady and a handful of framed sepia photographs. We made a bit of small talk. He told us he volunteered at the nursing home. Mercifully, he never asked if we knew Margaret's children. As he was about to leave the room, he turned to ask if he could have a photo of us together. I gave him a quick smile. 'Yes, of course,' I lied cheerfully. 'I'll come and find you.' There was no way I was being photographed. What if Margaret's children saw the photo and recognised me?

With our hearts beating ever faster, we waited for just a few more minutes, listening to the man's footsteps retreating along the corridor and back down the stairs, before we decided to leave. Luckily, we had kept the taxi waiting and so, with our heads down, we made our way out of the nursing home. Carefully avoiding the 'office' near the main entrance and smiling blandly at any staff, we slipped through a side door and hurriedly made our escape. Tumbling into the taxi, we were almost hysterical with laughter and relief. Although, talking about it later, we decided that if it really had been one of Margaret's sons or if we were accosted by a complete stranger again, we should stick to our guns. With Margaret's small figure hardly visible beneath the bed sheets, it was highly unlikely that anyone would notice the strong physical likeness between Margaret and myself. We both wondered if the encounter in Margaret's room would get back to her children. Because, if they took the time to Google me, they wouldn't have any difficulty in identifying exactly *who* had been in their mother's room. Fortunately, however, there was nothing on my voicemail at work and no emails arrived, so it looked like we had got away with it.

In fact, we both went back to Selly Wood House a couple of times after that and each time I wore dark glasses and a baseball cap, which in hindsight was a pretty pathetic attempt to preserve my anonymity. It could even be that I made the situation even worse. A bloke in a dark blue suit, wearing a baseball cap and sunglasses in the middle of a bleak Birmingham winter? The staff probably thought, and probably said, 'Who on earth is that prat?'

I continued to see Margaret at least twice a year, if not more. And on each visit, I noticed that she had declined further. The last time I saw her was a few months before the lockdown due to Covid-19. She was fast asleep again. But, when I spoke to her, she stirred, even if her eyes remained closed. As usual, her hands, tucked under the blankets, began to edge upwards. Slowly but surely she moved her hands out from under the covers until she extricated them. She was clearly searching for my hands, for some physical contact. As I clasped my hands around hers, she sighed and smiled. I chatted away about nothing significant, while her eyes remained firmly closed. But just as I was about to go, she opened her eyes, stared up at me and smiled broadly as I said, 'Hello, Margaret, it's Andrew. You used to call me Patrick.'

She seemed to be listening, and as I repeated that I used to be Patrick, she smiled once again. As was my habit, I kissed her on the cheek several times as I prepared to leave, while she squeezed my hand hard. I kissed her cheek again. She was trying to speak, to articulate a few words, but nothing came out. I wondered if she was trying to say 'Patrick'? Or maybe 'Andrew'? Before walking out of the room, I said a final goodbye to her – not knowing that it would be the last time I ever saw her.

It was November 2019. Within a few months, the Covid-19 pandemic would strike and nursing homes like Margaret's would be closed to visitors for a long, long time. Knowing I couldn't visit her, I used to telephone the home for an update. It was always the same message: 'She's smiling. She's cheerful, but she is very frail.' This went on for over two years.

In the interim, I had got to know Margaret's parish priest, Father Denis McGillycuddy, who had been at St Edward's in Selly Oak for more than twenty years. I confided in him about Margaret being my birth mother. Father Denis was cool, calm and collected when I explained our relationship and never batted an eyelid when I told him about the situation between Margaret and myself. Catholic priests have seen and heard so much in the confessional that they are rarely shocked or surprised by what may have happened in their parishioners' earlier lives. He told me that he was very fond of Margaret, although she had never confided in him about me. But when she was living up the road, she attended mass every day and was often there when he unlocked the doors in the morning. Father Denis kindly promised to let me know if and when anything happened to Margaret. From time to time I would call him to check up on her, and he would also call me.

When I was researching the church where Margaret worshipped, I stumbled across details of the Woodville mother and baby home which opened in 1943 and was run by the Sisters of Charity of St Paul the Apostle. It was virtually opposite St Edward's church. The home could accommodate up to fifteen young women and their babies, but it closed in 1973 and was reopened as a hospice. I often wondered if there were any sad stories behind those walls. Then, in Ireland, Prime Minister Micheál Martin issued a public apology in February 2021. This was after a five-year investigation revealed that approximately 9,000 children had died at eighteen mother and baby institutions between 1922 and 1998. As I read about the terrible abuse in the homes, I shivered. Especially at the fact that a number of young children had died and been buried in makeshift graves in the grounds of the homes. I had been with Margaret in St Raphael's mother and baby home in Bristol, which had been abruptly shut down with a total news embargo on what went on there. In fact, the file remains closed, because of its sensitive contents. After the official apology in Ireland, it made me wonder, all over again, about what went on in St Raphael's. I can only thank God that Margaret and I were there for just a few weeks.

Like Margaret, Father Denis McGillycuddy was Irish. Hailing from Milltown in County Kerry, he was charming and looked much younger than his seventy-six years when he celebrated his golden jubilee as a priest in January 2021. Whenever I was in Birmingham, I would always visit him and light a candle in his church for my birth mother. Father Denis told me that she, too, had always lit a candle when she was in the church. I smiled when he told me that because, when entering a new church in whatever part of the country or world I found myself in, I would always light a candle and offer it up for my mum Betty, who died in 2015. Or for my dad who had died in 2002. And, of course, for other people I had known, loved and who had sadly passed away. This seems to be another habit that I have quite unknowingly picked up from my birth mother.

During this time, I also took it upon myself to do some further research about Margaret. I had always been suspicious of the vagueness surrounding her age. She had failed to give her birth date to the adoption agency and all they had been able to tell me was that she was 'approximately' twenty-nine years old at the time of my birth. So, I sent off for her birth certificate. Opening up the envelope, I audibly gasped. There was the truth staring at me from the piece of paper. Margaret had been born on 25 May 1926, making

CHAPTER TWELVE

her just weeks away from her thirty-fifth birthday at the time of my birth – a big difference from the twenty-nine years she had told the nuns.

After I'd recovered from my initial shock, I found it hard to condemn her for what could easily be termed a 'white lie'. Especially as it's something we've all done at various times in our lives. Still, it was just yet another thing to add to the list of things Margaret had been evasive and misleading about to do with me and another sign that she had taken every effort to make sure she could not be traced.

• • •

In January 2021, Father Denis called and told me he was hoping to go into the nursing home to see Margaret. Visits were still severely curtailed because of the pandemic. A few days later he called again. I thought it would be to say that he had seen her but actually, it was to tell me that her health had sharply deteriorated and she was nearing the end. By now, Margaret had reached a mighty ninety-four years of age, so Father Denis had arranged with Margaret's daughter Anne to hold the phone to her ear so he could give her a blessing. I was out on my daily walk when my mobile rang. I couldn't answer it in time but it was Father Denis. He left a simple message, saying Margaret had died. It seemed that she'd slipped away peacefully in the early hours, with the night nurse by her bedside.

I was hit by waves of sadness for her family and, of course, for myself. My sadness came out of regret that, despite our quality time together in the various care homes, I had never really got to know my birth mother. Unfortunately, she never gave me that chance. I'm not sure that she ever really understood that I genuinely hadn't wanted a second 'mother'. Moreover, I came to realise that she was so consumed by fear of her children discovering my existence that she simply wasn't capable of dealing with the wider issues within our relationship, such as leaving me in the Nazareth House Orphanage until I was almost three years of age. And I was never able to explain fully that there had only been one 'real' mother in my life: Betty, in Swindon. When she died in her sleep in July 2015, I wept for days and remained inconsolable for a very long time.

But I only shed a few tears over Margaret. As one of my closest friends said at the time, 'It's such a shame that she never got to know you, Andrew. Because I'm quite certain that if she had, she would have really liked you. And not just that. You could have both had a lot of fun together. She would have been very proud of your achievements, and also, you'd have made her laugh! What better mixture for a mother and son could there possibly be?'

CHAPTER THIRTEEN

Margaret had died on Wednesday 2 February 2021, the ancient feast day of Candlemas, which, for Roman Catholics, commemorates the ritual purification of Mary, forty days after the birth of Jesus. I knew that Margaret prayed to Mary. I also knew that she prayed with a rosary, which Catholics believe is a remedy for temptation and the hardships of life, so it felt appropriate that she should pass away on that day. I hope that would have been a source of comfort to her children.

Even before Margaret had taken a turn for the worse, I'd told her local priest, Father Denis, that I would like to go to her funeral. If it happened during Covid restrictions and was subject to those restrictions, I planned to watch from outside the church. At that time, there were very strict, almost draconian limits, requiring there to be only thirty attendees at a church service. Moreover, I had just been through the heartbreak of a Covid funeral for my wonderful sister Shirley. She had died in hospital in Swindon in November after a short illness. She was only sixty-four.

Shirley and I had always been extraordinarily close. She was a cherished sister, who had privately offered to act as an intermediary with my mum Betty if ever I decided to try to track down my birth mother. It was so kind and thoughtful of her, as despite anything I said to try to reassure Betty that she was my *real* mum, she feared losing me to a completely unknown woman: my birth mother. I had always planned to tell Shirley about tracking Margaret down when I finished writing this book. But that was not to be. I was utterly devastated when she died so young. There had been only thirty of us in the crematorium in Swindon because her little church, where she was a spiritualist medium, was closed due to the pandemic.

But, as it turned out, when it came to Margaret's funeral, Father Denis McGillycuddy wasn't prepared to have anyone telling him what he could or couldn't do, especially not in his own church. He was adamant that he was not imposing limits on the size of the congregation at the service and was unequivocal about the fact that I should be there.

'You were, and are, her first-born son,' he told me decisively. 'As far as I'm concerned, you have a perfect right to attend your birth mother's funeral.' So, I agreed to be there. I also arranged with Father Denis that Amanda Platell would also attend and that we would sit discreetly at the back of the church. I was particularly worried that I might be recognised, since I frequently appear on television. Besides which, I'd already been identified several times – although not accosted by anyone, other than the guy in Selly Oak – when visiting Margaret in her nursing homes. It occurred to me that some of the staff from her final home might also be there and they could recognise me as an occasional visitor.

My main concern, however, was to avoid any contact with Margaret's close family. As far as I was aware, she had done her best to ensure that I remained a guilty secret, a deliberate policy she had maintained for sixty years so that her family would have absolutely no idea of my existence. This was why I was so anxious

CHAPTER THIRTEEN

not to encroach, or cause any upset, on their mother's final journey. While she was technically my birth mother, I had not been brought up by her. This was an experience that belonged solely to my two half-brothers and sister, Sean, Patrick and Anne, and was also why I'd firmly decided not to attend the family burial.

I understood from Father Denis that Margaret had originally intended to be buried in a double plot at Sutton Coldfield cemetery with her husband Patrick (Paddy) Lennon, close to the Good Hope Hospital, where he died in 1996. It was about four miles from Oscott cemetery and the cemeteries were equidistant to the one where someone used to pay weekly visits, bearing a bunch of flowers, to the grave of James Coffey. I would never know if it was Margaret who made that weekly pilgrimage. It was yet another of the many secrets she would be taking to her grave.

The funeral was due to be held at 10 a.m. on Friday 5 March 2021 at St Edward's Church, so Amanda and I were on the first train out of London Euston at 6.15 a.m. We reminisced about the first time we had gone to Margaret's house, just around the corner from the church, which was now more than twelve years ago. It had been quite a journey, and now we were nearing the end of it. Very unusually, Amanda was anxious about the funeral in case I was recognised, although I thought that, as a very distinctive and strikingly good-looking woman, she was far more likely to be noticed than me. She was also worried that someone might work out that I was a blood relation. What if I looked like one of her sons or her daughter? But, fortunately, as Father Denis had pointed out, thanks to Covid, everyone in the church would be required to wear a mask. So I believed there was no need to worry. Masks were then mandatory when appearing in public places and they enabled many Hollywood stars and other celebrities to enjoy the simple but rare pleasure, of being able to move anonymously through crowded streets. I also recall wondering if the printed order of service leaflets would contain photographs of Margaret, maybe as a younger woman, from around the same time she had me at the age of thirty-four.

The so-called 'early fast train' to Birmingham proved to be extremely slow and stopped everywhere. Then, as we pulled into Northampton, we were thrown off it because of a technical fault, leaving us to wait forty-five minutes for a connection. At that point, I was very worried that we might be late for the funeral. However, we arrived at Birmingham New Street in good time, going straight to the church where Father Denis was waiting with a pot of strongly brewed tea and homemade cakes. Delicious!

In keeping with Irish Roman Catholic tradition, Margaret's coffin had been received into the church the night before the funeral. Amanda and I chatted away with Father Denis and then, just before we went into the church to join Margaret's family, who had already arrived, he handed each of us a freshly printed order of service.

My reaction to the coloured photograph of a much younger Margaret on the front cover was not at all what I expected. Finding myself assailed by a sharp stab of panic, I couldn't prevent an involuntary gasp of fear and alarm, my hands trembling as I stared down at the woman's picture. It was somehow familiar, and then I recalled that there had been a smaller, much fuzzier photograph of exactly the same woman on the mantelpiece in Margaret's room at her final nursing home. When I'd first seen it, I'd assumed it was a picture of Margaret's only daughter, Anne. How wrong I was. It was a photograph of Margaret. Only this time, it was a clearer and more flattering image on the front of her funeral order of service. In retrospect, I think the photo may have been taken when she

CHAPTER THIRTEEN

was in her mid-fifties, definitely some twenty-five to thirty years before I saw her for the first time. Then, aged eighty-three, she'd been a little old lady walking back to her house in Birmingham after an early morning service at her church. The very same place of worship, in fact, where Amanda Platell and I had just finished having a delicious breakfast with Father Denis while waiting to attend her funeral.

Following Jane Moore's excellent detective work, Amanda had been the first to contact Margaret, knocking on the older woman's front door only to be met by outraged denials about my birth and adoption before the door was slammed in her face. But Amanda, who has a heart like a hotel, had never stopped trying to help Margaret. Not only a constant support to me during the trials and tribulations of attempting to form a relationship with my birth mother, but also joining me when I visited both her nursing homes, Amanda had also insisted on accompanying me to Margaret's funeral. But now, she was unusually apprehensive in case anyone from the family might be suspicious about why I was there. Which, despite Father Denis's assurances that there would be no problem, since everyone present would be wearing a mask, was why I held back from entering the church until just before the service was due to start, when the family and other principal mourners would already be in place.

Later, Amanda told me that as I stared, for the first time, at the photo of my birth mother, I'd clearly muttered out loud, 'Is that Margaret? Oh, no! It can't be Margaret.' Why was I so determined that it couldn't be her? And why, when I'd first looked at the photograph, had I felt a stab of anxiety and fear in the pit of my stomach?

When we'd first met at the BHS café in Birmingham, my initial impression of Margaret was that she was a sweet little old lady; a kindly soul who chatted away, smiled a lot and cared deeply about her late husband. 'He was a fine man,' she'd said more than once, 'who the Good Lord took away from us far too soon.' And while it was frustrating that she told me nothing about our time together in Bristol and at the mother and baby home, or even about visiting me in Nazareth House, I'd thought that she was basically a kind woman. She was also very proud of her Gaelic roots and her family in Ireland, as well as her grown-up children and grandchildren, who were all living in England. On the telephone, Margaret spoke constantly to me about her three children in Birmingham: her sons, Sean and Patrick – the latter being the only one who wasn't married – and her clearly much-loved daughter Anne.

Now, as I stared down at Margaret's photograph on the order of service, my mind seemed to be all over the place. Why on earth did I feel so anxious and fearful? Was I reliving the searing pain I felt when Margaret had left me standing three times – literally in the freezing cold wind – outside BHS in Birmingham, having faithfully promised me that she would come to see me? Or was it more deep-seated? Was the pain linked to mine, or rather Patrick's, time in the orphanage?

When Margaret visited me in Nazareth House, I was obviously too young to remember if she was ever irritable, cross or even frustrated. Was the little boy in front of her a potential threat to her prospect of marital happiness? Might he consign her to a lonely spinsterhood for the rest of her life? Back in the cold and unforgiving social climate of the early 1960s, Margaret must have been fully aware that not only would her parents have been utterly ashamed of her but they were more than likely to disown her and her child. Moreover, she couldn't be sure that any potential suitors would be any more understanding of her predicament, or willing to take on and adopt her illegitimate child. This was probably why – as she told me emphatically the first and only time we met in the BHS café – she hadn't even considered the possibility of telling her parents about her pregnancy. And she most certainly hadn't ever told her husband, she'd added, emphasising again the fact that Patrick Lennon, her husband of over thirty years, had known absolutely nothing about me.

When Father Peter Burrows had put me through the regressive therapy which had caused me considerable mental pain, it had never occurred to either of us that he should probe my relationship with Margaret when I was a toddler. Yet he had, in fact, raised the prospect that Margaret might have resented me. He'd also pointed out that other women in her position might well have opted for an illegal abortion, especially when, as an experienced nurse, Margaret would have known exactly who to contact if she'd decided to pursue that alternative. But it seems as if her deep Catholic faith meant that she would never have countenanced it. When she learned that she was pregnant, and if the father really was James Coffey, Margaret would have hoped that they would marry. After all, when I arrived at the orphanage, she had told the nuns that there was a 'prospect of marriage'.

So, while the Margaret who I met in BHS, and later in various nursing homes, radiated Irish warmth and charm, the Margaret who left me – worried and waiting for her in the cold outside BHS – was not kind. She had, in fact, been as cold as ice towards me, which clearly illustrated that there was a tough, single-minded streak of self-preservation running through her. All of which would explain why she had given birth to her illegitimate child nearly 100 miles away from where she lived and worked. In addition, unless I can manage to discover otherwise, she did so entirely on her own, without any help from friends or family and with no one knowing anything about either her pregnancy or her child. She had also, apparently with no assistance, organised my placement in Nazareth House. Maybe there was a secret hand behind the scenes pulling all the strings, but I have considerable doubts that there was ever such a person.

The majority of babies in Nazareth House were typically placed there after a priest had intervened on behalf of the pregnant woman. When we first met at the café in the Birmingham BHS, she told me that she had never confided in a priest. When she had gone to confession, even within the privacy of the confessional, she had only ever referred to a terrible sin she had committed. 'But I could never bring myself to tell any priest what I had done,' she told me. 'I just said it was very bad, and I would have to pay for that sin for the rest of my life.' If I had heard about Margaret's case from a stranger, I would have had huge admiration for her survival in spite of the terrible difficulties that women who found themselves at odds with the social conventions of the early 1960s faced. But unfortunately, like so many other illegitimate children born at that time, it now appeared as if I had also been damaged by the experience.

In the funeral photograph, which had startled me so much, there was a ghost of a smile on Margaret's handsome face, which was otherwise dominated by a large pair of glasses. But there was also another, almost hidden expression that I had obviously found very scary when I'd first seen it. Sometime after the funeral, I showed the photograph to a good friend without letting on who it was. 'Study that photo,' I said. 'What does it say to you?' After a few seconds, he replied, 'It says to me that the person is steely and hard, and it looks as if there are troubling secrets behind those glasses.' He was dumbfounded when I told him it was my birth mother. Yet his response reflected my own unleashed fearful and anxious feelings

CHAPTER THIRTEEN

when first setting eyes on it. All these feelings raced through me as we waited for the sign from Father Denis that the funeral service was about to begin.

Just before we entered the church, I turned the pages of the order of service and almost yelped again when I saw the photo on the second page. It was of Margaret, probably in her twenties and looking very serious. But obviously, and unmistakably, my birth mother. There were the same eyes. The same high cheekbones. The same dark hair and the thin, angular face exactly like my own. I wondered what those bright, intelligent eyes were thinking. Had she just arrived in Birmingham, which was to cause such dramatic changes in her life?

As Amanda and I finally entered the church, clutching our orders of service, I took a deep breath to brace myself against the first sight of the coffin. I find it's the finality of it all, far more than anything else, that affects me time and again. Leaving the presbytery with Amanda, I led the way as we walked through the main entrance of the church. If I had taken the priest's route, leading from the presbytery and straight into the church, it would have brought me to the front of the altar in a rather conspicuous arrival, which I was most anxious to avoid since I wanted to be as unobtrusive as possible. As I'd hoped, wearing masks because of the Covid pandemic was proving to be a great help.

Amanda and I took our seats in a pew at the back of the church on the family side. We shook our heads as we refused the offer from a steward to move near to the front. I noticed that Margaret's family were already in place. They would have held a prayer vigil at the coffin when it was brought into the church the night before. On top of it, I could see the same photograph of Margaret, with that flicker of a smile, her rosary and a solitary mauve orchid, which was clearly her favourite flower. The same spray of orchid decorated each page of her order of service. As the familiar strains of 'Abide with Me' filled the church, signalling the start of the service, I finally understood why I felt so uptight and nervous: because this was, for so many reasons, a hugely important day in my life.

A funeral is seen by many as a rite of passage or a celebration of someone's life. But it also serves another purpose. It enables those left behind to truly examine their thoughts and the feelings they had for the departed. I was sitting just a few yards from my Irish family. They were oblivious to my existence, let alone my presence at the back of the church. But as the service progressed and I was bitterly regretting the gaps in the story I shared with Margaret, two facts slowly dawned on me. Not only did I begin to realise that, very unusually, none of her children were going to speak about their mother – a fact confirmed by a quick scan through the order of service – but also, while Margaret had talked time and again, with great pride, about her children and grandchildren – and Bobby the small yappy dog, of course – both in person and during our frequent phone calls, I didn't get the impression of a great deal of sorrow or upset from her family. But then, Margaret had been lost to them for many years because of her dementia, and maybe some of her younger grandchildren couldn't recall the time when she held a larger and more central place in her family's life, especially when they had lost their beloved grandfather, Patrick Lennon, back in 1996.

Safely in our pew, I looked at the order of service again, noting that the various readings and prayers were due to be delivered, I assumed, by Margaret's grandchildren, since I didn't recognise any of the names. Father Denis had told us earlier that Margaret had always known what hymns, prayers and poems she'd wanted at her funeral, having ensured that everyone, especially her own family,

CHAPTER THIRTEEN

was fully aware of, and understood, her final wishes. I thought how remarkably sensible it was that she had planned everything so carefully, and long before she was struck down by dementia. It was clearly a lesson for us all, I told myself, as I glanced again at the order of service, noticing that the last poem was due to be read by someone called 'Peter'. Wondering who he might be, I noted that the poem 'Remembered Joy' by an unknown author was one I'd heard before when attending other funerals.

For the first time, I raised my head to study the family who, of course, I could only see from behind. I swiftly worked out which one was Anne, Margaret's only daughter, and guessed that the other two men sitting closely together nearby would probably be Margaret's sons, Sean and Patrick. However, my wandering thoughts were interrupted as the final notes of the first hymn died away and Father Denis turned to address the congregation. Welcoming all the mourners, and especially the deceased's close family, it was only when a 'Peter Lennon' was introduced by Father Denis that I found myself sitting bolt upright, my stomach churning with shock. Had Father Denis *really* just said that Peter Lennon – *Margaret's eldest son* – would be doing the final reading?

What…? Had I misheard what the priest had just said? Turning to Amanda, I lowered my mask and muttered, 'What son…? Who on earth is Peter…?' But Amanda could only shrug as she glanced back at me in equal confusion. I had never heard this name before. At our first meeting, Margaret told me that Sean was the eldest son: the eldest of her three children. She was clear and unequivocal. But now it seemed that there were four children from her marriage to Patrick Lennon. Unless, of course, Father Denis was mistaken. But how could he be? He'd known Margaret for about twenty years. Moreover, she'd been to pray at his church every day until she moved into her first nursing home. He can only have assumed that I, of all people, would have known all about her 'Lennon' children, and since I had never mentioned Peter Lennon, there was no reason for Father Denis to do so either.

My mind was whirling as I did my best to understand that Margaret had given birth to four children: three boys and one girl, but for some strange reason of her own, she had decided to tell Amanda and me that she only had two sons and one daughter. Why on earth would she do that? Did she forget? But even as that thought flickered through my brain, I immediately realised it was nonsense. How could any mother, even well before falling victim to dementia, forget giving birth to a child? And if he was the first child from her marriage, I'd have thought it was impossible for her to do so. I know that Margaret claimed to recall nothing about my birth, including the identity of my father, but I never really believed her. For one thing, it was all far too convenient. Also, even I could see that from all our conversations about her happy marriage to Patrick Lennon, she was being highly selective. Despite having no problem remembering the date, place and every detail of her marriage ceremony onwards, Margaret appeared to develop sudden amnesia when I reminded her that I was still in the orphanage when she got married.

The funeral service proceeded with various hymns, readings and prayers by Margaret's grandchildren, while I was trying to comprehend the fact that Margaret had – God knows why – deliberately and consistently lied to me. I became aware, however, from Amanda's looks of concern that during the last hymn I was swaying on my feet. In fact, for a few bewildering moments, it seemed as if the world of Margaret Lennon, née Connolly, was spinning on its axis, leaving me reeling with shock and feeling like I had been

CHAPTER THIRTEEN

punched very hard in the stomach. Regaining my composure, I was eventually able to sit down and try to calm myself as the congregation listened to some charming reminisces about Margaret from Father Denis McGillycuddy. She had attended mass every day at his church and was often already outside, waiting to go in, when he unlocked the church doors in the morning. She liked to perform domestic chores, such as doing the washing and ironing, for him. He said that if there was any justice, Margaret was already in heaven. I didn't doubt it.

I was still struggling to pull myself together as I gazed across the church at Peter Lennon, who was walking forward to read the poem. I wasn't really absorbing a word he was saying. But I do remember thinking, as I stared intently at the complete stranger – a man I'd never seen before – that we were as different from each other as chalk from cheese. Not only was he fair-haired, whereas I am dark, but there wasn't even a vague facial or physical likeness between us. Then, I heard a couplet from the poem. 'My life's been full, I've savoured much. Good times, good friends, a loved one's touch.'

'Well! Your life certainly *was* full,' I mentally told Margaret, by now feeling slightly hysterical, because it was definitely even fuller than I'd thought. So, she had four other children, not three, and I had three half-brothers, not two. But, if I hadn't been at her funeral, would I have ever known the truth? Why did she hold the information back? Which, quite honestly, is my euphemism for 'why on earth did she tell me such whopping lies – and blatantly continue to do so until dementia finally claimed her mind?'

Margaret was very proud of her children and I clearly remember her telling me that Sean lived 'south' of Birmingham, which I later discovered was the Bromsgrove area where I had worked all those years ago. Patrick was a taxi driver who called in on his mother most days, while Anne lived near to Margaret and worked in an office. Amanda was also clearly at a loss to understand what was going on. Undercover of the hymns, she confirmed my recollection of Margaret's conversation about her *three* children. So why was there no mention of the first child from her marriage to Paddy Lennon? Why was there no mention of Peter, her second-born son, if you accept that I was the first?

Sean and Patrick are good Gaelic names. Áine, meaning 'brightness' or 'radiance', is accepted as Anna and Anne. Saint Anne is also the patroness of unmarried women, housewives, women in labour or who want to become pregnant, so I could see why Margaret would have chosen that name. But what of Peter? He was of course the first pope and, according to scripture, he was the rock (from *petra* meaning rock or stone) on which the church was built. Perhaps the name was Paddy Lennon's choice? His father, a labourer, was called Thomas. Margaret's father was John – or Sean to give him the Gaelic version of his name. So where did the name Peter come from? Was it particularly significant to the family for some reason?

And then I suddenly had the most astonishing thought. Was it possible that 'Peter' was my birth father's name? The name of the unknown man who Margaret had told the nuns at Nazareth House she was hoping to marry in July 1963? Had Margaret kept his memory alive in her new family? Or was that idea complete and utter nonsense?

Should I even have been at the funeral? Why was I there? I never knew the real Margaret Lennon, née Connolly, despite my best endeavours. But the answer to my first question was a resounding YES. I should be there. I had decided long ago that I wanted to be at the funeral but not because of any sense of entitlement. She was my birth mother, after all. I also hoped that the ritualistic nature of the funeral would help me to deal with the long-buried emotions that had surfaced through my counselling.

I had thought the funeral would enable me to fill in the blanks of our brief life together and also her life post-Patrick and the orphanage. I could listen to the tributes to Margaret, soak them up and get to know a little more about her. I also thought – and hoped – that it would bring me some closure and signify the end of a long journey. For years, I had thought and wondered about my birth mother. And I had, sadly, put off trying to find her for a long time until I eventually tracked her down. Then I was highly frustrated when she deliberately prevented me from even trying to scratch the surface of any possible relationship with her. Crucially, by attending the funeral, I would also be able to say goodbye to her, something she had never had a chance to do with me when she finally decided to give me up for adoption.

Now, I finally realised that I was not grieving for the 94-year-old woman in the coffin. If I was grieving for anyone, it was for the unmarried 34-year-old nurse who gave birth to me in February 1961 and, more than two years later, signed the papers that brought me into a new, loving family. I would always be overwhelmingly grateful for that. I was so lucky with my adoptive parents and I hugely appreciate the warmth and stability they gave me, so in one way, I owe her everything – this woman who, I imagine, did plenty of grieving for the first-born son she must have assumed she would never see again.

Of course I had my own share of guilt too. Being a Roman Catholic, there was always guilt to contend with. I knew I should have searched for Margaret earlier. But, like so many other adopted children, I hadn't done so because of the fear of upsetting my real mum in Swindon. I should have made contact with Margaret when she retired at the age of sixty, when she would have had time on her hands and might have been more willing to talk to me.

If I had shed any tears at the funeral, they would have been a mixture of sadness and regret, but continuing to study that haunting photograph, while the funeral slowly drew to a close, I reluctantly forced myself to face some brutal facts. Even if I had found Margaret when that photograph was taken, some twenty to thirty years ago, she would almost certainly have provided me with no more than the pathetic crumbs she'd doled out in the BHS café and during our many phone calls. It would still have been a case of her controlling information and dispensing it strictly on her own terms.

While trying to concentrate on the prayers and the hymns during the service, I couldn't prevent myself from staring across the large church at the many members of my Irish family in front of me: my blood family. My brain was racing as I tried to work out what I really felt about being in such close physical proximity to them for the first time. It was all very confusing. Should I feel something? And if so, what?

When Amanda and I visited Margaret in her care home, I used to worry that our paths might cross with her children and always wondered whether my flimsy story about Amanda's Aunty Dee, working with Margaret in the NHS, would withstand their scrutiny. Now, here I was just yards from them as they mourned the death of their mother. But even as my eyes searched the pews in front of me for clues, for a likeness to me or a familiar-sounding voice, I never felt the urge to speak to or embrace them. Apart from anything else, it was definitely the wrong time and the wrong place. I certainly had no intention of doing or saying anything to intrude on their grief or their mother's carefully planned funeral service. My sole emotional and physical link was to their mother, who'd carried me for nine months and hoped to retrieve me from the orphanage for more than two years before giving up the fight. The link was not with them, not least because they had a different father, while I still didn't know who mine would turn out to be.

I shed no tears. But if I had, surely her family would have thought it very odd that someone would shed tears for a stranger. Yet... that stranger was the person who gave me life and it was sad to realise that a link to our joint history had died with her. There were now things that I would never get to know, which is why my heart ached that morning in the church. As for Margaret, I was grieving for how the relationship could have been, should have been or would have been, had things been different. Grief over the loss of someone you didn't know, or hardly knew, can take many forms. If her family had known I was there and were aware of the link, they might well have said to me, 'She's our mother who left you when you were two, so why do you care about her?' or, 'You didn't know her, so why do you care whether she died?' And I asked myself the same questions: 'Why am I struggling with grief over someone I didn't know? Do I even have a right to grieve?' However, whether it was 'right' or not, I felt a genuine, palpable, sense of loss.

Afterwards, Amanda told me that as the mass ended she'd found herself struggling with her own emotions. She thought it was because, over the years, she'd invested so much time and effort in Margaret. First of all, in the protracted search for my birth mother and then in accompanying me to visit Margaret in various nursing homes. She also confessed that at one point, she was overcome by a mad urge to march to the front of the church and announce, 'There are not four children of the deceased here – there are five! And the firstborn is right there, at the back of the church.'

She didn't, of course. It was just a crazy impulse, waves of which kept sweeping over her during the long service. Also, since she knew that I could be quite emotional at times, I learned later that Amanda had made a secret wager with a friend, regarding the odds of me breaking down or, at the very least, crying during the service. She'd put it as high as 80 per cent. There was, however, only one moment when I thought I might indeed 'lose it', which occurred at the very end of the service.

I was deeply touched by the sheer poignancy of the occasion as, coming slowly down the nave towards me, Margaret's coffin was carried out of the church, carefully guarded by smartly dressed undertakers with her family walking slowly and silently behind, all preparing to accompany her on her final journey to the cemetery. I fought off the tears, however. I was determined not to lose control of my emotions in front of Margaret's children. Moreover, I felt it would have been sheer self-indulgence on my part, because any tears I shed would have been shed for me or Patrick, the son she had abandoned, not for Margaret herself. And then it struck me. I hadn't heard anyone crying, or even seen anyone raising a handkerchief to their eyes during the service. Absolutely no one at all, which, upon reflection, both Amanda and I found very strange.

As the family were exiting the church, I saw that Anne, Margaret's only daughter, was suddenly looking visibly distressed. Instinctively, I'd always felt, even though I knew so little about Margaret's children, that Anne was likely to be very close to her mother. I'm sure her sons were too, of course, but I could somehow sense the bond between mother and daughter and I almost wanted to literally reach out and touch her hand, which would have been highly inappropriate. She turned and gazed at us. Was she wondering who the strangers were at the back of the church? She lingered but never

CHAPTER THIRTEEN

came over to speak, which was a relief. I offered up a silent prayer for Anne as she exited the church.

When Amanda and I left the church too, we waited as Margaret's immediate family joined the funeral cortège for the ten-minute drive to the cemetery. Lying in the first sleek black car there was a large floral tribute with white flowers spelling out the word 'MOTHER'. I said to Amanda, 'I know I never use that word to describe Margaret, but for more than two years of my early life she was just that: she really was my mother.' Then, as the cars pulled away I made the sign of the cross and muttered under my breath, 'Goodbye, Margaret. Safe journey.'

I imagined the coffin finally being released into the grave under the freezing grey skies of that March day. There would be no cathartic moment for me and yet I was content. I knew that I had done the right thing by attending Margaret's funeral, and apart from the shocking discovery that I now seemed to have an extra half-brother, Peter Lennon – about whom Margaret had never said a word – I thought that the funeral service had passed off fairly smoothly, with no one being upset by my and Amanda's presence.

A few months after the funeral, I decided to return to Birmingham, and to the cemetery, to leave some flowers on Margaret's grave. Standing in front of her grave and thinking about her early life in her beloved Ireland, I resolved to visit County Mayo just as soon as I could. An added incentive, of course, being that I now knew, without a shadow of a doubt, that I was at least half-Irish! But of course, any trip abroad was likely to be many months away, due to the many rules and regulations surrounding Covid-19.

For now, I realised that my long journey with my birth mother had finally come to an end. I had found her and talked to her but she went to her grave with almost all of her secrets intact. I'm fairly sure now that from the moment she agreed to meet me, Margaret had privately resolved to never, ever open the Pandora's box concerning my birth and the subsequent time I'd spent in Nazareth House Orphanage, mainly because it would bring back far too many harrowing memories for her. Perhaps even more importantly, I'm certain that it was her intention that details of her past life – shrouded in secrecy and locked away for over half a century – should remain permanently hidden. And her biggest secret, of course, was the name of my birth father. And if it wasn't James Coffey, who was it?

CHAPTER FOURTEEN

As the thick mist started to clear, I gazed out of the window and realised I could just about make out the runway thousands of feet below, at which point my heart jolted, my stomach churned, my mouth became dry and I felt physically sick. As the plane descended, I thought about the runway below, which was once a sea of swaying bog cotton.

That runway belongs to what is now a thriving airport, which is the gateway to the little town of Knock, home to what is arguably Ireland's most important Roman Catholic shrine. It is also the conduit to the place where my birth mother, Mary Margaret Connolly, was born and grew up and which I was about to visit for the very first time.

My heart was pounding, mainly because I was anxious about what I would find at the end of my long journey. A journey which had effectively begun when, as a young reporter, I had first seen a faded newspaper cutting about a demolished orphanage, Nazareth House, when working for the *Gloucestershire Echo*.

So, after spending so many years trying to track down my birth mother, I was now travelling to County Mayo in the west of Ireland where Margaret's family had lived for decades. I was excited to experience what would be my first glimpse of my Celtic heritage. I hoped the trip to the town where she had lived from her birth until her mid-twenties would add some colour to the landscape of her life.

I knew from my research that Margaret Connolly was born and brought up at Stonefield in Carrowteige, an obscure Gaelic hamlet, or village, on the Rossport Peninsula in County Mayo, in the extreme west of Ireland. I had been to Dublin many times. Also to Belfast, and to a little town on the Irish/Northern Irish border called Castleblayney with some Irish friends. But I had never travelled so far into rural Ireland, which was where Margaret was from. What would I find? My head was buzzing with questions: would her home still be standing? And, if so, who might be living there? Also, were any of her relatives still living in the area, and was the Connolly family well known?

Margaret had proudly told me that her parents, John (or Sean, as he was known in Gaelic) and his wife Mary Connolly, were sheep farmers. But I had an instinct that it might not have been much of a farm: County Mayo was often described as one of the most desolate and deprived parts of Ireland. Apparently, around 1954, Margaret's family had moved from Stonefield to Baltinglass in County Wicklow, on the opposite side of the country. It seemed that her parents had been made an offer they couldn't refuse by the Irish government. They were given fertile land to establish a new farm, and it had proved a sensible move to accept the offer, because today, the farm is still thriving in the capable hands of Margaret's nephew Sean, the son of her older brother John, who died at the grand old age of ninety-three in May 2016.

On the flight, I'd thought long and hard about the few nuggets of information Margaret had given me about growing up in Ireland.

CHAPTER FOURTEEN

It sounded wonderful, but by then I knew that she was prone to exaggeration about her past and her family. She had told me that one of her brothers was a lawyer. It wasn't very important, of course, but as I later discovered, none of them were members of the legal profession.

The timing of the government's offer must have been a godsend for Margaret. As her family left Stonefield for a new life in Baltinglass, which is on the border with County Kildare, Margaret took her chance to forge a new life and moved to the Midlands of England to train as a nurse. She could never have imagined that within six years of arriving in England, she would fall pregnant and have an illegitimate child she would call Patrick James. The pregnancy and birth seemed to cause her so much pain and shame that she chose to hide it from everyone, especially her God-fearing family. I would soon find confirmation in Ireland of why she kept me a secret from the family she loved so much.

As the plane finally taxied on the runway, the windows spattered with heavy drops of rain, I chatted to an elderly woman called Mary, who told me she was back in County Mayo for a family funeral.

'I left in the 1950s to go to England as there was no work here,' she told me. She had travelled on a ferry to Holyhead, the major Welsh seaport serving Ireland.

'You never flew?' I asked naively.

'Oh, no,' she said. 'No one I knew ever flew in an aeroplane. There were not that many flights and it was far too expensive for ordinary folk.' She stared at me keenly and said, 'Are you back visiting your family, too? Did your parents move to England?'

I smiled and said, 'Why do you ask that?'

'Oh,' she said, 'you're clearly Irish – through and through.'

An elderly man, who'd overheard our conversation, chipped in:

'Oh, I remember that Holyhead ferry,' he said. 'Passengers on the top of the ferry, the cattle below.'

Her face lit up. 'That's right. The cattle were always underneath. It was known as the cattle ferry.'

That exchange gave me the first inkling of what life must have been like for Margaret in the 1950s when she'd emigrated to the UK. I was absolutely certain that she would have taken the same 'cattle ferry' from Dublin to Holyhead when she embarked on the voyage that was to change her life.

As I drove the hire car out of the airport and spotted the pair from the plane, my mind raced again. The man and woman were deep in conversation and sheltering from the persistent rain under an umbrella. I offered them a lift, but they politely declined. They were waiting for the bus. 'We always go by the bus,' she said. Driving on, I saw a landmark which I had read about as I prepared for my trip. It was a bronze statue of a priest with his hands extended upwards, as if to heaven. It was the statue of Monsignor James Horan, who had conceived the idea, more than forty years ago, of building Knock airport on the top of a hill that was usually shrouded in mist. Horan raised millions of pounds to build the airport, which he believed would make Knock a tourist destination, and draw pilgrims from around the world to an important shrine to Our Lady which was featured on the International Catholic Heritage map.

The International Eucharistic and Marian Shrine is believed to be the site of an apparition in 1879, when fifteen local residents claimed to have seen the Virgin Mary, St Joseph, her husband, and St John the Baptist – quite the holy trio! The Monsignor eventually got his wish for the airport, despite the misgivings of many in the Irish government. It was, moreover, a huge success. Even the Monsignor had grossly underestimated the number of pilgrims, who he hoped would visit in their tens of thousands. The first plane to land, Aer Lingus flight 4962, touched down in October 1985 and in that first year, 9,200 passengers made the trip. Nowadays, an estimated 1.3 million pilgrims make the journey to Knock each year, most of them arriving at the little airport. Even Pope Francis was there in 2018. The wily old Monsignor, who died at Lourdes (another Marian shrine) a year after the airport opened, would have been absolutely delighted.

As I walked to the church at Knock, I suddenly felt it was a racing certainty that Margaret, who said the rosary every day and whose rosary beads were placed on the top of her coffin, would have been there as well. Maybe in her youth? Possibly on one of her many return visits to Ireland? I was convinced that for the first time in my life I was walking in her footsteps in her native country. It was a strange feeling. I wondered how many other children who'd been given up for adoption by Irish mothers in the 1950s and 1960s visited the shrine to pray for guidance and inspiration as they tried to retrace their own birth mothers' early lives.

I drove to Westport, a town about an hour from where Margaret was brought up, which was where I was staying. The guide books described it as a lively and cosmopolitan town, full to bursting with bars mostly hosting performances of traditional Irish music. Nearing the town, I saw the dramatic outline of Ireland's 'holiest' mountain, Croagh Patrick. It's a shrine to St Patrick, the patron saint of Ireland. Dramatic and imposing at over 2,500 feet, it's regarded as a holy mountain because according to the *Book of Armagh*, a manuscript written in the eighth century, St Patrick fasted on its summit for forty days and nights in 441. The remains of a church he supposedly built are still on the mountain. Although previously regarded as something of a myth, it seems that during an archaeological excavation at the summit in 1995, the foundation of a stone oratory dating back to between 430 and 890 was unearthed. So maybe St Patrick really did build that first church? Every year, on the last Sunday of July, there's a pilgrimage to the peak. Pilgrims come from across Ireland and far beyond, with 30,000 to 40,000 of them making the trip. Many of them are rumoured to make the trek up the mountain in bare feet, but not me. I opted for sensible walking shoes – not least because it was November and very cold, wet and windy.

As I clambered up the mountain, with its spectacular views over Mayo, I strongly felt Margaret's presence again. I was sure that she would have joined a pilgrimage to the mountain at some point in her life as well. Her faith was so important to her. The name Patrick also played a central role in her life. After all, she christened me Patrick, she married a Patrick Lennon, and they called their third son Patrick. The round trip to the top of the mountain and back down again took me more than four hours. I felt truly invigorated at the end, but also in urgent need of a chilled pint of Guinness. My first but certainly not my last of my visit to Ireland.

After checking out a few bars back in Westport, I decided to have dinner in an Italian restaurant. The credit card machine wasn't working and unfortunately, I didn't have any cash. And yet the staff couldn't have been nicer. The bright-eyed waiter simply asked if I could, at some point, put some cash in an envelope through the letter box as they were closing for the next two days. I was taken aback. They had never met me before. They didn't even ask me where I was staying or for a telephone number. They just treated me with blind trust. Then, they asked me if I was in Mayo visiting relatives.

'Why do you ask that?' I said, conscious that I was echoing my words at Knock airport.

CHAPTER FOURTEEN

'Well, you sort of look local,' the waiter replied. I gulped at the observation and the next day I paid my debt, along with an extra-large tip for the trusting waiter.

The next morning, bright and early, I was on my way to Stonefield to find the tiny community where Margaret had grown up. I had looked it up on the map and realised that it was no more than one mile in length. As I drove, the scenery became ever more spectacular. The north coast of Mayo is one of the most remote corners of western Ireland, with the sound of the sea never far away. It is bounded by majestic cliffs, rugged headlands and rocky coves, a vista that has hardly altered since England's Lord Protector Oliver Cromwell's invading army rampaged across the terrain in 1649–50. The landscape is utterly glorious; wild and unspoiled. Near to Margaret's old home are the 11,000 hectares of mountain and blanket bog that form Wild Nephin National Park – a special protection area – and the white sandy beaches of the Mullet Peninsula. I kept stopping the car to absorb the views and enjoy the wonderfully invigorating and crystal-clear air.

As I got closer to Stonefield, I noticed that the fields were golden brown and dotted with sheep but that there was a conspicuous absence of crops swaying in the chilly Atlantic wind. Maybe winter was the wrong time of year for any wheat, barley or oats to be sown? But I wondered if one of the reasons the Connolly family had moved away, more than sixty-five years ago, was because the agricultural land in Carrowteige was too poor to make a decent living. I also noticed that all the road signs were now in Gaelic. It appeared I was moving deeper and deeper into the old Celtic territory. When I called in at a Roman Catholic church, Our Lady Star of the Sea at Cornboy, which was built in 1914, a mile or so from Margaret's original home, I found myself pondering whether she had been a regular member of the congregation. Her mother Mary, née Gallagher, was born and brought up in Cornboy, so may well have attended the church.

The parish priest, Father Joe Hogan, was charming and helpful. I had been in touch with him prior to my trip, telling him that I was going to be in the area, researching my family's Irish roots. He had been an ordained priest for only eight years, but he knew Margaret's youngest brother Padhraig, who had taught at the local school in Stonefield. Father Joe remembered, 'Padhraig was a great character and passionate about education. He was very strict! It was the cane and the stick to enforce discipline – but that was the way in the 1950s and 1960s.' He added, 'The area had no secondary school until 1959, and Padhraig was one of the driving forces behind it finally opening.'

As Father Joe told me more about the secondary school, I did some swift mental arithmetic. If, as I thought, Margaret had left for England in 1954, I wondered what had happened with her education. Did it just stop at the end of primary school? Or did they carry on teaching her in classes alongside the primary-school age children? As I was considering how to politely frame that question, Father Hogan seemed to read my mind. 'Back then, in this area, most people never had a secondary education. They had to teach themselves, which is why so many people who left Ireland for a new life in England in the 1950s could barely speak a word of English. Because they had been brought up speaking Gaelic, and that's all they knew.'

Before this, I'd never given any thought to Margaret's education. Had she gone to England barely able to speak English? Or had she, with the help of her youngest brother Padhraig, taught herself before she went? Either way, it showed me yet again how determined she was to make a better life for herself. Because, within a few years of arriving in the Midlands, she had qualified as a nurse. Maybe she had polished up her English at night school?

When I asked Father Joe how the local community would be likely to react, back in the 1960s, to a local girl falling pregnant outside marriage, he replied slowly, 'No one would ever know. The girl would go away to have the baby. Often to England. It would definitely be covered up, because if it became public knowledge, it would be the cause of great scandal and shame for her family. Times have changed today, thank goodness,' he added. 'But back then, it was a very harsh life for young girls who got pregnant.' I wondered what he would have thought if I had told him that Margaret was thirty-four, hardly a young girl, when she gave birth to me in Bristol in 1961. But Father Joe had merely underlined the cruel facts of life in '60s Ireland. Margaret, who was no fool, would have known that she risked social ostracisation – even total rejection by her own family – if she'd ever dared to tell them that she had become pregnant.

Then, Father Joe dropped a bombshell. 'I have here,' he said, 'a copy of a video of Padhraig's wedding. Would you like to see it?' I was utterly amazed. I had assumed the wedding had happened decades ago, long before video recording was popular. 'Oh yes, they married sixty years ago,' he said with a grin as he noted my astonished expression. 'This is a rare film of its day. Very few people videoed their weddings.' It turned out that Father Hogan's uncle was then the parish priest and a keen cine photographer. It was he who had married the couple and also made the film.

And so, I sat in the church, astounded to find myself watching the black-and-white film of Margaret's little brother's wedding – my uncle's wedding! Padhraig was marrying Maureen O'Connor, another quintessentially Irish name. They were teachers at the same school. Maureen was an attractive woman who towered above her new husband. She was dressed in a traditional white dress that fell just below the knee, which was apparently all the rage at the time, and she had two bridesmaids.

As I scanned the faces of the guests, I realised that I was looking for someone who might be Margaret. Would I recognise her? Was she even there? I suspect she was. The wedding certificate revealed that both the bride and groom were from Carrowteige, so they had been childhood friends. They married on Tuesday 30 December 1958. Padhraig was twenty-eight, his wife twenty-five. Her sister Bernadette was a witness, as was Padhraig's friend Liam Boland. Margaret would have been thirty-two and well into her nursing training.

There were around twenty-five to thirty guests at the wedding at St Muredach's Cathedral in Ballina. I felt myself drawn to one of the guests, a smart-looking woman with high cheekbones wearing a hat (as all the women were) and who had a broad smile, just like Margaret. Was that my birth mother? There was an older couple, clearly husband and wife, beaming and smiling. Was I watching Margaret's parents, John (Sean) and Mary, my grandparents? Yes, I think I was. The video featured a traditional three-tier wedding cake. My uncle looked very happy as his new wife toasted their union with a glass of milk. I was struck by just how many of the women guests were puffing away on cigarettes at the wedding breakfast table. Later, I watched the video again with a friend. He kept playing and replaying it, exclaiming, 'Just look at the groom! It could so easily be you, Andrew. There's an incredible likeness. The two of you even have the same smile.'

Padhraig Connolly rose to be the principal of two schools and

CHAPTER FOURTEEN

he remained in teaching until he retired in Ballina in 1994. The youngest of the four Connolly children, he had contemplated becoming a priest before deciding to train as a teacher. Like Margaret, he had also succumbed to Alzheimer's at the very end of his life. I was given a copy of Padhraig's death notice. His funeral service, on Christmas Eve 2019, was held in the same cathedral where he was married. His wife had died before him, while Margaret was confined to bed in a Birmingham nursing home when he died. With the promise of a copy of the video being emailed to me, I set off on the last part of my emotional journey to Stonefield, Carrowteige.

The village was even smaller than I imagined. A couple of dozen houses, many of them single-storey structures, were built on either side of the solitary road that cut through it. I parked the car and was struck by how quiet it was. I could hear birdsong, there was a faint whiff of coconut-scented gorse and the Atlantic breeze whipped against the houses, carrying the cries of the sheep grazing in the fields. The solitude of Stonefield was in stark contrast to Margaret's new life in Birmingham, England's second city. Even in the 1950s, the hustle and bustle of a cosmopolitan city would have been extraordinarily different to the simple agrarian lifestyle she had been accustomed to in Stonefield. How did she cope with the change from rural backwater to swinging metropolis, especially if her English had been limited to the point of being virtually non-existent?

Carrowteige is home to the Comhar Dún Chaocháin Teo, which takes its name from the local peninsula. It is a community development cooperative that has developed a wide range of community and Irish language-based projects. The organisation has won several awards for its work running summer camps and also has a pre-school service, organises festivals and promotes walks along the area's magnificent cliffs. It is contained within the same building in which Margaret and her siblings were taught their first lessons. As I was heading to the visitor centre, I noticed one or two people who were parked in their cars winding down their windows. They were all smiles. I assumed they weren't used to many strangers; after all, we were miles off the beaten track. It was the parents waiting in the cars who spoke first. They told me the centre would reopen in thirty minutes and then they asked why I was there. It was disconcerting. I never expected anyone would ask me questions or even notice me. One or two of the people I spoke to said that they were delighted to meet me. It seemed that they had been watching me on television for years, since I reviewed the papers on Sky News. They had also heard me on RTÉ Radio 1 in Ireland and often read my articles in the *Daily Mail*, which has its own Irish edition. So much for travelling incognito!

The couple who ran the visitor centre, Teresa and Vincent MacGearraigh, could not have been more friendly and helpful. They, too, knew that I was coming as they'd been alerted in advance. Teresa had founded the centre in 1995 and the walls were lined with wonderful black-and-white photographs of Carrowteige in the 1950s – and some from even earlier than that. The couple showed me what used to be the school building, which was established by a Connolly who, despite the name, was not related to Margaret's family. They also told me that in Margaret's day, boys and girls had separate entrances to the school and they were kept well apart at playtime. That division was a sign of the influence the all-powerful Roman Catholic Church had wielded back then.

They also showed me a written history of the area which examined the grinding poverty that led so many families to leave and try to secure a better life in America. Many of those who emigrated had lived in 'hovels' near the school. After they had left, the bricks from those dwellings were used to build a wall around the school that is still there today. At the visitor centre I could delve deeper into Stonefield's history. The first Connolly in the area was reportedly a teacher, who was known as a 'hedge' schoolmaster. This was seemingly because, when the English, under Cromwell, occupied the area, teaching was banned and so the first Connolly taught behind hedges and ditches to escape detection. Following the execution of Charles I, Oliver Cromwell regarded an educated population as a dire threat and a likely cause of trouble. Due to Cromwell's fanatical Protestantism, the celebration of mass was also prohibited. The service therefore took place in isolated places, usually with a large rock being used instead of an altar, hence the term 'mass rock' occurring in several places throughout Ireland.

Teresa and Vincent also took me to Margaret's family home, which was just a few minutes' walk from the school. Margaret's father, John Connolly, who they referred to as Sean, was apparently a skilled stonemason. He built the family home, which was two rooms divided by a wall, with one window, no second storey and which was originally thatched. The family lived and slept in one room, while the other room was used for storage. The furnishings would have been simple: chairs, small wooden stools, a cooking pot, a kettle and a tea pot and some crockery. The house is still standing today, overlooking the Atlantic and the mountains. No one has lived in it since 1977 and for a while it was used as a shelter for the sheep. When Margaret had lived there, there was no electricity, gas or running water, so it was no wonder she wanted to move to England. In fact, hot running water and electricity were only introduced to Stonefield in the mid-1960s.

So much for Margaret's tale of growing up on a 'large farmhouse', then. In reality, it was a tiny smallholding that consisted of barely three acres of land on which they raised sheep, geese and chickens. Any digging was done with shovels as very few farmers could afford tractors in those days. Margaret grew up in such a remote part of Ireland that obtaining food supplies from the neighbouring towns was problematic. It's why she and the other local children often caught their own lunch and dinner. They would fish for lobsters – a specialist local catch – and search for crabs living among the rocks. This involved putting the full length of their arms into holes in the rocks that were barely wide enough to extract the creatures, sometimes with devastating consequences. According to local legend, one man was unable to free his arm from the hole and drowned when the tide rose. The crab holes were at, or near, low tide and far away from the village, so any cries for help would have gone unheard.

While the house was even more basic than I had imagined, the views were extraordinary. The moody Atlantic Ocean sparkled against a backdrop of craggy, slate-blue cliffs and felt like it was within touching distance. In the distance was the beautiful Achill Island, which was once voted to possess one of the best beaches in the world, even beating competition from Polynesia and the Greek islands. But, when the rain cascades down from the blackened sky and a thick mist engulfs the region, it is undoubtedly a bleak and uncompromising landscape. As far as I could see, despite growing up blessed by such spectacular scenery, there would have been few opportunities for a young woman whose ambitions transcended the simple life of her parents and grandparents. It was also no wonder that when they were offered the chance, the Connolly family relocated to live and work in Baltinglass, a far more prosperous area.

Back in Birmingham I came across another fascinating book. Published in 1987, its Gaelic title was *A Mhuintr Dhú Chaocháin*,

CHAPTER FOURTEEN

Labhraigí Feasta and it proved to be a treasure trove of memories from Margaret's childhood. Incredibly, it included many photos of the Connolly clan, including some of a teenage Margaret and her brother Michael, or Micky, who later went to Birmingham and often worked as a farm labourer. It also featured her parents. There were photographs of Margaret's father John Connolly (or Sean, as he was known in Carrowteige) looking very dapper in a smart waistcoat and her mother Mary, who despite her harsh surroundings was known for always smiling: just like her daughter.

The time to leave the north coast of Mayo came all too soon, and upon my departure I felt truly sad. I'd fallen in love with the gloriously wild landscape. The windswept Atlantic coast is ideal for surfers, while the sheltered coves facing the east are perfect spots for family outings. Plunging into the Atlantic, all along the north Mayo coast, are the rugged, pewter-coloured cliffs that offer glorious walks and the chance to watch dolphins and puffins, gulls without number and regal peregrine falcons. It is a bird-lover's paradise. And on top of that, I'm told, if you are *very* lucky you might even see some minke whales.

I only had time to scratch the surface of this wonderful part of the world, which is why I fully intend to return for a much longer holiday. After all, now I know that I am definitely at least half-Irish, I'm keen to explore more of this stunning landscape with its majestic cliffs, weather-beaten headlands and rocky coves that has barely changed over the past thousand years.

CHAPTER FIFTEEN

As the early morning sun was rising, nine-year-old Jimmy Coffey crept out of his mud-built home to join his best friends, the Lohan brothers: Laurence, thirteen; James, nine; and Patrick who was just seven. The boys had hatched a plan the night before to go to the River Shiven at Ballinamore Bridge in County Galway, which was about 1.5 miles from their homes in the village of Cloonabricka. Also joining them on their early morning adventure was a young friend and neighbour, Matthew Keane, aged eleven.

According to contemporary reports, it was a Sunday, 10 July 1904. A warm and sunny day, with the smell of newly mown hay filling the summer air as the five young boys raced through the fields. Birdsong echoed in the early morning as the boys did their best to avoid stinging nettles and cowpats, laughing as they ran, each one determined to be the first to see the river. Finally, their ears filled with the rasping sound of corncrakes as the river came into sight. The boys, whose families had been friends for years, had promised their parents they would be back after their swim and be ready to put on their Sunday best for mass, which was held at St Brendan's Church in Toghergar. Tragically, it was a promise that four of the boys would not be able to keep.

All five of the youngsters had been repeatedly warned by their parents, and by their teachers, about the dangers of the River Shiven, which stretched for just over 21 miles and teemed with trout. All the boys knew about the perils of the sink holes, known locally as swallow holes, and the strong and dangerous currents. But they were young, and fearless. They were boys!

When they got to the river, Jimmy Coffey had the idea to strip off and dive into the water, which was about 4 feet deep from the bank. The boys had no qualms about following him. After all, they knew the Shiven really well. In fact, they used to walk to Killyan National School via stepping stones in the river. They never even had to worry about getting their shoes wet, because they never had any. Their families were far too poor for such luxuries.

But, as the boys waded into the water, one of them, Matthew Keane, held back. Did he fear the water? Or did he have a terrible premonition of an accident…? Whatever the reason, the other boys didn't hesitate. Jimmy Coffey swam out the furthest but he rapidly got into difficulties. As he cried for help, Laurence, the oldest Lohan brother, swam to the aid of his friend. But he also got into trouble and disappeared below the water's surface. His brothers, who must have been terrified, swam across the water to try to help him. They, too, disappeared. All three boys had been sucked into a lethal, 10-foot-deep swallow hole.

As Jimmy Coffey fought for his life, Matthew Keane, who was still on the bank, raced up and down desperately shouting for help. His cries were heard by a local man, John Carr, who quickly stripped off, ready to dive to the rescue. But before he could enter the icy water, three officers from the Royal Irish Constabulary, whose station was next to Ballinamore Bridge, heard the commotion and

CHAPTER FIFTEEN

immediately took charge. By which time, Jimmy Coffey had also sunk beneath the surface.

The three policemen dived deep down into the water to try to rescue the boys. But their efforts proved to be in vain. Despite finally managing to pull all the boys out of the water, all four of them had drowned. Their lifeless bodies were eventually taken by pony and trap to be laid out in the old police station, which today is a popular hostelry. When word got back to Cloonabricka, the screams of the boys' mothers rent the air as the families set about the horrendous task of having to bury their young children. It was an utterly dreadful and shocking tragedy which left an indelible mark on the close-knit rural community.

At the inquest, the jury returned a verdict of accidental drowning. Young Matthew Keane, just eleven and known affectionately as Matty, was called as the main witness. The coroner's report, featured in the *Southern Star* newspaper, said, 'The boys went to bathe early in the morning in about 4 feet of water. James Coffey got into a deeper part of the river and cried for help. Laurence Lohan, who went to his assistance, sank. Lohan's two younger brothers tried to rescue him, but they too were carried into the deep water, and all drowned before assistance could be summoned.' The jurors singled out the three police officers who'd made such a desperate attempt to save the boys for praise. They were Acting Sergeant William Maher, Constable Jeremiah Nelligan and Constable Peter Molloy.

After the inquest the village prepared for the boys' funeral. The sight of such tiny coffins must have provoked a huge amount of distress. One account of the tragedy, written much later, said:

We can only ponder the emotional scenes of shock, anger and

disbelief, guilt and profound sadness as the boys were carried along the old road, after wakes in Cloonabricka, to their eternal resting place. Akin to a ship battered against the jagged rocks on a stormy night while hoping to survive, the families and community were now left battered with a grief like no other. Their faith in God tested but not broken, they summoned up an inner strength to carry on.

The boys were buried at Killyan cemetery in Newbridge with timber crosses. Unfortunately, the crosses disintegrated a long time ago, which means that their final resting place is unknown. The pain caused by the boys' deaths was so deeply ingrained that, after a few years, the locals stopped talking about it. The enormity of the loss appeared to be too much for many of them to comprehend.

I discovered this remarkable story when, in 2023, I went to County Galway to look into the family background of Jimmy Coffey, the man my birth mother had claimed was my biological father. I wanted to try to get a feel for the area where he had apparently grown up and see whether there were any family members still living there or anyone who might have known him. I was well aware, of course, that the chances of meeting anyone who knew or who'd met Jimmy Coffey were highly unlikely. After all, he'd died in April 1961, a full sixty-two years previously. But then, I stumbled on the extraordinary story of nine-year-old James Coffey who was born on 3 June 1895. Could it be that the two James Coffeys, with the same Christian and surnames, were somehow related to one another?

They were! The Jimmy Coffey who had drowned in July 1904 was one of six children. His father, Thomas, was a labourer and his mother, Catherine, a domestic servant and cook. They lived in a

CHAPTER FIFTEEN

bleak house made of mud which has long gone. Jimmy's brother Eddie, known as 'Big Ned', was born in 1896, two years after Jimmy, and was utterly devastated by the loss of his older brother.

In 1924, Big Ned married a local girl, Agnes Hynes. Like his parents, he and Agnes also had six children: Jimmy, Eddie, Bob, Kathleen, Patrick and Tommy, who is still alive at the time of writing this book and living in County Limerick. The first boys, born in 1926, were twins. Jimmy Coffey, the elder twin, was named after the uncle he never had the chance to meet, the boy who'd perished in the river. I could hardly believe such an extraordinary twist of fate. Because if Jimmy Coffey really was my birth father, I would have a direct connection to the tragedy that had scarred a tiny Irish community over 120 years ago.

My introduction to the boys' story came from a stalwart of the Newbridge community: Denis Delaney, aged eighty-three. Not only did he know the story of the drownings but he had also known Jimmy Coffey, my possible birth father. It seemed that they had worked alongside each other, first in Galway and then again when they were both in Birmingham, where Jimmy Coffey met his untimely death in April 1961.

I had arranged to meet Denis at the local store, next to the pub in Newbridge, just a couple of minutes' drive from the cemetery where the four little boys are buried. I had made some calls before I arrived in Ireland, telling the people I'd spoken to that I was searching for information about my birth relatives. And, just as in County Mayo, when I was looking into the background of Margaret Connolly, I received the same extraordinarily kind level of help and cooperation.

Denis was delighted to meet me, happy to give up his own time to show me round. As he got out of his car, his face was wreathed in smiles. Although I had come to Galway with a friend, Denis ignored my companion and walked straight up to me, extending his hand as he said, 'Well, I know which one of you is a Coffey. Very nice to meet you, Andrew. I knew Jimmy Coffey very well. I knew him when I was growing up in Galway. I also knew him in Birmingham. There's a strong family resemblance. Oh, yes! You definitely look like a Coffey all right. But, strangely, you don't look like Jimmy.'

And then came the biggest surprise. 'I was at your Jimmy Coffey's funeral in Birmingham.' I couldn't believe my ears. Had I misheard him? I had come to Galway in the hope of getting to know a little bit about the community the Coffey family hailed from. Instead, I had stumbled across a haunting story about the drowning of the nine-year-old Coffey boy, who might possibly be my great-uncle. But now, here I was, actually face to face with someone who had grown up with the man my birth mother had claimed was my real father. She'd certainly told the nuns at Nazareth House exactly the same story. And now, Denis Delaney was informing me that he'd been with Jimmy, right to the very end of my potential birth father's 36-year life!

Uncharacteristically, I was lost for words. I stuttered and stumbled and then my urgent questions began to pour out of me. 'You actually knew him? Did you like him? Were you really at the funeral? Did you ever hear that he had a child? Did you know he had a girlfriend called Margaret who thought she was going to marry him?' On and on the questions flowed. Looking bemused, Denis, a well-preserved 83-year-old who'd proudly told me that he had six sons and four daughters, plus twenty-seven grandchildren, said at last, 'Oh yes, I knew him. But I don't know anything about a girlfriend.'

CHAPTER FIFTEEN

'What was he like?' I asked.

'He was wild!' Denis replied.

Why didn't that surprise me? I listened with fascination as Denis proceeded to relate how, in the early 1940s, the Coffey family had moved from their very basic house in Cloonabricka into a single-storey three-roomed house in Rookhill, which lay a few miles away from their original village. The property included a proper kitchen and a galvanised roof. Jimmy Coffey left Ireland for Birmingham in the mid-1950s to find work and decent wages. At around the same time, my birth mother Margaret headed across the Irish Sea from the neighbouring county of Mayo. I asked Denis if they could have known each other before they left for England. Ever the romantic, I wondered aloud if they had planned to elope to England together. But Denis shattered my illusions of any romance between the young Irish couple.

'No, not a chance,' he said vigorously. 'We never went travelling to other counties. I'd be amazed if Jimmy Coffey had ever been to County Mayo. You never went far beyond your own home. Frankly, you couldn't afford to. So I reckon that if they did meet up, it would have been more likely to be in Birmingham where they would probably have both been looking for work.' Denis recalled that around 1959, Jimmy Coffey returned from England for a while and lived with his parents Big Ned and Agnes, known as Addie, in Rookhill, where they farmed a couple of acres of scrappy land. They also possessed a cow.

'Where they had originally lived, in Cloonabricka, it wasn't a real house,' Denis explained. 'Today it would likely be called a "hovel", and one which was not in great repair. Cold, damp and tiny, it was a case of utter poverty. But although the house in Rookhill was very basic, it was a big improvement on what they were used to.

There was no running water at their new home, nor any mains gas or electricity. They caught all the water off the roof and filled up at the nearest well. In fact, the water from the well was the best you could drink.' But, despite their poverty, it was apparently a very happy home. Big Ned loved to play cards and rarely lost a game. 'He was such a big man. So funny! And extremely hard-working. He was also a crack shot, which meant they very seldom went hungry,' Denis added, explaining that Ned went everywhere with his shotgun. 'You would often see him with his bag, which might have a couple of turnips, some potatoes or a cabbage peeking out of the top. But you knew what was underneath. Pheasants! The family's dinner.'

Denis himself had moved to Birmingham in 1960, when he was twenty-one, and he settled in Selly Oak. Coincidentally, that was also where Margaret was living when I'd finally managed to track her down, in the little house she had shared with her late husband, Patrick Lennon. 'Some of my children were born in the hospital in Selly Oak,' Denis added. Which led me to wonder if maybe Margaret, who was a nurse, might have been involved in their births.

It seemed that Denis had often worked with Jimmy Coffey and, more frequently, with his twin brother Eddie. They installed suspended ceilings and this job took them back and forth across the country, which is why Denis felt that he knew Eddie better than his brother, Jimmy. I then asked Denis if he had any recollection of meeting Margaret. Or whether he knew if Jimmy had been in a serious relationship with a nurse, who was about the same age as him and from a similar Irish background? Or whether Jimmy was likely to have fathered a child? 'I reckon that I would have remembered. I certainly never knew he even had a girlfriend. And I definitely never heard anything about a baby. Believe me, I wouldn't

CHAPTER FIFTEEN

have forgotten that bit of news!' Denis said with a snort of laughter. 'And I'm quite sure that his brother Eddie never knew anything about a girlfriend or a baby. Because he would surely have told me.'

Although more than sixty years had passed since Jimmy's fatal accident, the recollection of that dreadful day still remained vividly clear in Denis's memory. 'Jimmy was hit by a van in Erdington. He suffered really terrible, terrible injuries. Eddie told me all about it. He was, naturally enough, deeply upset, especially as Jimmy was his twin brother.' The night before the funeral there was a traditional Irish Catholic wake. 'It was held at Eddie's house. People came around to see Jimmy in the open coffin. They came to pay their respects. We had a few drinks. Jimmy was well liked. He was a real character.' Denis smiled at the memory.

'He was definitely a bit of a chancer,' he added. 'As I've said, he was a real harum-scarum type of man. You'd never know what he might get up to. But Jimmy was well-known for liking to have a flutter on the horses. I always reckoned that he kept the bookies in business. The day after the wake, there was a big funeral at the local Catholic church. Then, it was off to the cemetery for the burial. His twin, Eddie, and another brother, Tommy, paid for the headstone. Jimmy never had any money. He liked the horses too much.

'It was all so sad.' Denis uttered a heavy sigh. 'He was so young and we always thought that he had no family of his own. There wasn't even a whisper to suggest that he might have fathered a baby. It… well, it feels very strange to only realise now, after all these years, that I'm discovering he may have had a son.'

Although it was highly unlikely, I asked Denis if he had any recollection of seeing a slightly built Irish woman, who might have been standing alone during the funeral. I was trying to determine whether Margaret had been at the funeral or not. Because, if Jimmy really was my father, her prospects of marriage had been shattered by the death of her fiancé, barely two weeks earlier. On the other hand, if she hadn't known about the funeral, it suggested that he knew nothing about her pregnancy or that he had walked out of her life when he discovered she was carrying a child. Denis slowly shook his head. 'I really couldn't say. It was such a long time ago. But I do remember that Jimmy's parents weren't there. They didn't have the money to travel to England.'

Back in Ireland, the same grieving process was underway. Denis's own younger brother Joe, who's now seventy-seven, went to the small Coffey house in Rookhill on the night of the wake in Birmingham, to pay his respects to Jimmy's family. Denis told me that he had eventually returned to live in Galway with his growing family and remained close to Big Ned and Agnes, who might well have been my grandparents.

Agnes had always walked with a pronounced limp, although Denis didn't know whether it was caused by a problem with her hip or one of her feet. When people tactlessly referred to her impediment, Big Ned always made light of it. 'He used to say, "Well, she's not going to be jumping across ditches, is she?" Big Ned was a good family man,' Denis said. But, while mobility was obviously a consideration, dignity was not. It seemed that Ned used to take his wife to visit their neighbours with Agnes either perched on the crossbar of his bicycle or sitting in a wheelbarrow. 'No one would take any notice,' Denis remarked. 'Lots of people had health problems back then.'

And it seemed that whenever the twins, Jimmy and Eddie, or their sister Kathleen, who'd also moved to Birmingham (she died in 2011), wrote letters home to Rookhill, a kindly neighbour would read them to Agnes, who was illiterate. Agnes died, aged seventy-four, on 14 October 1972 and Big Ned was seventy-nine when he passed on 20 March 1977.

I found it very touching to hear that Denis's devotion to Big Ned did not end with his passing away at the family home. His adult children had asked Denis to perform one last favour for his old friend. 'Ned hadn't shaved for a couple of months. But I cut his hair, shaved him and generally smartened him up,' Denis explained. 'So that when they laid him out in his coffin for the wake, the dear old boy looked very respectable.' The husband and wife are buried side by side in the family plot with Big Ned's parents, Thomas and Catherine. I visited their grave in Killyan cemetery. The inscription read, 'In loving memory of Thomas Coffey, 20 October 1940, Catherine Coffey, 19 September 1943, their daughter-in-law Agnes, 14 October 1972, their son Ned died 20 March 1977.'

After my trip to the cemetery, I went to Killyan National School where Jimmy had studied. In its heyday, around 100 pupils were taught there, with most children receiving only a primary education. Some, however, never even completed that. Being part of a farming community, they would have been pulled out of their classes to work with their parents. The school closed down about fifteen years ago because there were too few children in the local area. Now, it is a home for Ukrainian refugees. A Ukrainian flag flutters from the old school gate.

Denis then took me to the bog where he'd worked with the Coffey brothers cutting turf. 'We had our own bogs. Our bog was next to the Coffey one. I used to cut the turf alongside Jimmy and Eddie.' Back then, Irish people heated their homes and cooked their food using turf as fuel. The turf was extracted from bogs using a two-sided spade called a 'sleán'. Often, entire families worked on the bog, turning each sod to ensure that the sun and wind aided the drying process. Turf was invaluable. It not only heated rural people's homes, it was also sold across the country to heat houses in towns and even in Dublin. To this day, turf is still used to heat homes, ovens and water in Newbridge, although environmentalists have criticised the ancient tradition. Burning smoky fuels has been banned in Dublin, and in 2018, the Bord na Móna, a semi-state-owned body set up to develop Ireland's peatlands, began phasing out commercial turf cutting. Then, the government banned the sale of turf and wet wood. Fearing a backlash from rural voters, however, the Irish government made an exception for those families who still live next to the remaining bogs and allowed them to cut turf for domestic use, and around 15 per cent of households still do so. Denis himself told me that, even today, he can still be found working in the bog with his grandchildren.

I then travelled to Galway with the aim of trying to find the exact spot on the River Shiven where the boys had drowned in 1904. There were no headstones in the local cemetery and the story about their tragic deaths had been almost completely forgotten, until it was resurrected in 2019 by the author Michael Martin. He wrote a book about the history of the area, *From Ballinamore to Ballygar and Newbridge*, in which he included a short report on the boys' tragic deaths, along with a section of the coroner's report. However, the story has since been brought back to life in a far more poignant way, by the Ballinamore Bridge Heritage Group, which was founded in 2022. For their first major project, they decided to conduct more research into the fate of the four youngsters, together with an investigation into the boys, their families and how they would have lived.

Based upon their findings, the local heritage group decided to commission a plaque to commemorate the loss of the four boys. It was unveiled in September 2023. Tommy Crehan, a local man and member of the heritage group, then wrote a moving account in an illustrated booklet that was called simply 'A Local Tragedy'. He acknowledged:

> The tragedy remained with the people. But the pain of their loss was so intense, that they stopped talking about it completely. Rather than remember, they chose to forget. It was their way of dealing with the trauma. In a wider context, there appears to be a clear correlation between this tragedy and that of the Irish Famine. In general, people did not want to speak of the famine. In the same way, they wanted to forget this immense local tragedy.

Before the plaque was finished, members of the heritage committee went to the River Shiven, to visit the spot near to where it's believed that the boys drowned. In the 1950s the river had been cleaned and the 10-foot-deep hole, in which the boys had perished, was finally filled in. As an act of symbolic remembrance, the committee had arranged for a single flower to be cast into the water for each boy. Flowers may not be able to speak, but their silent presence said everything as they slowly floated down the meandering river. In fact, I found the whole idea incredibly moving. Not only as an act of commemoration but also because the day they cast the flowers into the water, in February 2023, just happened to be my birthday. Yet again, I felt a very strong connection to the young Coffey boy who'd so tragically drowned.

The committee had commissioned a local craftsman to create a 1 metre-square granite plaque that depicted the four young boys arm in arm, with their backs turned away from the world in an eternal embrace. It was unveiled in summer 2023 to commemorate their short lives. Under the Latin word *Resurgere*, which means 'to rise again', there is a brief verse above an image of Ballinamore Bridge. It reads:

> A warm summer day
> The river ran cold
> Our four young boys
> Shall never grow old

As Tommy Crehan wrote:

Like all children, every one of us has experienced warm, lazy summer days, with the natural instinct to visit a nearby lake or river. But, as the result of a simple action, those boys would never reach adulthood. It describes the mood of what it means to experience loss; giving a voice to the complex emotions that come with grief.

As I walked up and down the river, past the spot where the boys drowned, I became entirely lost in the mists of time. The River Shiven had always been vitally important to the area. Indeed, as far back as the first settlers, it had provided fish and a mode of transport. Its water was also harnessed for power; its force used to drive the flour mills along the banks of the river. Sadly, Water Safety Ireland says that in each of the last ten years, approximately 120 people have died by drowning in Irish rivers. When the young boys died, the numbers were much higher. Matthew Hughes, from the heritage group which owns the pub where the boys' bodies were laid out all those years ago when it was a police station, said, 'There were no headstones for the boys. Their families wouldn't have had

CHAPTER FIFTEEN

the money. They were timber crosses which perished long ago. The worst thing about dying is being forgotten. So we decided to do a memorial to them.'

The boy who didn't go into the water, Matthew Keane, went on to live a long and happy life. He married a local woman named Julia and had three children, two boys and a girl, Patrick, Kathleen and Thomas. Matthew, always known as Matty, carried on living in Cloonabricka where he worked the land as a farmer and a thatcher. He taught his children how to drive tractors, tying a belt around the seat so they wouldn't fall off. He also taught them how to fish and hunt rabbits. But more importantly, he made sure his children, unlike himself, never missed a day of school. Besides his three children, he had eleven grandchildren, fifteen great-grandchildren and numerous great-great grandchildren. But he never talked about the swimming tragedy. Perhaps the pain was just too deep. In fact, most of his grandchildren knew nothing about it. When Matthew Keane died in June 1985, aged ninety-two, he was also laid to rest in Killyan graveyard. The cottage where he first lived is now in ruins. A pair of rusty wrought-iron gates stand proudly at the entrance, perhaps waiting patiently for a family to return.

When I arrived back in England, I kept thinking about how Denis Delaney had said I was definitely a Coffey but that I didn't look like Jimmy. Earlier that year, I'd met Rhona Coffey and her brother Phil. They were the children of Patrick Coffey, Jimmy's younger brother, who'd also moved to England for work and had divided his time between Manchester and Birmingham. Rhona and Phil had waited to meet me on the forecourt of Birmingham's New Street station. As I approached, he'd turned to his sister and exclaimed, 'Oh, my God, it's Dad! That bloke looks exactly like our dad. I can't believe the likeness! Look at the cheekbone structure.

Just look at those eyes…' So I began to wonder, as I did so often, about my birth mother, Margaret. Was I really Jimmy Coffey's son? Or could she have had a relationship with Patrick Coffey – the man who was affectionately known to the family as Parc, a shortened form of Pádraic, the Gaelic version of Patrick?

I'd learned that for years, Patrick Coffey's children had known that their father was once engaged to a girl in Birmingham. But it never worked out, so Patrick asked for his engagement ring back when he started dating Philomena, the woman who was to become his wife and the mother of his four children, the first of whom was born in August 1963, when I was two years old. My birth mother Margaret had named me 'Patrick James'. I'd always assumed the reason she chose the name Patrick was because it's a very popular Roman Catholic name. Not only is Saint Patrick the patron saint of Ireland, but Margaret was always very proud of her Irish ancestry. Besides which, when I'd finally managed to contact my birth mother, it was clear that she had a very strong Catholic faith and that the Church was an extremely important part of her life.

But perhaps it was not quite that straightforward. Maybe… just maybe, Margaret had developed a relationship with Patrick, whom she almost certainly would have met through the other Coffey brothers. Maybe Patrick could be my birth father? His first fiancée – possibly my mother? – only discovering that she was pregnant *after* he'd requested his ring be returned because he intended to propose to another woman? If so, was that the real reason I was called Patrick?

Patrick Coffey's family have always known the story of the Birmingham girl whose heart was broken when he asked for his engagement ring back. But unfortunately, his children never knew that girl's name. So, leaving aside the fact that Patrick could be seen

CHAPTER FIFTEEN

as a bit miserly over the ring and thus did not come out of this story smelling of roses, I could only think of one vitally important question: Would it be stretching coincidence too far to seriously consider the fact that Patrick's ex-fiancée in Birmingham might have been my birth mother, Margaret Connolly?

CHAPTER SIXTEEN

My big sister Sue is a dead ringer for Mum. They look alike, sound alike, are both headstrong and straight talkers, and they were also very close. For years, I struggled over whether to tell Sue that I had found Margaret. The same guilt which kept me awake at night over Mum also applied to my sister. It's probably because we are so close that I hesitated to tell her. I didn't want to disappoint her. As the eldest of Betty and George's three children (she was nearly ten when I arrived on the scene), Susan was a huge part of making me a happy and welcome addition to the family. All her life she has put family first. Always. In fact, she has done lots of work on the Pierce family tree, as she is fascinated by the history of Dad's family, going all the way back to the fishing industry in Brighton. So, realistically, I knew she would understand why I had done it, but I knew she would be upset, especially when she discovered that I first met Margaret while Mum was still alive.

Only a small handful of people had been in the loop about Margaret, but I knew the time was coming when I had to tell my sister. But when? The family celebrated her seventieth birthday in January and sadly I couldn't be there. But I promised Sue I would take her and Ian, her husband of fifty years, to lunch a few days later. Just the three of us. A rare treat. A few days before I went to Swindon, I asked her to dig out some old photos of me from soon after I arrived in the family.

On that day, over tea and biscuits in her neat flat in Swindon and with Mum and Dad's wedding photograph displayed above us, we leafed through the photos. They were mostly black and white. There was my third birthday party, my first as part of the Pierce family, a few months before the adoption was finalised by the courts in the summer of 1964. Dad obviously took the photograph as he is the only one missing from the dinner table. All four of us children were there, as were Mum and my grandparents.

There were photographs of our family holiday at Butlin's in July 1964, around the same time I legally became a member of the Pierce clan. How I loved those holidays, one at Butlin's Bognor Regis and the other at Butlin's Minehead: the Redcoats; the beach; the fun fair; bumper cars; candy floss; toffee apples. The family also had a strict rule. Fizzy drinks were only permitted on high days and holidays. For me, at Butlin's, it was always Tizer with a dollop of ice cream dropped in, a knickerbocker glory. We always did well in the Butlin's Happy Family competition, and that's because we *were* happy and we had the photographs in Sue's collection to remind me. Mum's parents, Anne and John, joined us too. I have vague recollections of the 'Redcoats' and of my screaming blue murder at the side of the indoor swimming pool, terrified by the sight of the plastic tropical birds that overhung the water. I can also recall sharing a bed with Christopher in the tiny chalet and the messages, broadcast loudly over the Tannoy, telling us when it was time to get up and go to breakfast or signalling when lunch or dinner was about to be served. In fact, for anyone who can recall the popular television programme, it was all very *Hi-de-Hi!*

CHAPTER SIXTEEN

Mum's parents, my new grandparents, had moved to Swindon in 1960 from Dagenham, where Mum had grown up. Granddad had not been enthusiastic about Mum and Dad adopting a stranger, a boy they knew so little about. It's hardly surprising that Granddad was so concerned. Naturally, he worried that I might bring 'bad genes' into the family. After all, Mum and Dad knew next to nothing about my birth parents nor my family history. Yet Granddad was delighted his early misgivings about adopting me were misplaced. In fact, according to Mum, we were very close right from the start, when Granddad put a protective arm around his second grandson.

I loved both my grandparents, whom we saw a lot. We walked or, as we got older, cycled to their terraced house at 30 Wolsely Avenue on the Park South council estate. Sunday afternoons were our favourite. Nanna and Granddad had a lovely old Labrador called Lassie who we would hear padding up the hallway lino even before we knocked the door. We perfected a mischievous Sunday tea routine. We agreed in advance that one of us would say, 'Nanna, Mummy says we must not ask to stay to tea but if you ask us, then we can stay.' It always worked. And tea was always a tin of John West red salmon with salad. We lost Nanna to cancer in 1970. I wrote the sympathy card from her four Swindon grandchildren that went on her coffin. I also served on the altar at her requiem mass and somehow, aged nine, managed to get through it without crying. Granddad approved of that. He died in 1984. We were close until the very end.

Happily chatting to Sue and Ian about our memories of our grandparents, I had almost forgotten that I had something important to tell her, but Sue hadn't.

'So, why do you want them? The photographs. What do you want them for?' she said. Straight to the point. She is her mother's daughter after all.

I told her that they would be going into a book. Her face lit up in the broadest of smiles and all I could see was my mum.

'Are you writing your life story?' she asked.

I laughed out loud, saying, 'Don't you think I'm still a little young for that?! And anyway, who would buy it?' Then, I took a deep breath and told her the truth, which had been a long time coming: 'I'm writing a book about finding my birth mother.' You could have heard a pin drop.

Momentarily, but it seemed longer, there was silence, which she broke by saying, 'You did it. You found her? I've never understood why you haven't done it before. I was thinking only the other day why hasn't Andrew tried to find her. He would know people who could do it.' Then, she paused, before saying, 'I've never understood why you wouldn't want to.' But my relief over Sue's unfazed reaction was short-lived. She then asked the question I had dreaded: 'Did you start looking for her after we had lost Mum?'

Tears welling up in my eyes, I spluttered, 'Mum was alive, which is why it was such a secret. You're the first member of the family to know.'

There was another silence before she reassured me, 'Mum would have understood why you did it. She would have been OK about it. You could have told her.'

'No,' I replied. 'I wasn't risking it. I never, ever wanted to hurt her or you. I worried then, I worry now, that you might think I tracked down Margaret because there was a vacuum in my life. A yawning gap. A large hole in my life which the Pierce family could not fill. That's not it. That's not why I did it. I started the process of tracking her down because I genuinely wanted her to know that I was OK. I thought she might have been worrying about me, tortured about what had happened to her first-born son. As I was approaching

CHAPTER SIXTEEN

fifty, I thought she would be in her sixties. Time could be running out. I knew Dad's Alzheimer's had started in his early sixties. If I was to find her and talk to her I thought time might be running out too.'

How little did I know.

'I never told Mum because I couldn't bear the idea that she might think that somehow she hadn't been enough for me, that she had failed me in some way or had been a disappointment and that's why I was trying to track down the woman who brought me into the world. I also worried that she might fear that I would forge a special relationship with Margaret, that she might feel eclipsed or overlooked in some way. I couldn't bear to put her through that.'

I reassured Sue and Ian that while Margaret and I had often talked on the telephone, I had met my birth mother on equal terms only once. It was the meeting in the BHS cafeteria all those years ago. I told them how, after that, she had failed to show up four times. That then I had found her again in the nursing home where we had cosy chats but I knew she was already in the grip of dementia, which was why she no longer lived in her own home. I always knew that Margaret felt a connection with me on those visits but sometimes conversation was difficult, indeed, almost impossible as her powers of communication faded. But her smile was as wide and generous as ever. As we chatted about Margaret, Sue suddenly interrupted me to say, 'But I'm so glad she never knew. I'm so glad you never told Mum.' Tears were pouring down her cheeks as she said it and I began to fight back the tears again.

Then, of course, the questions came flooding out: Who was she? What did she do? Where did we meet? What was she like? Did I like her? To that last question I answered, 'Yes. I did like her but she never gave me a chance to get to know her, not even a little bit.' When I told Sue that a key part of my decision to look for Margaret had been our own dad, her tears flowed again. I told her that on several occasions, at least three or four, and while clutching my hand, which he would squeeze tightly, he had said, 'Find her, son. Find your birth mother. She deserves to know that you're OK.'

As we continued to chat, I told Sue and Ian about Margaret coming to England from Ireland in the 1950s to train as a nurse. I also told them that Birmingham had always been her home. Sue was astonished. 'But she lived in Bristol. That's where you were born. I'm sure there was a piece of paper saying your birth mother lived in a Bristol nurses' home.' If there was a piece of paper, it was news to me, and there was no evidence to support Sue's recollection in the Nazareth House file. Sue was so convinced that Margaret had lived in Bristol she even asked if I'd got the right woman. Had I been given the wrong file and been reunited with the wrong mother? Impossible. Margaret admitted she was my birth mother and there was the paperwork, and letters in her own handwriting, to support it. Sue said she had grown up thinking that Margaret lived in Bristol and that the father might have been a doctor, although she says Mum and Dad never talked about the adoption.

To this day, I've never been able to fathom why Margaret chose to have me in Bristol, nearly 100 miles from Birmingham, where she lived and worked. Even today it's a ninety-minute journey on the train and would have been much longer back in 1961, and a car ride back then would have taken at least two hours, as it was before the country's vast motorway network opened. Bristol offered her anonymity, of course, and this would have been in short supply in Birmingham, where she was a state-registered nurse. But, if my birth father was not James Coffey, had Margaret enjoyed a romance with a man who then moved to Bristol? Could that man have been

CHAPTER SIXTEEN

the mysterious doctor Mum and Dad had heard talk about at the time of my adoption, or was that just gossip from the nuns?

Was that, then, how my birth in Southmead Children's Hospital and my spell in the mother and baby home came about? Was there someone in Bristol who had organised it, who knew their way round the system? Knew people? Someone like a doctor, or some other kind of medic perhaps? Usually, the mother's Catholic priest would organise the placements, but the forms in the Nazareth House file show that this was not the case with Margaret. On the form where there were spaces for the name of a priest, there were instead conspicuous blanks. Mum had told some of my friends that the nuns had mentioned the doctor but she wasn't sure she believed them. Were they trying to glamorise Margaret's story? Sue had certainly never heard the story of an Irish pipe layer, who was killed only days after I entered Nazareth House, being my birth father.

I told Sue and Ian about the regressive therapy I'd had with Father Peter and the problems with my sore legs. She couldn't remember there being an issue with them, but she had one clear memory: 'When you first came to us and used to sit on the loo, the door had to be kept open. You told us they used to shut you in the cupboard.' Did that explain why Betty and George used to say to me, 'Patrick's in the cupboard'? Was it their way – in hindsight not the best way – of explaining to me that my old life, Patrick's life, was in the cupboard but that Andrew's new life was different? Patrick was no longer in the cupboard and Andrew was at the centre of a noisy and loving family. Maybe.

Sue was visibly upset at the thought of me being punished in the home for wetting the bed and by the images of the steel bath, the urine-soaked sheets and the bleach in the water. Then she told me something I had completely forgotten: 'If you were sick at night, you were sick in the bed. Always in the bed. You were probably in a cot in the home with high sides. You wouldn't have been able to get out.' Did the staff leave me in the cot overnight even when I had wet the bed or been sick? Was that part of my punishment?

As we set off for lunch, I felt like a heavy burden had been lifted from my shoulders. Sue and Ian were the first family members I had told about my birth mother. They took it in their stride and were curious and supportive. But most of all, Sue's tears at the thought of Mum knowing about my search convinced me that my decision not to tell her anything about Margaret Connolly had been the right one. Margaret had never been a threat to Mum. I only ever had one mum. I only ever wanted one mum, Betty. The woman who risked turning her family upside down to adopt a lost soul in an orphanage whose birth mother had tried to do the right thing but in the end had to bow to the inevitable and give her son up for adoption. Margaret rightly took her chance at happiness by marrying a man who made her happy and who could give her a family she could love without guilt and without having to constantly look over her shoulder. I'm so glad Margaret gave me up, otherwise there would have been no Betty and George.

CHAPTER SEVENTEEN

While Margaret had a happy childhood, it became clear, when talking to Father Joe Hogan and the wonderful people at the visitor centre in County Mayo, that career prospects for clever young women in the mid-1950s to 1960s were just about non-existent. There wasn't even enough work for men, who were always first in the queue for jobs, let alone their wives or sisters. Margaret clearly didn't relish the idea of being a farmer's wife, nor of working on her parents' smallholding, which could barely support the family. So I can completely understand why she left it all behind and decided to go to Warwick, in England, to train as a nurse.

At that time, Margaret was part of a 500,000-strong exodus of young unmarried men and women who left Ireland to live and work in England and was among 25,000 who eventually settled in Birmingham. Many of her contemporaries followed her into nursing, a profession they were encouraged to enter as it was deemed appropriate by Ireland's rigid class and patriarchal structures in the 1950s. Nursing simply extended the normal practice of female self-sacrifice from the domestic realm into the sphere of women's employment. A mid-century manual for trainee nurses says as much:

> There must be a very real love for the sick; a strong sense of obedience; loyalty to authority and to one's fellow nurses. She must be trustworthy and unselfish. She should have a pleasant manner and be perfectly natural without affectation. She must be prepared to give up many things, even to make sacrifices for the good of her patients.

When she was thirty-one and working at the local hospital, Margaret qualified as a state-registered nurse (SRN). But, ambitious and keen to get on, she moved to Birmingham to train as a district nurse. When she arrived in the city after her basic training in Warwick, Margaret moved into the subsidised accommodation which was provided for young nurses. Like today, recruitment in the NHS in the 1960s was difficult. If she had tried to rent a room she might well have encountered the infamous wording on 'To Let' boards in newsagents back then: 'No Blacks, No Dogs, No Irish'. Nursing in England would have exposed Margaret to anti-Irish prejudice, no matter how good she was at her job.

This section from a report written in 1950 by the president of the Catholic Nurses' Guild lays bare the discrimination my birth mother faced in the NHS: 'Although three-fifths of our Catholic nurses are from Ireland, I record it as a fact that they are not popular with the matrons, who find that they do not conform readily to hospital regulations. Their numbers are greatest in the least attractive types of nursing; chronic fever, sanatorium and mental.' Even when living in England, Irish women could never completely escape the shackles of the omnipotent Roman Catholic Church. Missionary priests were sent to follow them by Archbishop John Charles McQuaid, the powerful Primate of All Ireland and Archbishop of Dublin from 1940 to 1972. McQuaid had the ear of successive

CHAPTER SEVENTEEN

Prime Ministers, irrespective of their political party, and wielded huge power in questions of morality.

Admittedly, this was long before the appalling child abuse scandals which shattered the Catholic Church's moral authority in Ireland. In the 1950s and well into the 1960s, Catholics like Margaret regarded the Church with a mixture of awe, reverence and deference. Archbishop McQuaid sent the missionary priests to England to protect Irish women's 'spiritual sanctity'. The priests loitered in the reception areas of hotels in London and other major cities. They were there to ensure that young Catholic girls never got into trouble, particularly with men. Obviously, however, they weren't always successful.

Various books about the influx of Irish nurses in the 1950s and 1960s mention the resentment that they experienced from their English colleagues. The trigger for this hostility was the belief that by leaving home and suspending their duty as nurturing mothers, Irish women were undeserving of a place in the maternally oriented world of nursing.

Margaret qualified as a district nurse in 1961, the year I was born, when she was thirty-four. I can't help wondering how on earth she managed to combine her nurse training with being pregnant and giving birth – especially as the latter would require her to be absent from work for at least five to six weeks. When she handed me over to Nazareth House Orphanage in March 1961, she was just two months away from her thirty-fifth birthday.

It must have been in Birmingham that Margaret met James Coffey. If she ever did meet him, of course. Because, although I have seen two official forms, signed in Margaret's distinctive handwriting, that claim James Coffey is the father of her child, I have found no other evidence that they knew one another at all. Moreover, although I would happily embrace the idea of becoming part of the Coffey family, neither members from the present or past had any knowledge that Jimmy ever met my birth mother, let alone became the father of her child. The only real similarity between them that I can find is that Margaret's family background was not dissimilar to that of James Coffey himself.

According to his family, Jimmy Coffey was a slim-built and dark-haired Irish charmer, with an overwhelming interest in having a daily flutter on the horses. Did he also have an eye for the ladies? If so, how long were any of them in some kind of relationship with him? If, indeed, he was ever really interested in anything other than gambling? Jimmy was born and brought up in Rookhill, Ballinamore, Ballinasloe in County Galway. The county is next to Mayo, where Margaret grew up. Did they ever meet when they were in Ireland? It seems unlikely.

As I mentioned earlier, I had first contacted Rhona and learned all about the Coffey family while searching for any details I could find about Jimmy. Unfortunately, however, this was all in vain. The main problem was that my birth mother Margaret had clearly stated in two official documents that James (Jimmy) Coffey was my father, but she only did so some two years *after* his totally unexpected death, which took place when I was merely five weeks old.

Tommy Coffey, who is in his eighties, and the only one of Jimmy's siblings who was still alive when I was first making my enquiries, was astonished to discover that his long-lost brother might have fathered a son, back in the 1960s. 'He was stunned to be informed that his older brother Jimmy might have had a child he never met,' his niece, Rhona, told me. 'He was even more stunned', she added with a laugh, 'when he was told it might be you, Andrew. He's been watching you on TV for years!'

CHAPTER SEVENTEEN

Like Margaret, Jimmy went to Birmingham in the 1950s to find work. Reportedly, he told some friends in Birmingham that his family was once so poor he had to walk to school in his bare feet. My enquiries showed that he worked on various building sites in Birmingham and lived in rented accommodation. It was said he never seemed to have any money, but that's not surprising considering that he was said to have spent most of his spare time at the bookmakers. Frankly, I've never seen or heard of a hard-up bookie.

When Jimmy died in the terrible accident – struck down by an out-of-control van in April 1961 – it was his twin, Eddie, and Tommy, his youngest brother, who paid for his funeral and the simple yet dignified headstone at Oscott cemetery. Jimmy died broke and left no money. So, if he really was the father of her child, and if Margaret had been expecting him to contribute towards my accommodation at Nazareth House Orphanage, she would have been disappointed.

My enquiries also showed, as far as I could tell, that Margaret's supposed affair with Jimmy Coffey and the birth of his son were totally unknown to any of his workmates, or anyone in the Connolly family, both in Birmingham and back in Ireland. However, Margaret did perhaps provide one intriguing clue about Jimmy when she returned to Ireland shortly after I was born. Leaving me to be looked after by the nuns in Nazareth House Orphanage, she went back to the family farm in Carrigeen, Baltinglass, for a short holiday to visit her parents and three brothers. A letter to the orphanage arrived from her family home. My adoption file said that one brother was a farmer, another was a teacher and another one worked in engineering. The report added, 'Margaret's parents do not know of Patrick.' She sent a month's money to the nuns, so presumably it was a long visit to Ireland and I would have had no visitors for four weeks.

While there, she confided in her mother that she had recently enjoyed a close friendship with a man. She pointedly never used the word boyfriend or lover but just referred to an unnamed male friend. This conversation was overheard and was relayed to me by a friend of the family.

When I met them, they told me what they had overheard that day: 'Margaret told her mother that she was great friends with a man she lived close to in Birmingham. But all of a sudden, she'd stopped hearing from him. Weeks and weeks went by and she kept going backwards and forwards to where he lived to try to find him. But although he'd been a good friend, it seemed that he had moved on and left no forwarding address. No telephone number. No work address. Absolutely nothing.'

Margaret apparently told her mother, 'I was baffled. There was no sign of him. Nothing at all.' As she was telling the story, Margaret showed her usual self-control, giving away no sign of distress or emotion. Of course, there was no mention of the fact that this might have been the man Margaret had named as the father of her child. The child who was currently being cared for by nuns at Nazareth House Orphanage in Cheltenham. But, by her own admission, Margaret had always been very secretive and had clearly never told a living soul about her newborn son. Her mother could never have known the truth behind the story. The missing man had made her daughter pregnant and they'd had an illegitimate son. Her grandson.

Unfortunately, this story ends with a brutal jolt. Because Margaret then proceeded to tell her mother what had happened when she was walking along a familiar Birmingham street and bumped into a mutual acquaintance who knew the (nameless) man. She related to her mother, 'I said to the woman, I'm so pleased to see you. The fact

CHAPTER SEVENTEEN

is, I'm a bit worried. I haven't seen our mutual friend for months. He seems to have disappeared. Do you know what's happened to him?' There was a short pause while the other woman delved deep into her handbag and fished out a sheet of paper. It was the order of service for a funeral. But it wasn't just any funeral. It was the order of service for the funeral of the man Margaret had known and was looking for. Once again, there was no mention of his name. Was it James Coffey?

So… if Jimmy Coffey really was my father, the shock and distress must have been enormous. Cool as a cucumber, all she'd said to her mother was, 'The funeral explains why I couldn't find him.' But of course, it wasn't that simple. When Margaret put me into Nazareth House in early March 1961, the address she gave for Jimmy on the registration forms was Slade Road. When he died, on 15 April, barely five weeks later, the address on the death certificate was Hunton Road. It seemed that he had moved and simply hadn't told Margaret about the change of address. Had he, in fact, done a runner? But Margaret never mentioned the mystery man to her family again.

Later, the same person said to me, 'I am really amazed that Margaret had a baby out of wedlock. Believe me – it was a huge crime in those days. Her parents were *very* strict Catholics when the family was younger. To tell the truth, I think the family had sort of given up on her ever getting wed. Because it was a big surprise to all of us when she said she was getting married to Patrick Lennon. After all, she was well into her thirties. And we hadn't heard of any previous boyfriends that she might have had in Birmingham. But I have to say that Patrick was a very nice man. And they visited Ireland regularly, often coming over here to stay for a week at a time. Of course, Margaret's parents never went to her wedding to

Patrick Lennon. They simply didn't have the money. In 1963, people were not flying around the world or across the Irish Sea like they do today. But I know that her youngest brother – Padhraig, the schoolmaster – gave her away. He travelled to Birmingham during his school's summer holiday.'

On at least one trip back to Carrigeen, Margaret sent money to Nazareth House for my accommodation. In my adoption file there are handwritten notes, on scraps of paper, that usually accompanied the money she sent to pay for my board and keep. The first one is poignant in its simplicity. It says, 'Enclosed £4 from 5th March to 19th March for baby Patrick Connolly who is in Nazareth House, Cheltenham. Would you kindly let me know if I should pay weekly fortnightly or monthly.'

The letter in the adoption file addressed from her parents' farm was dated 29 June 1961, by which point I was nearly five months old and had been in the home for more than three months. Was that when she told her mother about the disappearance and death of a friend whom she never actually named during the entire conversation? If so, she knew within weeks or months of his death. So, precisely why she kept me in the home for another two years is a complete mystery.

There is one last written communication from Margaret in July 1963, two years to the month since she was supposed to withdraw me from the home because of her marriage. The letter came with £5 for my housekeeping and a note saying, 'I am commencing my holiday on Friday, July 19 for two weeks and I am changing my address.' Well, Margaret certainly was going on holiday. But what she never told the nuns at Nazareth House was that the holiday was in fact her honeymoon. She was marrying a man who knew absolutely nothing about her secret son. On 20 July 1963, she married Patrick

CHAPTER SEVENTEEN

Lennon at Corpus Christi Church in Stechford. The congregation and her husband were oblivious to the fact that she had a son in an orphanage – but she knew that I would be adopted soon.

How did the nuns explain her absence to a two-year-old whose birth mother had, according to the files, been his only visitor? I'm sure I looked forward to Margaret's visits, not least because they were the only ones I ever had. I often wonder whether I called Margaret 'Mummy'. Was that my first word, as it certainly can't have been Daddy?

Not so long ago, I handed over Margaret's entire adoption file to a priest whom I've known for many years. He has advised the Vatican on a range of issues, as well as some well-known authors when their work has involved the Roman Catholic Church or the papacy. He has also been consulted by bishops and even cardinals, especially if there is a sensitive issue which might be about to enter the public domain. Thus, few things about the Church would be likely to surprise him, so I knew that if anyone could make any sense of the possible relationship between Margaret and James Coffey, it would be him. When, early on in the file, he saw that James Coffey was killed in a car crash only weeks after I was born, he looked up slowly and said, 'Oh, dear – it's one of those. A toe-tag father. No. No, he's not your father,' he added, without any hesitation.

I had no idea what he meant. But, before I could ask him, he continued, 'Bear with me. I'm just going to read the file through to the end.' And I waited, somewhat impatiently I must confess, while he did so. When he finished, he closed the file, handed it back to me and said slowly, 'I obviously don't know how much work you've done on your birth parents. But James Coffey is not your father.'

'What...?' I exclaimed, wondering how he could be so confident in saying that. How on earth could he be so certain? Besides, I'd hardly told him anything about my unsuccessful attempts to build a relationship with Margaret.

He ignored my protest and said, 'Look. I've seen this so many times. The priests, the nuns, the church and often the doctors all connive to give the unmarried Catholic mother a toe-tag father.' Which, I have to say, was an entirely new expression as far as I was concerned.

Sensing my confusion and uncertainty, he gently added, 'When an unmarried man of a suitable age is taken to a local hospital – particularly following serious car accidents and also, more often than not, when it's a case of DOA or "Dead on Arrival" – a tag is fixed to his toe. This is commonly known as a "toe-tag", which is used to identify him on his way to the mortuary. Whereupon, the dead man then magically becomes the fiancé or the intended husband of an unmarried mother. No one knows anything about it, of course, other than the nurse or doctor who has tipped off the nuns, where the orphan baby has been, or is about to be placed in their care. Thus, no one knows anything about it, apart from the nuns and the mother. In fact, the mother may not even be told if she gives the baby up straight away.'

'But I still don't see…'

'It's very simple. The dead man's name stays on the forms when the baby is registered with the orphanage. So, when the baby comes up for adoption, the father is dead and the name won't surface in the adoption papers as no consent is required. The church did it again and again. I'm well aware of it. I've heard a lot about it. And what's more, I've been told about the various ways it can function. Frankly, I suspect that in your case, the doctor who arranged this might even prove to be your true birth father, who was almost certainly married – or engaged to someone else. I'm sorry if it is disappointing or

CHAPTER SEVENTEEN

upsetting. But, there is – certainly as far as I'm concerned – a 100 per cent likelihood of it being exactly what happened in your case.'

So, if my friend the priest was right, it would explain why Jimmy Coffey's workmate, Mr Kilmartin, who was with him when he died, knew absolutely nothing about a girlfriend, let alone a baby. And it would also explain why none of Jimmy Coffey's family knew anything about Margaret or her baby son, either. An important point, which my friend the priest thought was enough to clinch his argument, was that Jimmy's body was taken to the hospital in Birmingham, where Margaret was training as a district nurse. So, if the priest was correct, could Margaret have been involved in the plot? And if so, no wonder she was claiming total amnesia concerning anything related to my conception and birth.

Every time I spoke to Margaret, she ended our conversation with the same words. She had said them in BHS when we first met, on the telephone to me and also to Amanda when she called to check that Margaret had remembered she and I were supposed to be meeting up in the Birmingham BHS café. The words never changed: 'Please keep this a secret until the Good Lord takes me. After that, I will be in God's hands and He knows everything.'

Over the years, Margaret had obviously become an adept and experienced keeper of secrets. I often think of her carefully guarding her tongue, while sifting the whole truth, partial honesty, unreliable facts and outright lies as if she were laying out a deck of cards. Maybe her biggest secret was the name of my birth father. Because if it wasn't James Coffey, who was it? And was there a chance that whoever it was might have still been alive when I first contacted her? On the whole, I hope he wasn't. Because to actively deny me the (admittedly unlikely) chance of meeting him, would be – after all these years – almost unforgivable. But, when I first tried to talk to Margaret about my birth father, she could have easily explained that it wasn't James Coffey without giving me his real name and explained the circumstances, especially if he was a pillar of the community, hence the need for secrecy. As I was born in the socially strict and uptight early 1960s, I would have totally understood. Also, why was she still protecting his good name? Because he was either married – or engaged to someone else – when I was born?

When I began the journey to Margaret's front door in the Birmingham suburbs, I was only interested in finding her and making sure she knew that I was very happy and settled in my private life, and lucky enough to thoroughly enjoy my job. Also, that if she had ever worried about me at any point during the previous fifty years, I wanted to reassure her there would have been no need to do so. Although, to be honest, I've long since come to the conclusion that she had deliberately decided, for her own peace of mind, to try to forget about me as soon as she could. I completely understand this. In fact, under the circumstances, it was probably the best decision she could make. With a new husband and a future family consisting of four children, I'm sure she was tough enough to force herself to be pragmatic. Because there was no way she could have mourned her lost child while looking after a husband and a house full of children.

I had also wanted her to know that I'd had a wonderful upbringing by really amazing and loving parents. But the more I've delved into my birth and adoption, the more I've come to realise that it's now time to make a far greater effort, and finally discover the identity of my father. My journey to find out exactly who I am is still only semi-complete and I will be starting out, once again, on the search for my birth father. Following some good advice, it seems that first of all I should resolve the obvious question of

CHAPTER SEVENTEEN

whether Jimmy Coffey was, or was not, my father. Since there are so many potential Coffey cousins willing and able to help me, the most sensible course of action would be to take a DNA test. And, if that proves I have no link to Jimmy, then it looks as if my search will begin all over again.

So now, it's clearly a case of 'watch this space'!

CHAPTER EIGHTEEN

In the Lodge Hill Cemetery in Selly Oak, Birmingham, bathed in warm wintry sunshine, I walked past the protected special burial site of 500 soldiers who had laid down their lives for king and country in the First World War. Many of the men who'd died in local hospitals, mostly from the terrible injuries they sustained on the killing fields of Flanders, were, according to the inscriptions on their headstones, only nineteen years old. Mere teenagers. I found it impossible not to feel deeply moved by their fate. A cross of sacrifice, with the words '*Their name liveth for evermore*', marks their final resting place. Nearby is a small burial plot which is surrounded by a golden privet hedge. Here, fourteen German prisoners of the First World War are also buried. On each of the graves is a flat memorial stone shaped like an Iron Cross, which is Germany's highest military honour. I also passed the large crematorium, which has a bronze plaque honouring the forty-eight servicemen of the Second World War who were cremated there. Lodge Hill Cemetery and Crematorium are set in 61 acres of land which lie close to the ruins of Weoley Castle, once a medieval manor house. There is a Quaker section, which includes the graves of many members of the Cadbury family who created 'Bournville', the model village built specifically to house the factory employees.

I passed the memorial to children and babies, which was adjacent to a rose garden that formed a beautiful sanctuary for grieving parents. I was still seeking the section designated for those of the Roman Catholic faith, because I was heading for a final meeting with my birth mother, Margaret. I was carrying a simple wreath of flowers and berries, which I hoped would be rich pickings for the birds I knew Margaret had loved so much. Searching for the grave, I walked up and down endless rows of brooding sculpted angels, elaborate marble headstones and simple crosses, some festooned with flowers, for several minutes. Following a recent rain shower, the wet grass squelched loudly under my shoes and I was nearing the point of giving up the search… when, suddenly, there she was!

The brown marble monument was inscribed with gold text bearing the simple message:

In
Ever Loving Memory of
Patrick Lennon
Father and Grandfather
Passed Away
10th January 1996

Margaret Lennon
A Devoted Wife,
Mother and Grandmother
Passed Away
2nd February 2021
Rest in Peace
Forever In Our Thoughts

CHAPTER EIGHTEEN

Gently, I placed my wreath of berries on the headstone and bowed my head in prayer. My reverent birth mother would have approved of that, I told myself, before saying a Hail Mary. It was not only my own favourite prayer but, as I'd discovered over the years, it was a prayer close to Margaret's heart.

Father Denis McGillycuddy, who had been her priest at St Edward's Church, slowly made his way to join me at the grave. He had come with me to the cemetery but had deliberately fallen back, leaving me to find my birth mother's grave and also to say some private prayers for a few minutes. The parish priest had known Margaret for many years. In fact, he'd liked her very much and had also personally conducted her funeral service. Following his advice that I had every right, as Margaret's eldest son, to attend her requiem mass, I'd deliberately stayed away from her burial, which I believed should be just for her close family.

Now, as Father Denis blessed the headstone with holy water, we prayed quietly together. It was all so peaceful, with the silence only broken by the occasional muffled sobs of a husband laying flowers on his late wife's nearby grave. Otherwise, I felt entirely alone with my thoughts. Straining every emotional sinew, I tried to concentrate on sensing my mother's actual presence. In my mind's eye, I could see her face wreathed in that familiar, lovely, big smile and I almost heard those peals of infectious laughter, which had so often lightened the atmosphere in her care home. But try as I might, I was unable to conjure up any sense of her actual presence.

I'd decided to come here to her graveside only weeks after my trip to County Galway and my visit to the old home of Jimmy Coffey, the man who was named as my father on my adoption forms. But, as I gazed at her headstone, I was glad that she was reunited with

Patrick Lennon, her husband and the father of her other four children. She had married him in 1963, but he had died far too soon in 1996, leaving her to grieve his loss for twenty-five years.

However, as I thought about her life, feelings of deep regret flooded through my mind. Regrets over the extraordinary story she could have told me, about her secret trip from Birmingham, when heavily pregnant, to check into the harsh and unforgiving mother and baby home in Bristol. Or the story of her lonely labour in Southmead Children's Hospital, about which I knew virtually nothing. I never discovered, for instance, how long it took for the midwives to deliver me. But I do know I tipped the scales at more than eight pounds in weight. And I knew hardly anything except the barest of details about my baptism a few days later. It must have been a very cold and austere occasion, with strangers as witnesses and a completely unknown female 'godparent', no doubt drafted in by the local parish priest and whom I would never see again. Definitely not the celebration that Margaret would have wanted for the christening of her first-born son. No happy day surrounded by friends and family and, most importantly, the father of her child. I could imagine that even during that service, she would have been on edge, looking over her shoulder in case someone might recognise her. When the priest read out the names Patrick James, what did she think? Were they a clue to the identity of my birth father?

I will never know why Margaret was so unwilling to give me the answers to my questions. Questions I felt were quite normal under the circumstances. After all, when Amanda had first knocked on the door of her little semi-detached house, Margaret had vehemently denied that she was anything to do with me. I had, of course, known it was likely that her first reaction would be to deny the truth. Because she must have been in total shock on being tracked down

CHAPTER EIGHTEEN

almost fifty years after giving me away. But, when Amanda returned to her house a little later the same day, Margaret had cried and given thanks to God because, as she'd said, 'It is me. Please tell him it really is me and I will see him.'

However, when she eventually spoke to me, she had no recollection of either Bristol, Nazareth House or of the long journeys to see me from her nurse's accommodation in Birmingham. But there had been plenty of time, from that first knock on her door and the cup of tea at BHS in the centre of Birmingham, to think about what had happened to her and her first child all those years ago. Could she really have buried so much pain? It seems that opinion is divided. Some experts claim that the scars are so deep that very often when women are forced to give up their newborn children for adoption, they will instinctively bury their deepest feelings; to the point where they can genuinely no longer remember what happened.

A friend recommended that I read the book *Love Child: A Memoir of Adoption, Reunion, Loss and Love* by Sue Elliott, which was published in 2006. It was based on the author's personal experience as she was given up for adoption by her mother Marjorie in the 1950s. For Elliott, the shocks came thick and fast, including the discovery that she was not the only child her mother had given away. The book contained so many desperately sad interviews with Roman Catholic women in the 1950s and 1960s, who were forced to give up their babies. Mostly in their late teens, the expectant mothers had to leave their own families and enter mother and baby homes. Following the birth of their child, they were then expected some six weeks later to sign it over to a complete stranger. None of these women had ever forgotten their babies. In fact, quite the opposite. Each and every one of the interviewees recalled thinking about their lost child every day; the child which society would not let them keep. One of the women described how, when she told her boyfriend she was pregnant, his only reaction was to reply that he was already married with a family. To say that she was utterly shell-shocked was an understatement. She was shattered by the discovery that she was now totally alone, as the baby's father, in true 'Pontius Pilate' style, proceeded to totally wash his hands of her. In fact, she only agreed to sign the forms allowing her son to be taken from her and put up for adoption when she was cruelly threatened with the alternative of being admitted to a psychiatric hospital. Every single one of the women interviewed for this book could still clearly recall the precious moments when they were permitted to spend time with their child before the baby was adopted. Elliott records the devastating fact that most of the babies were secretly taken from their cots by the nuns as the mothers slept.

As I finished the book, I knew there was one marked difference between Margaret and the women in *Love Child*, which had proved to be such an agonising read. Margaret was thirty-four when she gave birth to me, and with my alleged birth father Jimmy Coffey being thirty-six, they had a combined age of sixty years. Surely that would have provided them with enough knowledge and experience not to make a mistake over an unwanted pregnancy.

For years I had wrestled with guilt over upsetting my adoptive mum Betty, the only real mother I had ever truly known, about my decision to search for my birth mother. But, as I stood over Margaret's grave, I realised that I had finally resolved another emotional tussle. I decided there and then that I should contact my Lennon half-brothers and sister. I would tell them about my meetings with their mother and my regular visits to see her when she'd developed dementia and was living in various care homes in Birmingham. If they were prepared to talk to me, they might be able to tell me something about her. I knew she was a devout Catholic. I also knew how much she'd loved her husband and her family, because she frequently told me before Alzheimer's claimed her mind. They might be able to tell me what she was like as a mother. Was she strict like my mum Betty? Or was she a softie, just like my lovely dad George? How surprised were they likely to be when they discovered that their mother had managed to keep such an important secret for so long?

Of course, there was always the chance they might not want to have anything to do with me, which would also be perfectly understandable. But I knew the time had come to find out.

THE HISTORY OF NAZARETH HOUSE

Fair-haired and with large blue eyes, the two-year-old girl was wandering forlornly near the tradesman's entrance of the large, imposing Victorian building. Around her neck, there was a piece of cardboard on which was written in red lipstick, 'I cannot keep this child. I have not work nor money. Thank you.' On the other side of the board were the words, 'Look after her. Thank you.'

The child, with her thick wavy hair, appeared to be well nourished. But she could only speak a few words. 'Mummy' was her favourite. Her clothes were scruffy and sewn into her green woollen knickers was a white tag bearing the name 'C. Smith' in Indian ink. By the child's side was a faded white pillow slip stuffed full of clothes. It was 1945, the end of the war, and the girl had been abandoned at the door of Nazareth House in Cheltenham by the very mummy she kept calling for.

The story of the little girl, which is told in a history of Nazareth House, was typical of that belonging to the 3,000 or so children who passed through the orphanage after it was founded by the Poor Sisters of Nazareth. They had arrived in 1884 and served the local and wider communities until the home closed in 1965, exactly one year after my own adoption was formalised.

The nuns had travelled to Cheltenham from their main convent in Hammersmith, west London, where to this day the archives of the Nazareth House Orphanages are kept. They were part of a religious order which was founded in London in 1851 by the Frenchwoman Victoire Larmenier (1827–78).

The community of sisters had a 'Foundation Book', which traces the development of Nazareth House to the end of the First World War. It notes that after changing trains at Gloucester, the Mother-General began to recite the rosary and the Litany of the Blessed Virgin Mary and the sisters finished this devotional exercise just as the train pulled in to Cheltenham railway station. There, they were met by four Catholic women and escorted across the road to St Gregory's Church, in the town centre, where they spent a few minutes praying before the Blessed Sacrament. To this day, St Gregory's is one of the most popular churches in Cheltenham and I often attended mass there when I worked for the *Echo* as a trainee reporter. The future orphanage's first incarnation was situated next to the church.

According to the Foundation Book, the house was furnished with 'new beds, armchairs and every convenience for the comfort and happiness of old men and women'. In the upper part of the new Nazareth House, the sisters found small beds and cots for the little children who were destined to live there. The furniture had been provided by wealthy inhabitants of the Gloucestershire spa town.

Like other Nazareth Houses, the Cheltenham orphanage provided accommodation for the aged poor and also for orphans and

CHAPTER EIGHTEEN

destitute children – primarily Roman Catholic girls. A report from December 1884 disclosed that sixteen children resided there, all of whom, except for two or three, had come from the workhouse. The accommodation consisted of nine rooms, with the aged and infirm of both sexes in one part, and abandoned infants in the other. In 1886 the nuns decided to open a soup kitchen for the large number of unemployed people in the town. Their charitable work was largely financed through the sisters themselves, who went out knocking from door to door in Cheltenham. They also built a chapel, complete with sacristy, as well as a schoolroom.

The St James's Square house had become too small for its growing number of residents. So, fundraising began again, with the aim of financing a much larger building. In 1888, the home moved to new premises on Bath Road opposite Cheltenham College. The Sisters of Nazareth continued to expand their premises and, in October 1906, they bought the neighbouring house for £1,800. Ten years later, they bought another building for £2,000. The now much-extended Nazareth House was used to house boys from the Catholic Children's Rescue Society. This was the building which was to become my first proper home, some fifty-five years later.

In the succeeding years and decades, most children arrived at the home as babies, their mothers given no more than five or six weeks before having to hand over their precious infants. The majority of infants didn't stay long at the orphanage, as most couples preferred to adopt a newborn child. The general belief was that a baby, only a few weeks or months old, was too young to have any memories of the home or its birth mother. As such, the baby would be totally unaware of ever having been in the orphanage, a large, bleak building which was, by now, a dominant feature of Cheltenham town centre.

When I arrived at Nazareth House in March 1961, there were

already thirty-eight children waiting to be adopted by new parents. This apparently included fourteen girls, who were toddlers, while I was one of the twenty-four babies. The formidable Sister Aloysius Magdalen O'Brien was the Mother Superior, with thirteen nuns reporting solely to her, while seven nuns looked after the children.

Nazareth House itself used to be opposite the renowned Cheltenham College, which was founded in 1841. It was one of the leading Victorian public schools and continues to occupy an equally prestigious position today. The contrast between the privileged Cheltenham College boys, studying in an institution founded in 1841 with the motto *Labor omnia vincit* ('Work Conquers All'), and the waifs and strays of Nazareth House could not be more marked. When I was in the orphanage, it was every child for themselves. You didn't even own the clothes you stood up in.

I'm still sad that, as an adult, I was never able to look round Nazareth House, if only to see whether the building's interior might jog any memories, either happy or sad. When I started seeing Father Peter Burrows for therapy in 2010, some of which took me back to my long-buried memories of Nazareth House, the idea of writing a book about my search for Margaret was the last thing on my mind. It was only after my mum Betty died in January 2015 that my feelings of guilt about my many abortive trips to Birmingham to try to see Margaret finally began to fade. The more I thought about the remarkable, if at times arduous journey, to trace and find my birth mother Margaret, the more I came to see that I should document it. Primarily to encourage and inspire other people who, like me, were troubled by, and torn with guilt about, attempting to trace their birth parents.

In 2018 I heard on the radio about a child abuse inquiry into what had occurred in various Nazareth children's homes in

Scotland, between 1933 and 1984. The inquiry was chaired by Lady Anne Smith, a former Supreme Court judge, and exposed some shocking allegations of abuse by the nuns. The investigation heard evidence from seventy former residents, along with former staff from Nazareth House centres in Aberdeen, Glasgow, Midlothian and Kilmarnock.

Over five decades, children in the homes were subjected to physical punishments on an almost daily basis. In Nazareth House homes in Glasgow, Aberdeen, Ayrshire and Midlothian, children were regularly humiliated, insulted and denigrated by the adults who were charged with their care. In some cases, the children endured 'particularly depraved' sexual abuse by adults they should have been able to trust.

The inquiry also heard that children were hit with belts, canes, sticks, broom handles, hairbrushes, shoes and wooden crucifixes. Carbolic soap was forced into their mouths, their heads were banged together and they were made to kneel in corridors for long periods of time. For many young children this became normal and those who tried to escape were harshly beaten when they returned. Those who reported their abuse to the police were not believed. Children were force-fed. They also had to queue for baths in a state of total undress, only to be forced to share bathwater that was too hot, too cold or dirty. Emotional abuse, including humiliation, coercive control, insults, denigration and unjustified punishment was rampant. Children were routinely locked in cupboards. And the ultimate mental cruelty: they were routinely separated from their siblings and faced harsh punishment if they tried to make contact with them.

The section of the report that made my blood run cold was the one referring to how children who wet the bed were subject to special humiliations: 'They were locked into dark cupboards or forced to "wear their wet sheets" for long periods of time.' It was the same story that emerged years later from my regressive therapy sessions with Father Peter. I couldn't help but wonder, is that what happened to my legs? Was that the reason they were so raw and painful until I was adopted? And was that why it took my new mum Betty such a long time to cure the problem?

One woman told the inquiry how she and her two sisters were beaten until they bled on their first day at Nazareth House in Aberdeen. She was ten years old when she arrived at the orphanage in 1967, while her youngest sister was just a toddler. When giving formal evidence, she said that the nuns pretended to be nice and kind in public but that they were apt to become violent as soon as the sisters' social workers left the building. In another incident, she described having her head smashed against a radiator until she was 'foaming at the mouth'. A 76-year-old lady said that nuns at the institution in Cardonald, Glasgow, told her that her parents had died and that now she had no family. Consumed by unhappiness and despair, she finally discovered decades later that her mother and father were very much alive and that she also had five brothers and sisters. It appears that the reason it took so long for her to trace and eventually see her family again was that she'd been sent – aged ten – to a Nazareth House facility in Australia, where she was abused physically, emotionally and sexually.

Lady Smith firmly rejected claims that some witnesses to the inquiry may have fabricated their stories. She said:

> It has been suggested, in evidence, that applicants may have colluded to present fictitious accounts about their time in the care of various Nazareth House orphanages ... I totally and utterly reject

CHAPTER EIGHTEEN

any and all such suggestions. I have absolutely no doubt that the Nazareth Houses in Scotland were, for many children, places of fear, hostility and confusion. Desperately unhappy places, where children were physically abused and emotionally degraded with impunity.

There was sexual abuse of children which, in some instances, reached levels of the utmost depravity. Children, in need of kind, warm, loving care and comfort did not find it. In fact, children were actively deprived of compassion, dignity, and also any comfort or care.

The inquiry was established in 2018 and in 2020, it disclosed how the nuns' vow of obedience meant that they did not question existing practices. Most of the sisters who gave evidence denied having seen any abuse take place. The report concluded with the firm statement that while the nuns now found it hard to face up to 'the reality' [of what they saw and did] 'that does not mean that the abuse did not happen'.

In a statement, the Sisters of Nazareth said, 'The report details the suffering and abuse endured by some of the children in our homes and for that we are deeply ashamed. As we have said before, we apologise wholeheartedly and unreservedly to those who suffered any form of mistreatment.' The statement concluded, 'From listening to their testimonies and reading the report, we know how deeply the experiences of those years in care have affected their lives. We realise that no apology can do justice to their childhood experience or heal these lasting memories, and we are profoundly sorry for having failed them at the time.'

It all sounds utterly shocking and terrible. And it was. Because the Sisters of Nazareth had, for more than 100 years, cared for children, orphans and abandoned babies – as well as children thrown out of their family homes because they were engaged in crime and/or were unmanageable. They were just children, like me – all of us placed in the hands of nuns who, to all intents and purposes, were assumed to be the very essence of compassion and Christian charity.

Some years ago, while on a relaxing river boat cruise in Germany, I met three nuns from Australia who were on holiday. From their dress and their general demeanour, one would never have known they were nuns. They were in ordinary civilian clothes and looked just like three girlfriends having a nice holiday away from their husbands. But I noticed that they were all wearing identical rings. My old Catholic instincts kicked in, and sure enough, within a few minutes one of them told me that she was a nun. I heard myself telling them that I had been brought up by nuns in a Catholic orphanage in England. They looked pensive before they asked me the name of the orphanage. When I told them 'Nazareth House', all three of them blanched. 'Whatever is wrong?' I asked. This was just months before the inquiry into abuse at Nazareth children's homes in Scotland was established. At that time, I had no idea about the inquiry itself or what its dreadful outcome would be. One of the nuns quickly replied, 'There have been problems reported with some Nazareth Houses in Australia. But I don't think that should worry you. It was historical stuff.'

Immediately, however, I was instinctively on high alert. But I judged it best to avoid the subject until the holiday was over and I was back in Britain. Once back home, I started to investigate. It wasn't difficult to find reports of the many claims of dreadful cruelty that had allegedly been carried out at some of the Nazareth Houses in Australia. I also uncovered a report from 2011 that listed allegations of abuse and brutality at one of the homes in

CHAPTER EIGHTEEN

Queensland, Australia, over a ninety-year period ending in 1976. The report, by Professor Bruce Grundy of Queensland University, described how one girl had her legs burned with a red-hot poker to exorcise the devil, while another child almost lost her feet and legs, which became infected, after her ingrown toenails were pulled out with pliers by a nun. Yet another child was badly scarred after being scalded by a nun – who'd complained that the child didn't use enough hot water when washing.

In his report, Professor Grundy wrote,

> Ruthless and sadistic madness, on the part of at least some of the nuns, and a depthless depravity on the part of some priests … are the defining characteristics of at least some of those who ran the orphanage. There was no limit to the sexual deviance that could be engaged in, especially with those unlucky enough to be singled out as 'the chosen ones'.

One girl told the 2011 Australian inquiry:

> I was a bed-wetter until the age of seven. Every morning, one of the nuns or senior girls would come around and check our sheets. If any of us had wet our beds, we would have our faces rubbed into the bed – sometimes until our noses bled. We would then be told to get dressed and go to mass. I can remember that during the mass, blood would still be dripping from my nose, with my sleeves covered in blood as I tried to staunch the flow.
>
> After breakfast, we would do our chores and go to school. The home had its own school up to grade six, so there was no escaping the nuns. In the morning, before class began, the nun would call out the names of those who'd wet their beds; if you

were guilty you had to stand up on top of your chair. If there were a lot of us, she would pace up and down the aisles of desks and, if she poked her stick into you, it meant you had to go and stand at the front of the class, where she had buckets of hot water lined up. We were forced to stand in this hot water until it had cooled. Whereupon, she would tell us to put our shoes and socks back on over our burning feet. What made it a far worse punishment, was that most of the time our shoes were already much too tight – it being very rare that we had proper fitting shoes – so it was agony to try and force them on.

This extract comes from the Australian report and it bears a close resemblance to the mental and physical torture endured by Charlotte Brontë's eponymous heroine Jane Eyre, also a penniless orphan.

One former inhabitant of Nazareth House told the Australian inquiry, 'Bed-wetting was about the worst thing you could do. The punishment was being forced to stand in front of a nun's cell with the soiled linen on your head or being sat in a galvanised steel bath while two assistants poured buckets of cold water over your head.'

At the very mention of 'buckets of cold water over your head', I wondered whether this had actually happened to me. And, if so, maybe it could explain why I was terrified of having my hair washed when I was adopted and went to live in Swindon. My mum Betty, obviously with the best of intentions, and in order to save money by not heating any extra water, always used to make sure that after your hair was washed, the shampoo was gently rinsed off with cold water. And once I was able to understand why my mum was being so frugal, I eventually got used to it. But it's no wonder that those lovely nuns on the river cruise had blanched with fear when I mentioned the dreaded words 'Nazareth House'.

CHAPTER EIGHTEEN

Although I've searched high and low for reports of any abuse at Cheltenham, I've never found any. But clearly, violence and abuse were commonplace in some of the Nazareth House establishments. I wondered whether Margaret had heard the same reports on the radio in her little house in Birmingham, or seen anything on the TV news. Had she wondered whether the same abuse had been carried out at the home where she'd left me with the nuns? I thought again about my old friend Sir Charles Irving, the late Tory MP for Cheltenham. In one of our many conversations, he gravely admitted that he'd been extremely worried because he'd heard that 'things had been not at all OK at Nazareth House'. But as the orphanage had closed soon afterwards, he'd felt that it was too late to do anything about the rumours. And he said nothing else to me on the subject.

In a very long telephone conversation, I also shared the findings of the report with Father Peter Burrows. Having read the reports on the internet, however, he knew all about it. For the first time, he told me that he had halted the regressive therapy when we encountered my fuzzy memories of ice-cold bath water and urine-soaked clothes and sheets. He recalled that as I'd talked to him about it – even though I was in a trance – tears poured down my cheeks and my body shook. He'd deliberately never told me anything about this before because, when I came out of the trance, I was perfectly calm. My tears had gone and I appeared to be totally oblivious. 'That's precisely why I decided not to press the regressive therapy any further,' Father Peter told me. 'I had heard quite enough.'

Nazareth House Orphanage was my first home. It was where I, as 'Patrick', learned to speak, although by all accounts I never spoke very much. Nowadays, my friends wouldn't hesitate to tell anyone who's interested that over the succeeding years I definitely seem to have made up for lost time. However, basically it was, and perhaps still is, a hugely significant part of my life. When I embarked on this journey, all roads seemed to lead back to my earliest days in Nazareth House. Were there any other answers buried in the ruins of that building? Will I ever know why Margaret kept me in the orphanage for two and a half years when the man she'd told the nuns was my father had died only five weeks after my birth? I seriously doubt that I ever will. Principally because Margaret made sure that she took the answers to those questions – along with so many others – to her grave in Birmingham.

POSTSCRIPT

As I tore open the brown envelope, three small black-and-white photographs, which were wrapped within a single sheet of handwritten paper, slipped on to my desk. I gazed at the photos and thought my heart might miss a beat. I was staring at a familiar chubby child. He was smiling and standing up in a play pen, hanging on to the side to ensure he didn't topple over. Dressed in a white baby suit, he was next to a cute little blonde girl who didn't look as happy. He was barely a year old. I stared and stared.

There was another photo of the same toddler sitting down on a blanket on a lawn, playing with two other boys. The little blonde girl was there too. The children's names were written in black ink on the back of the photos. The blonde girl's name was Ann. The black boy who was kneeling down in the photo was called Nigel. The other boy was called Adrian. In the background, there were two large, old-fashioned prams.

I had nearly missed a heartbeat because the chubby child was clearly me. I was incredibly moved. I had never seen photos of me so young. Before that, the youngest I'd seen was me aged two and a bit, wearing my trademark red duffle coat and Rupert Bear checked trousers, in the days when I was first introduced to Betty and

George in the Nazareth House orphanage. I knew straight away that no one in my family had ever seen these photos. I couldn't wait to share them with my big sister Sue, who knew straight away it was her little brother when she saw them.

I hurriedly read the handwritten letter. It was from a lady called Mrs Philomena Olver, who, coincidentally, lived in Bristol, where I'd been born in February 1961. She had been in touch with me when the hardback edition of *Finding Margaret* came out the summer before. She had worked in the nursery at Nazareth House in Cheltenham, which was my first home for nearly three years. Philomena told me that she was at the orphanage at the same time as me. She was adamant that she could remember me. I thought that very unlikely and said so.

In a long conversation on the telephone, with the photos in front of me, Mrs Olver (who told me to call her Philomena) said, 'It's you. No doubt about it.' She had been hunting around in the attic and stumbled on a sheaf of old photographs. As she leafed through them, my name jumped out at her, written on the back of the photograph. And there it was. Patrick. I had been baptised Patrick James Connolly just a few weeks before my mother, Margaret Connolly, moved me into Nazareth House in March 1961.

Philomena told me, 'I remembered you as a toddler when I read about your book. You were a shy little thing. You never said very much. I especially remember you because you never had any visitors, not like some of the other children.' I told Philomena that my birth mother Margaret, who had lived and worked as a nurse in Birmingham, had in fact visited me at the home. 'Well, if she did, I never saw her and don't remember her,' she said. 'There was one girl who visited her child every day. She was a nurse like your mother, but she rented a place opposite the orphanage so she could see her little girl. I never knew how things worked out for you. I was so happy to hear you had been raised in a loving family. You deserved that. All the children did, but sadly it wasn't like that for all our little children.'

Of course, Margaret, if she had wanted to see me more often, could have arranged for me to be put in the Nazareth House in Rednal, a suburb of Birmingham about eight miles from the city centre. The orphanage, opened in 1913, stood on a thirty-acre site and could house up to 200 children and some destitute, pensioner-age women. Margaret worked in the main hospital in Birmingham. She could have visited me after work or at weekends. But she opted for the safety-first option of Cheltenham instead.

Margaret, who to the very end of her life refused to give up any information about my experience in the orphanage or reveal who my father was, was always terrified that knowledge of her secret child would come out and would have been worried she might be spotted going into the orphanage to visit me. Very little chance of that in Cheltenham. Although she could have said she was going into the home to do voluntary work. There were many volunteers in the Cheltenham orphanage, after all.

Philomena had lived in various Nazareth Houses all her life until she was fifteen, when the nuns sent her to Cheltenham to work in the nursery. 'I loved the children,' she said. 'I would play with you, talk to you, and try to give you the love you were missing because you had been abandoned by your mothers. It was sad to see some children like you with no visitors. If there were potential adopters, the nuns would always dress the baby or child in their finest. It was like Sunday best. When your parents came to see you, they always put you in those long Rupert Bear checked trousers.'

She said the big prams in the background of one of the photos were to take the newborn babies to the local Catholic church to be baptised: 'I must have been godmother to hundreds of babies. We used to take them round to the local Catholic church, St Gregory's, to be baptised. It was a sad experience with no family there for this important moment in a child's Christian upbringing.'

My adoption went through in the summer of 1964 when I was aged three, but what of the other children in the photos? Philomena wasn't sure. She didn't know what had become of Adrian. Nigel was moved to the Bristol Nazareth House in 1965 when the Cheltenham home closed. He was eventually adopted by a couple, who also adopted a little fair-haired boy at the same time. And what of Ann? She wasn't sure. 'Ann's mother wanted to make a home for her little girl, but her parents, who were well to do, were not having any of it. So little Ann stayed in the system for a long time,' she said.

There was a third photo in the envelope, of three little boys gazing up at a nativity scene. The photo was taken from the back. One was a little black boy, possibly Nigel. There was one boy in the middle wearing those distinctive Rupert Bear trousers. Was it me? I wasn't sure. He seemed too tall. And anyway, no one owned the clothes they stood up in. It was a free for all.

Was Philomena aware of the allegations of routine cruelty by the nuns and some of the helpers? 'I never saw any of that,' she said. 'I heard about it. But if a child wet the bed, there was a terrible hullabaloo.'

I had been a bed wetter, a bad habit I took with me to Swindon. A habit that took Betty and George, my mum and dad, years to break, even after I had become a happy and integrated member of their family.

How I wished my mum Betty was still with us. She would have loved to see those photos. We had lost her aged eighty-one when she died peacefully in her sleep in the little council house in Swindon that was her home for fifty-nine years. And my home too until I left Swindon aged eighteen to start my journalistic career. In Cheltenham. Where else?

• • •

My birth must have been a brutal, emotional experience for Margaret, my birth mother. There were no friends or family with her when she arrived in Bristol at the turn of the new year in 1961. There would have been no Hogmanay celebration for the heavily pregnant Margaret. Instead, she checked into St Raphael's, a mother and baby home run by a Roman Catholic order of nuns a few weeks before I was due.

She was a single woman in the harsh, unforgiving social climate of early 1960s Britain and she was alone in Bristol by choice. She trusted no one. She wanted nobody to know about her pregnancy. She was having a child out of wedlock in defiance of the church's strict teaching about sex being restricted to marriage. For Margaret, there could hardly be a graver sin. Even though she had a loving and supportive family back in Ireland and an older brother in England, she told no one. Back then, the church was all-powerful, especially in rural Ireland. It was never even an option for Margaret to confide in her parents that they had a grandchild on the way. And it wasn't as if she could explain away her pregnancy as the result of a youthful mistake or her own naivety. She was only two months from her thirty-fifth birthday when she gave birth to me. So much for the 'gymslip' teenage mother I had always assumed had brought me into this world.

St Raphael's Home for Mothers and Babies was not kind to

its inmates. Initially, it was known as The Convent of the Good Shepherd at Henbury. There was the Convent House and Severn House Mother and Baby Home, which was renamed to St Raphael's. There was also Marian House, which housed women over the age of eighteen on a long-term basis. Many were over fifty years of age. They included women from the Good Shepherd Convent who had lived most of their lives in semi-seclusion and those termed as having 'dull intelligence'. Marian House was also used occasionally for girls awaiting placement within St Raphael's and sometimes for girls who had committed an offence or needed care and were being sent to approved schools as a result. These mother and baby homes offered short-term support to the unmarried mother, but their regimes were punitive, inflexible and often lacking in any empathy.

But I've hit an impenetrable brick wall in trying to find out more about St Raphael's, my first temporary home, with the file on the home closed until 2043. There have been some shocking stories about mother and baby homes that have come out over the last fifteen years. When the St Raphael's file is finally opened for public inspection, will it be another chapter in this horror story? Official inquiries into some of the homes have shown that there was violence and abuse inflicted on vulnerable young women in the very institutions that were supposed to protect them.

In the homes, the mothers would often go to the dormitory where the babies slept to give them their bottles in the morning, only to discover their babies had already gone. Some of the babies went back to Ireland to be placed into care. Others went as far afield as Australia. The mothers were often never told where their babies had gone.

Even in Southmead Children's Hospital, away from the moralising gaze of the good sisters of St Raphael's, Margaret could not escape her sense of shame. She was kept in a separate room from the other pregnant women. For the married expectant mothers, there was to be no guilt by association with the Irish woman whose child's birth certificate had a great yawning gap when it came to the space for the father's name. Instead of his name in bold, proud letters, there was a single word: unknown.

As ever, with Margaret, if there was evidence of a connection to Bristol, the childhood home of Billy Butlin who created the camp where I had my first holiday with my adopted family, she had buried it deeply. Just as she did with her emotions when it came to dealing with me face to face when we met for the first time in forty-five years. Was Bristol chosen by her for the simple reason that it offered her the anonymity she craved because of the terrible social stigma of being an unmarried mother in Britain in the early 1960s? Or was there another reason? Was there a link to Bristol and my father, whose identity Margaret never revealed to me? When we met, she said she couldn't remember who he was. I didn't believe her at the time, and with the benefit of hindsight I still don't, as I think she was trying to protect him and her own reputation to the end.

Was Bristol her idea? Or did someone else suggest it as a location? My birth father, perhaps? Did he live there? Or work there? Was he born there? Did he have medical connections enabling Margaret to have her baby there?

My time in Bristol was short. After a few days in the hospital, it was back to St Raphael's, where she had been for the two weeks before she went into labour. At the age of five weeks, I was transferred to Nazareth House in Cheltenham, some forty-odd miles from Bristol, where there were babies and toddlers and a separate wing for older people who had fallen on hard times. I could just have easily gone to Nazareth House in Bristol. I'm not clear why

I didn't, as it would have made more sense. The only clue I have is that the older children, abandoned by a parent or who had become orphaned, tended to go to Bristol. At the home, brothers and sisters were kept in separate houses and no information was ever given to them about their siblings' lives. Gratuitous and calculated cruelty, in my view.

At the end of 2024, I stumbled across an official report marking the 120th anniversary of CCS Adoption in Bristol, the adoption agency that effectively handled my own transition from orphanage to happy family life. The report pointed to acts of immeasurable cruelty in Roman Catholic orphanages at the very time I was a resident. One of the lines of the little-noticed report was chilling: 'Previous residents of the Nazareth Houses in Bristol and Cheltenham have reported mixed experiences and some complaints were raised, including in 2001, when reports of historical abuse, including being beaten and suffering sexual abuse from other residents and adult helpers, were reported in the *Bristol Evening Post*.'

I found the newspaper reports, which were composed of testimonies from children in the home at the same time I was there. The homes could cater for up to 100 babies and children until Cheltenham closed in 1965, barely a year after my adoption, and Bristol in 1970. In the early days, the orphanage had an outstanding reputation. In 1954, the *Evening Post* wrote, 'The sisters devote their lives to the care of the little ones, trying as far as it is possible to make it up to them for what they are losing not being members of a real family.'

Reading through the newspaper articles, again and again there were reports of beatings for wetting the bed. Punishments included being sat in a galvanised steel bath while two assistants poured buckets of cold water over the child's head. The urine-sodden sheets were wrapped around their legs or neck. At night time there were checks to ensure all the children slept on their backs with their arms crossed over their bodies so that, according to one person's story, 'if we died in our sleep we would go to heaven'.

Teresa Smith, who was still living in Bristol, was forty-one when she spoke to the newspaper about the 'ritual of abuse' that she suffered. I was forty at the time, so a direct contemporary of hers. She told the newspaper, 'With the exception of one nun their role seemed to be to punish. One of my most vivid memories was being locked in the cupboard and spending hours in the dark. I saw nuns grab hold of girls' hair and pull them upstairs hitting them with a hairbrush.'

John, aged fifty-five, told the newspaper about the 'regime of fear' that prevailed and the abuse that he suffered. 'You would have to sleep with your hands across your chest at night,' he recalled.

> I remember the nuns or helpers would pull the sheets off the bed and if your hands and arms weren't folded you were made to kneel on stone floors. If you wet the bed you were put in a bath of cold water and scrubbed with disinfectant. One of our duties was to clean a 200-foot stone hall floor. There would be two or four boys scrubbing on our knees. Standing above us would be another boy who would swing a broom to ensure that we didn't put our head up and stop cleaning. One of our helpers, not a nun, was particularly cruel. She told my brother and I that our mother didn't want us and nor did they.

John said the torment was exacerbated by the sexual abuse he suffered in the dormitory at the hands of the older boys.

Arthur was sixty-nine when he spoke to the newspaper, saying he was sent to Nazareth House as a three-year-old and remained there until he was thirteen. He too was scrubbed with disinfectant if he wet his bed. He still has no idea if he has any brothers or sisters. 'We had no protection, no cuddles, or anyone to care for us,' he said. 'At night I felt so lonely I cried. When other people talk about their childhoods I go very quiet. I am not as angry now but I will take these memories to the grave.'

Michelle Daly was a carer at the home and was shocked by what she saw. 'Babies were neglected and the nuns only made an effort for visitors,' she said. In her interview with the newspaper, she talked about a five-year-old girl called Marie who was still in nappies and fed baby cereal: 'Marie was left in a storage room and used to crash to the floor, banging her head, and making it bleed. I bit my lip hearing her screams in there.' After the home closed down in 1970, she tracked down Marie and became the youngest woman in the country to adopt aged nineteen. She went on, 'Marie wouldn't have been so bad if she hadn't been so utterly neglected. All they cared about was how clean the place was, no baby or child was ever cuddled or played with.'

Daniel, who had also been a resident at the home, added:

> Once when I was angry I flooded the bathroom. The nun stripped me naked in front of 100 boys and put me in a bath of icy water. I was shivering and crying and crying. Then she tied me to a shower and beat me with a stick which hung around her waist like a crucifix. I was nine years old.

He also recalled being locked in a cupboard for a day at a time: 'The nuns told us that we were a curse on the world.'

After the hardback edition of my book came out, one woman,

now in her eighties, phoned me to say she had been in the Cheltenham Nazareth House in the 1950s. According to her, the nuns slept at the end of the dormitory. The children were woken by the ringing of a bell and it was each to their own to find clothes, which may or may not fit. The nuns used to run hot baths and would order a child to dip their toe into the water. If they screamed with pain, or even pulled a face, she said, 'The nun would beat us until their handprint was left on our bottoms. They were so cruel.'

CCS Adoption records show that my orphanage was used as a dumping ground for children who were perceived as 'different' and therefore considered unsuitable for adoption. They included children with mixed ethnicity and disabilities. The anniversary report I referred to earlier said that during the 1960s, 'research was undertaken and different child care theories developed, which highlighted the harm caused to children by growing up in large, regimented institutions, with little opportunity to form key attachments to trusted adults'. The report went on to describe how social worker June Newport – whose name appears briefly in my adoption file after she met Betty and George, though they never spoke of her – was sent into the home for the first time in 1961, the year that I arrived:

> She found that the different orders of nuns ... continued to provide strict regimented care and were not receptive to modern child care methods and theories, including being unwilling to provide care for children in small family settings ... Newport persistently raised concerns about the need for higher ratios of staff to children in the Bristol and Cheltenham Nazareth Houses and the negative impact on children of the highly regimented care.

I'm certain Margaret was oblivious to any ill-treatment of the children in the home. Her visits had to fit in with her busy work schedule as a nurse in Birmingham and there were probably a couple of visits a month at most. And as the witnesses said, the nuns always ensured they were on their best behaviour in front of any visitors. I later learned Margaret was a stickler for housework, so I'm sure she would have approved of the obsession with hygiene and cleanliness – even though it seems the high standards were achieved by the nuns beating the children they were supposed to care for.

• • •

The joyous, never-seen-before photos of me in the home, proudly standing up in a play pen – albeit with a bit of help – came as a complete shock. But a very nice shock. In them, I looked happy and cared for. The only photos I had been aware of before were the one of me gazing wistfully at the flowers in the park near the orphanage and the one with Betty and George holding me on a weekend visit. So the two new photos were important in so many ways. They showed how I looked when I wasn't on parade for potential parents. I have shown Philomena Olver's photos to family and friends, who all agreed in an instant not only that it was me in them but that I looked happy.

Frustratingly, there were no photographs of me in the home. I have still never seen a photo of the interior of the rambling old Victorian building that was Nazareth House.

When those photos were taken, Margaret had absolutely no intention of giving me away. She was still clinging to the noble idea that one day she would be taking me out of the orphanage and creating a loving home for me. With my father? On her own? I suspect I will never know the answer to that. The photos helped to underline yet again how difficult it must have been for Margaret to walk away from me. It was hard enough for women to give up their babies at five weeks – which I've learned was the standard practice in Catholic adoptions in the 1950s and 1960s. How much harder the separation must have been for a mother like Margaret, who had forged a loving relationship with her son. I was a toddler. I was walking, talking, laughing. I had my very own personality.

When Margaret met Patrick Lennon, he proposed to her and she faced a choice: lose the man who offered her the chance of security and happiness and children she did not have to hide away or walk away from me. I completely understand why she made the decision she did. And so it was that her dream of a home with her son Patrick was shattered on the altar of her matrimony to the other Patrick. Looking at the photos, I thought how her wedding day must have been tinged with personal sadness over the son she thought she would never see again.

The devastating stories I uncovered in the *Bristol Evening Post* rammed home the fact that the abuse that I had read about in the two Nazareth House inquiries in Australia and Scotland also happened much closer to home. My home. Chillingly, some of the stories related to people who were similar ages to me at the time or were in the Bristol and Cheltenham homes at the same time as me. But it seems the worst abuse was inflicted on children who were older. Were the toddlers spared the wrath of the brutal staff members? All I know is that the stories about the punishments meted out to children who dared to wet the bed, involving urine-sodden sheets, had uncanny parallels with what I uncovered in the regressive therapy I had with my counsellor, Father Peter Burrows.

An eminent psychologist, Father Peter was born in 1940. He was always an overachiever, especially in academic circles. As a senior high school student, he was picked out as one of the brightest in southern California. Peter got his first degree at the University of Southern California and then went on to become a Master of Theology at the Episcopal School of Theology at Harvard University. He got his PhD at Hebrew Union College in Ohio. Undoubtedly clever, he was also compassionate.

I loved Father Peter and was devastated when he became very ill. He spent his last days being looked after by nuns in Nazareth House in Plymouth, which was now an old people's home run by the Sisters of Nazareth. I visited him there more than once. 'Our conversations started in Nazareth House,' he told me. 'And our last conversations will be in Nazareth House.' He died in June 2021, aged eighty, in the twenty-eighth year of his priesthood. The irony was never lost on him that he spent his last days in the same institution where I spent my first years.

Some of the home's former residents from the home still have nightmares and flashbacks. I don't. But what I do have now is two wonderful photos and three names: Adrian, Ann and Nigel. I hope that by publishing their photos, I may just trigger some more memories. Maybe someone will recognise these children. Nigel was adopted along with another little boy, but I'm not so sure about Ann or Adrian. I hope they met their very own Betty and George.

It would be nice to meet them. To talk to them. To see if they remember much about the home. To see if they, like me, have been astonishingly happy. In the end, I was very lucky Margaret gave me up for adoption, otherwise I would never have met my real parents. If Margaret hadn't met Patrick Lennon, I could have been in the home for many more years and I would almost certainly have missed my chance to be adopted by Betty and George, who instead would have found another little boy to make their family complete. I was one of the lucky ones. I would so like to know if Ann, Adrian and Nigel struck lucky too.

Andrew Pierce
March 2025

ACKNOWLEDGEMENTS

Where to start? First, I must thank Amanda Platell, not just for being with me on every step of my journey during *Finding Margaret* but also for first raising the idea of me writing a book at a boozy dinner with friends. Jane Moore, star of *Loose Women* and *I'm a Celebrity... Get Me Out of Here!* – if she hadn't found Margaret, there would have been no emotional journey, let alone a book. Vicki Field, my indefatigable agent, who never doubted there was a bestseller in the book. Her mother, Mary-Jo Wormell, who has been the best editor I could hope for. Denis Delaney in Galway provided fascinating and helpful information about the man who may be my birth father. Priests Peter Burrows and Denis McGillycuddy were so kind and understanding. Rhona Coffey and her extraordinary family in Birmingham, my colleague Sue Connolly who found some great photographs and the journalist Christian Gysin, who opened so many doors in the search. Last but not least, my long-suffering partner, Russell.

ABOUT THE AUTHOR

Andrew Pierce is a columnist, consultant editor for the *Daily Mail* and television presenter. He is a regular each week on *Good Morning Britain* on ITV and co-presents *Britain's Newsroom* daily on GB News.

Andrew would love to hear from you and you can find him at the following:

Website: www.andrewpierceofficial.com
TikTok: @toryboypierce
X: @toryboypierce
Instagram: @piercetoryboy